Com

A series edited
professor at the Universit



François Makowski

# French made easy

## A course for beginners

45 lessons

HACHETTE F.L.E.
58, rue Jean-Bleuzen
92170 Vanves

Contact

**FRENCH FOR EVERY POCKET!**

**A new series of self-study French courses**

*General course books and a range of materials designed to meet the specific needs of French learners, providing training in the language along with a mass of interesting information about France and the French.*

Already available :

**French made easy *(intermediate)***

**Allô, j'écoute, *French for the telephone***

ISBN : 2.01.018265.0

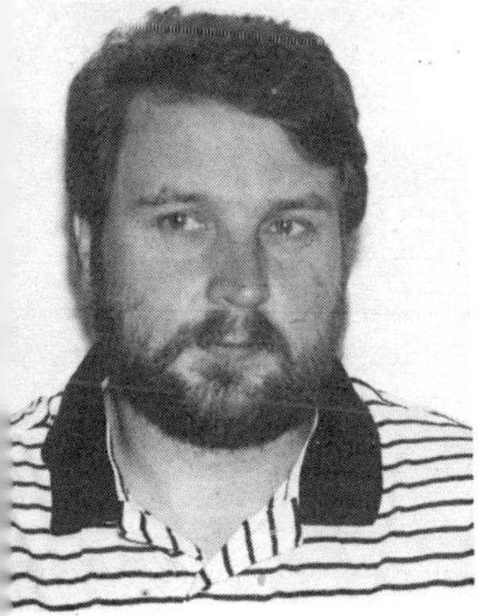

THE AUTHOR

**François Makowski** was born in Bourges (central France) in 1953 and has been teaching French to foreign students for more than 15 years.
A specialist in the theory and practice of teaching French as a foreign language, he regularly takes part in conferences in Greece, Italy, Poland, Portugal, Spain...
François Makowski is the author of several successful French courses for children and adults.


Artwork Chloé PARENT
Layout ENVERGURE

English-language version Malcolm SCOTT
Drawings Emile BRAVO

*Cover*
Artwork Chloé PARENT
Photos VLOO

*Cassettes*
Coordination Elisa CHAPPEY
Music Olivier BERNARD

# TABLE OF CONTENTS

# GENERAL INTRODUCTION

You are planning a business trip to Paris ... or have simply decided to take your holiday in France this year. Everything would be fine except ... you can't speak French. **French made easy** has been designed with you in mind, specifically aimed at people who have never had the opportunity to study French or who, having studied it at school, would like to refresh their command of the language quickly and efficiently.

Based on a lively functional approach, this practical course of **45 lessons** will enable you to make rapid progress by using the language, adopting the rhythm that suits you best.
You may, for example, prefer to take a more traditional approach, working through the book progressively, lesson by lesson (each lesson will take about 15 to 25 minutes per day). Alternatively, you can be more selective, focusing upon your own specific interests and needs. For this, we provide at the end of the book : a **grammar index,** an **index of themes** and an **index of language functions** (greeting people, giving advice ...).
The book is accompanied by **two cassettes**, enabling you to work effectively on your comprehension and to practise speaking and pronunciation.

## 1. How the book is organized

**French made easy** contains :

- a guide to pronunciation
- 45 lessons
- 7 sets of games and quizzes : "On the Brighter Side"
- 8 tests : "Check your progress"
- a grammar summary
- verb tables
- a French/English - English/French mini-dictionary
- a grammar index
- an index of language functions
- a thematic index
- a list of idiomatic expressions

• **Texts**

– Each lesson begins with a short reading passage (text or dialogue).
– The most common situations that you are likely to encounter when staying in France have been chosen as the themes of these 45 introductory passages : lunch in a restaurant, a train journey, an encounter ...
– You will be learning standard French but we have made a point of showing you the different ways in which French people express themselves. This varies according to their profession (a company director or taxi driver), their age, where they happen to be (at home, in the office, ...).
Each text is translated into English. This is not a simplified, "word-for-word" rendering of the French but a translation that sets out to convey the natural equivalent in English.
All the dialogues and texts have been recorded on the cassettes. Once again, we have aimed at authenticity in the articulation and rhythm rather than an artificial simplification...

• **Phonetics**

We suggest you start by quickly reading through the **Guide to Pronunciation** to familiarize yourself with French sounds. Do not hesitate to refer back to it whenever you have a doubt as you make progress through the book.
We have identified the most important words and expressions in each text from the point of view of pronunciation. They have all been recorded on the cassette but you will also find a transcription of their pronunciation in the International Phonetic Alphabet followed by an "imitated pronunciation" where you simply read the words as if they were English.

• **Expressions and vocabulary**

Each vocabulary section gives an additional list of words related to the theme of the lesson. You can also refer to the end of the book, to the French-English/English-French mini-dictionary containing more than 1000 entries.
Lastly, we have selected a series of important expressions listed in the section called "Variations". They are intended to give you practical assistance in a wide range of situations : what to say when you want some help, how to apologize, how to refuse an invitation ...

## • Grammar

One or two important points of grammar are explained on the page opposite the reading passage. If you want more detailed explanations, you will find them in the **Grammar Summary** and the **Verb Tables** at the end of the book.

## • Exercises

***Practice in writing :***
Each lesson includes a series of short exercises (with the answers at the bottom of the page):
– Grammar exercises to help consolidate new structures,
– Translation exercises to recycle vocabulary and expressions introduced in the text.

***Practice in invention :***
An exercise called "Say it in French" presents a series of common situations calling for meaningful communication. This is an opportunity for you to express yourself, to create sentences as if you were really there...

***Practice in listening and speaking :***
The sign ∩ tells you which exercises may also be done orally, using the cassette.

## • French culture and everyday life

Every 6 lessons, we introduce 7 sections to change the pace a little, called "On the Brighter Side" which are entirely devoted to specific details about life in France :
– the section "Did you know" gives you useful, practical information,
– a selection of games and quizzes refresh your general knowledge about France,
– a series of drawings illustrate popular expressions often used by the French.



## • Assessment and revision

You can test yourself every six lessons by doing the 8 exercises in the "Check your progress" sections.

## 2. How to use the book

*Five 2-page lessons at the beginning of the book deal with a practical subject – such as numbers or writing the address on a postcard (lessons 1, 3, 5, 7 and 9). All the other lessons contain 4 pages. We suggest you organize your work as follows :*

**1. Listen to the recording and read the text**

– Depending upon your previous knowledge and language-learning abilities, listen to the recording of the text with the book closed, trying to identify the words and expressions you already know (repeat two or three times, if necessary).

– When you feel you have identified everything you can, open the book and read the text aloud, using the recording to help guide your pronunciation. Don't worry if you feel slightly discouraged at first – this is quite normal during the early stages ! – Check your understanding with the help of the translation on the right-hand page.

*– **Idiomatic expressions** : for additional explanations about the construction of certain expressions, turn to the **List of idiomatic expressions** at the end of the book.

**2. Listen** to the words and expressions listed in the pronunciation section and repeat them aloud.

**3. Read the grammar section** carefully, referring to the grammar summary and the verb tables if you want further details.

**4. Do the exercises** (in writing) and immediately check your answers. Depending upon your level, prepare the answers to the exercise recorded on the cassette.

**5. Learn by heart the words in the vocabulary section and the expressions listed in the "Variations".** Practise creating new sentences by stringing the expressions together in different ways ...

**6. Invent sentences** corresponding to the situations presented in the "Say it in French" section. Do it aloud first of all, and then write out your answers in full. Compare your answers with the possible answers suggested at the bottom of the page.

**7. Finally, we suggest you go back to the text** of the lesson. Listen to it again and read it aloud. You will now find it a lot easier !

# Guide to Pronunciation

At the bottom of the first page of each lesson you will find a number of words or expressions taken from the reading passage, followed by two different phonetic transcriptions.
The first transcription, between brackets [ ], uses the International Phonetic Alphabet. It is the most reliable transcription but presupposes some knowledge of this alphabet.
Each symbol used in this alphabet corresponds to a single sound and you should therefore pronounce them all when you read the phonetic transcription.
For the second, so-called "imitated pronunciation", we have used the letters of the ordinary alphabet. It is the easiest to use but it is also the least reliable. It only gives you an approximate idea of the real pronunciation.

## French sounds and their transcription in the International Phonetic Alphabet

The following tables are not exhaustive ; there will inevitably be exceptions. We therefore suggest you use the cassettes as you work through the different lessons.
It is important to bear in mind that letters in French words are sounded (or not) depending upon their position in the word or their combination with other letters.

### 1. Vowels :

| sound | possible written forms | example | transcription | translation |
|---|---|---|---|---|
| [i] | i | si | [si] | *if* |
| | y | analyse | [analiz] | *analysis* |
| [ɥ] | u | tu | [tɥ] | *you* |
| [u] | ou | cou | [ku] | *neck* |
| [ɑ] | a | la | [lɑ] | *the (fem.)* |
| [a] | a | pas | [pa] | *step* |
| [o] | o | nos | [no] | *our* |
| | au | auto | [oto] | *car* |
| | eau | eau | [o] | *water* |
| [ɔ] | o | avocat | [avɔka] | *lawyer* |
| [ə] | e | leçon | [ləsɔ̃] | *lesson* |

| | | | | |
|---|---|---|---|---|
| [ø] | eu | feu | [fø] | *fire* |
| [œ] | eu | beurre | [bœr] | *butter* |
| [e] | é | été | [ete] | *summer* |
| | es | tes | [te] | *your* |
| | er | aller | [ale] | *to go* |
| [ɛ] | è | père | [pɛr] | *father* |
| | ê | tête | [tɛt] | *head* |
| | ai | mai | [mɛ] | *May* |
| | est | elle est | [ɛlɛ] | *she is* |
| [ɛ̃] | in | fin | [fɛ̃] | *end* |
| | ain | pain | [pɛ̃] | *bread* |
| | aim | faim | [fɛ̃] | *hunger* |
| | ym | sympathique | [sɛ̃patik] | *nice* |
| [œ̃] | un | brun | [brœ̃] | *brown* |
| | um | parfum | [parfœ̃] | *perfume* |
| [ɔ̃] | on | bonbon | [bɔ̃bɔ̃] | *sweet* |
| | om | ombre | [ɔ̃br] | *shade* |
| [ɑ̃] | an | tant | [tɑ̃] | *so much* |
| | am | chambre | [ʃɑ̃br] | *bedroom* |
| | en | lent | [lɑ̃] | *slow* |
| | em | temps | [tɑ̃] | *time* |

## 2. Semivowels :

Semivowels are never pronounced alone ; they are always accompanied by another vowel.

| sound | possible written forms | example | transcription | translation |
|---|---|---|---|---|
| [w] | | | | |
| [w]+[a] | oi | toi | [twa] | *you* |
| [w]+[ɛ̃] | oin | point | [pwɛ̃] | *point* |
| [w]+[i] | oui | oui | [wi] | *yes* |
| [w]+[e] | ouer | jouer | [ʒwe] | *to play* |
| | ouez | jouez ! | [ʒwe] | *play !* |

With [j], a large number of combinations are possible with all the other vowels. We only give a few examples below.

| | | | | |
|---|---|---|---|---|
| [a]+[j] | ail | travail | [travaj] | *work* |
| | aille | il travaille | [iltravaj] | *he works* |
| [ɛ]+[j] | eil | pareil | [parɛj] | *same* |
| | eille | oreille | [ɔrɛj] | *ear* |

| | | | | |
|---|---|---|---|---|
| [i]+[j] | ille | fille | [fij] | *girl* |
| [œ]+[j] | euille | feuille | [fœj] | *leaf* |
| [u]+[j] | ouille | rouille | [ruj] | *rust* |
| [j]+[a] | ya | voyage | [vwajaʒ] | *journey* |
| [j]+[o] | io | radio | [radjo] | *radio* |
| [i]+[e] | ier | papier | [papje] | *paper* |
| | ié | société | [sɔsjete] | *society* |
| [ɥ]+[i] | ui | lui | [lɥi] | *him* |
| [ɥ]+[ɛ] | uet | muet | [mɥɛ] | *silent* |

## 3. Consonants :

| sound | possible written forms | example | transcription | translation |
|---|---|---|---|---|
| [p] | p | papa | [papa] | *daddy* |
| [t] | t | ta | [ta] | *your* |
| [k] | c + a/o/u | cas | [ka] | *case* |
| | k | kilo | [kilo] | *kilo* |
| | qu | qui | [ki] | *who* |
| [m] | m | ma | [ma] | *my* |
| [f] | f | facile | [fasil] | *easy* |
| | ph | photo | [foto] | *photograph* |
| [s] | s | sa | [sa] | *his/her* |
| | ss | poisson | [pwasɔ̃] | *fish* |
| | c + e/i/y | cela | [səla] | *that* |
| | ç + a/o/u | garçon | [garsɔ̃] | *boy* |
| [ʃ] | ch | chat | [ʃa] | *cat* |
| [ɲ] | gn | ligne | [liɲ] | *line* |
| [l] | l | la | [la] | *the* |
| [r] | r | rapide | [rapid] | *fast* |
| [b] | b | bonbon | [bɔ̃bɔ̃] | *sweet* |
| [d] | d | dans | [dɑ̃] | *in* |
| [g] | g + a/o/u | garçon | [garsɔ̃] | *boy* |
| | gu + e/i | guitare | [gitar] | *guitar* |
| [n] | n | nos | [no] | *our* |
| [v] | v | vos | [vo] | *your* |
| [z] | s (between vowels) | raison | [rɛzɔ̃] | *reason* |
| | z | zéro | [zero] | *zero* |
| [ʒ] | j | jour | [ʒur] | *day* |
| | g + e/i | page | [paʒ] | *page* |

## • The alphabet and how to pronounce it :

It is important to learn how to pronounce the alphabet in French. You will certainly one day be asked to spell your name, your first name or address.

| | | | | |
|---|---|---|---|---|
| **a**→ [a] | **g**→ [ʒe] | **m**→ [ɛm] | **s**→ [ɛs] | **y**→ [igrɛk] |
| **b**→ [be] | **h**→ [aʃ] | **n**→ [ɛn] | **t**→ [te] | **z**→ [zɛd] |
| **c**→ [se] | **i**→ [i] | **o**→ [o] | **u**→ [y] | |
| **d**→ [de] | **j**→ [ʒi] | **p**→ [pe] | **v**→ [ve] | |
| **e**→ [ə] | **k**→ [ka] | **q**→ [ky] | **w**→ [dubləve] | |
| **f**→ [ɛf] | **l**→ [ɛl] | **r**→ [ɛr] | **x**→ [iks] | |

## • Silent letters :

Depending upon their position in the word, certain letters are not pronounced. We list the most frequent cases below.

– The final **-e**

→ facile [fasil] *(easy)*

– Final consonants

→ tabac [taba] *(tobacco)*

Note that when masculine nouns and adjectives are put into the feminine by adding an **-e**, the preceding consonant must be sounded.

→ étudiant [etydjã] → étudiante [etydjãt] (student)

– The **h** is normally silent

→ hôtel [otɛl] *(hotel)*

Except in the following combinations : **c + h** and **p + h**

→ chat [ʃa] *(cat)*

→ photo [foto] *(photograph)*

– When a word includes double consonants, the sound is only pronounced once

→ attention [atãsjɔ̃] *(attention)*

→ belle [bɛl] *(beautiful)*

→ assez [ase] *(enough)*

## • Tonic stress :

French words (or word-groups) are always stressed on the final syllable.

*Bonjour monsieur Dupont*

*Bonjour monsieur*

*Bonjour*

# LES SALUTATIONS

## ■ BONJOUR !

— *Salut, Paul ! Ça va ?*
— *Salut, Sylvie, ça va bien. Et toi ?*

— *Bonjour, monsieur.*
— *Bonjour, madame, ça va ?*
— *Ça va, merci. Et vous ?*

— *Au revoir, mademoiselle Martin.*
— *Au revoir, Pierre.*

## PRONUNCIATION

| | | |
|---|---|---|
| **Bonjour** | [bɔ̃ʒur] | bawngzhoor |
| **Au revoir** | [ɔrvwar] | oa rervwahr |
| **Salut** | [saly] | sahlew |
| **Monsieur** | [møsjø] | mursyur |
| **Madame** | [madam] | mahdahm |
| **Mademoiselle** | [madmwazɛl] | mahdmwahzehl |

## HELLO!

– Hi, Paul! How are things?
– Hi, Sylvie. Everything's fine.
And you?

– Hello!
– Hello! How are you?
– Very well, thank you.
And you ?

– Goodbye, Miss Martin.
– Goobye Pierre.

When greeting someone in French, you should make sure that the expression you use corresponds to the relationship you have with that person.
**Bonjour** and **au revoir** can be used with everyone.
**Salut** is much more informal and frequently used by young people, friends or members of the same family.
Note that **salut**, depending upon the context, can mean **bonjour** or **au revoir**!

## EXERCISES

### *1. How would you say "hello" to :*

a) Pierre, an old friend.
b) a lady that you do not know very well.
c) your boss.
d) your neighbour's son, called Paul.

### *2. How would you say "goodbye" to :*

a) Madame Martin.
b) your brother.
c) a young lady that you do not know.
d) a child.

**Possible answers :**

1. a. Salut/bonjour, Pierre. b. Bonjour, madame. c. Bonjour, monsieur. d. Salut/ bonjour, Paul.
2. a. Au revoir, madame Martin. b. Au revoir/salut. c. Au revoir, mademoiselle. d. Au revoir/salut.

## ■ *Qui êtes-vous ?*

— Bonjour, monsieur.
— Bonjour, mademoiselle.
— Vous êtes monsieur... ?
— Peter Brown.

— Vous êtes français ?
— Non, je suis anglais.
— Et qu'est-ce que vous faites ?
— Je suis avocat.

— Merci, monsieur.
— Au revoir, mademoiselle.
— Au revoir, monsieur.

## PRONUNCIATION

| | | |
|---|---|---|
| **Vous êtes monsieur... ?** | [vuzɛtmøsjø] | voo zeht mursyur |
| **Vous êtes français ?** | [vuzɛtfrɑ̃sɛ] | voo zeht frahngsseh |
| **Je suis anglais** | [ʒəsɥizɑ̃glɛ] | zher swee zahngleh |
| **Qu'est-ce que vous faites ?** | [kɛskəvufɛt] | kehsske voo feht |
| **Je suis avocat** | [ʒəsɥizavɔka] | zher swee ahvoka |
| **Merci** | [mɛrsi] | mehrsee |

## Who are you ?

— Hello*!
— Hello*!
— You are Mr ... ?
— Peter Brown.

— Are you French ?
— No, I'm English.
— And what do you do ?
— I'm a lawyer.

— Thank you.
— Goodbye.
— Goodbye.

## GRAMMAR

### Verbs :

**Je suis, vous êtes** → present indicative of the verb **être**
**Vous faites** → present indicative of the verb **faire**

### Nationalities :

| | German | American | English | Spanish | French | Italian |
|---|---|---|---|---|---|---|
| **Masculine** | allemand | américain | anglais | espagnol | français | italien |
| **Feminine** | allemande | américaine | anglaise | espagnole | française | italienne |

### Occupations :

| | lawyer | shopkeeper | employee | student | journalist |
|---|---|---|---|---|---|
| **masculine** | avocat | commerçant | employé | étudiant | journaliste |
| **feminine** | avocate | commerçante | employée | étudiante | journaliste |

**Je suis avocat :** occupations behave like adjectives in this construction **without** the indefinite article.

### The interrogative form :

The simplest way of expressing a question is by adding a **?** to the sentence when writing, and by using a rising intonation when speaking.

**written:** Vous êtes français. Vous êtes français ?
**oral:** ↗↘ ↗

## EXERCISES

### 1. *Masculine or feminine ? Place a cross in the appropriate column. (Watch out for the exceptions !)*

| | masculine | feminine |
|---|---|---|
| Je suis allemand. | ☐ | ☐ |
| Vous êtes étudiante ? | ☐ | ☐ |
| Vous êtes espagnole. | ☐ | ☐ |
| Je suis américain. | ☐ | ☐ |
| Vous êtes journaliste. | ☐ | ☐ |

### 2. *Find the questions. (Watch out for the gender !)*

Oui, je suis française. → Vous êtes française ?
Oui, je suis employé. → ..............................
Oui, je suis américaine. → ..............................
Oui, je suis journaliste. → ..............................
Oui, je suis Louise Martin. → ..............................

### 3. *Translate into French*

I am a clerk. Goodbye, sir. Are you Miss Lepont ? No, I'm (a) French (lady). Thank you, madam.

## VOCABULARY

| | |
|---|---|
| alors : then    et : and | à tout à l'heure → see you later |
| bonsoir → good evening | à bientôt → see you soon |
| bonne nuit → good night | à tout de suite → see you in a minute |
| bonne journée → good day | à demain → see you tomorrow |
| bon après-midi → good afternoon | |



**Key to exercises :**

1. masculine/ feminine / feminine / masculine / masculine or feminine
2. Vous êtes employé ? Vous êtes américaine ? Vous êtes journaliste ? Vous êtes Louise Martin ?
3. Je suis employé. Au revoir, monsieur. Vous êtes mademoiselle Lepont ? Non, je suis française. Merci, madame.

## VARIATIONS

**Pour saluer ou prendre congé :**

Au revoir, / Bonjour,
monsieur
madame
mademoiselle
Louis

***Greeting or taking leave of someone :***

*Goodbye / Hello*
*Mr ....*
*Mrs ....*
*Miss ....*
*Louis*

**Pour vérifier l'identité ou la nationalité :**

Vous êtes
monsieur ... ?
madame ... ?
mademoiselle ... ?
Louis ?
anglais ?
français ?

***Asking someone's name or nationality :***

*Are you*
*Mr .... ?*
*Mrs .... ?*
*Miss ... ?*
*Louis ?*
*English ?*
*French ?*

**Pour donner votre identité ou votre nationalité :**

Je suis
monsieur Martin
madame Dubois
mademoiselle Lepont
Louis Martin
anglais
français

***Giving your name or nationality :***

*I am*
*Mr Martin*
*Mrs Dubois*
*Miss Lepont*
*Louis Martin*
*English*
*French*

**Pour connaître la profession :**

Vous êtes ingénieur ?
Qu'est-ce que vous faites ?
comme profession

***Asking someone's occupation :***

*Are you an engineer ?*
*What do you do ?*

## SAY IT IN FRENCH

***You are in a train :***

1. Greet the person sitting opposite you.
2. Ask him/her if he/she is French.
3. Ask his/her occupation.
4. You arrive at your destination. Take leave of him/her.

**Possible answers :** (speaking to a young lady)

1. Bonjour, mademoiselle. 2. Vous êtes française ? 3. Qu'est-ce que vous faites ? Vous êtes étudiante ? 4. Au revoir, mademoiselle.

## UN, DEUX, TROIS...

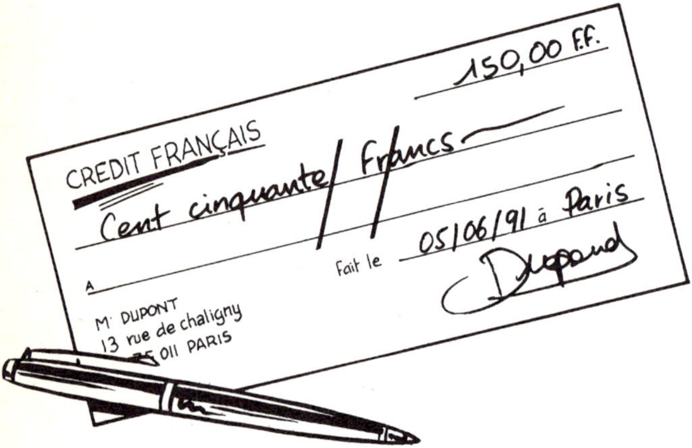


### PRONUNCIATION

| | | |
|---|---|---|
| **un** | [ɛ̃] | ang |
| **deux** | [dø] | dur |
| **trois** | [trwa] | trwah |
| **quatre** | [katr] | kahtr |
| **cinq** | [sɛ̃k] | sangk |
| **six** | [sis] | seess |
| **sept** | [sɛt] | seht |
| **huit** | [ɥit] | weet |
| **neuf** | [nœf] | nurf |
| **dix** | [dis] | deess |

## ONE, TWO, THREE...

| | | |
|---|---|---|
| 11 onze | 21 vingt et un | 70 soixante-dix |
| 12 douze | 22 vingt-deux | 71 soixante et onze |
| 13 treize | 29 vingt-neuf | 72 soixante-douze |
| 14 quatorze | 30 trente | 79 soixante-dix-neuf |
| 15 quinze | 31 trente et un | 80 quatre-vingts |
| 16 seize | 32 trente-deux | 81 quatre-vingt-un |
| 17 dix-sept | 39 trente-neuf | 90 quatre-vingt-dix |
| 18 dix-huit | 40 quarante | 91 quatre-vingt-onze |
| 19 dix-neuf | 50 cinquante | 92 quatre-vingt-douze |
| 20 vingt | 60 soixante | 99 quatre-vingt-dix-neuf |
| 100 cent | 1 000 mille | 1 000 000 un million |

## EXERCISES

### Write out, in full, the solutions to the following problems

cinq et quatre : 5 neuf
huit et neuf : dix-sept
cent et soixante : cent soixante
soixante-dix et vingt et un : quatre vingt et onze

**Key to exercise :**

neuf ; dix-sept ; cent soixante ; quatre-vingt-onze.

« Faire le premier pas »

*« Making the first move »*

## DID YOU KNOW?

When you meet someone in France, you usually shake hands. Close friends and members of the same family, however, will usually kiss one another on both cheeks... two, three or even four times.

When you leave someone, you can say *Au revoir* or *Salut*, but if you expect to see the person again before too long, you are more likely to say *À bientôt* (see you soon), *À tout à l'heure* (see you later), *À tout de suite* (see you in a minute), but you can also be more precise and say *À demain* (see you tomorrow), *À la semaine prochaine* (see you next week), *À lundi prochain* (see you next Monday).

**Look at the map and find the following countries, regions, cities, sea and rivers:**

1. Paris
2. La Seine
3. Lyon
4. La Corse
5. La mer Méditerranée
6. Les Alpes
7. La Belgique
8. La côte d'Azur
9. La Bretagne
10. Bordeaux

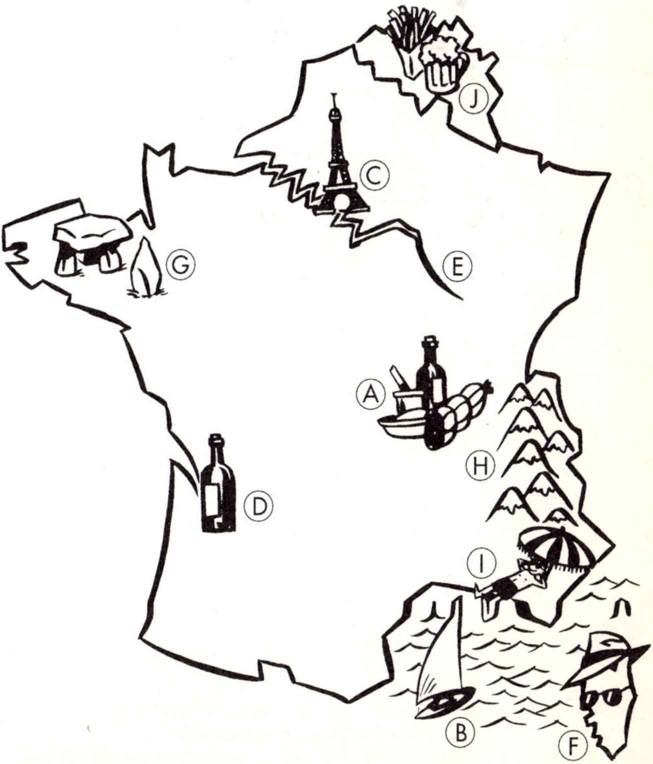




***Answers:*** 1.C - 2.E - 3.A - 4.F - 5.B - 6.H - 7.J - 8.I - 9.G - 10.D.

## ENCHANTÉ !

*Christian :* Papa, Maman, je vous présente Louis, un ami.

*Monsieur Joffre :* Ah, bonjour, Louis. Comment allez-vous ?

*Louis :* Très bien, merci. Et vous ?

...

*Madame Joffre :* Vous êtes de Bruxelles, je crois ?

*Louis :* Non, je suis de Namur. Vous connaissez ?

*Madame Joffre :* Oui, je connais très bien la Belgique.

...

*Jacques :* Louis, je te présente Isabelle, une amie.

*Louis :* Bonjour, mademoiselle.

*Isabelle :* Mademoiselle ? On se dit tu !

*Louis :* D'accord. Alors, Isabelle, comment vas-tu ?

*Isabelle :* Très bien. Et toi ?

### PRONUNCIATION

| | | |
|---|---|---|
| **Comment allez-vous ?** | [kɔmɑ̃talevu] | kommanhng tahlay voo ? |
| **Très bien, merci** | [trɛbjɛ̃mɛrsi] | treh byang, mehrsee |
| **On se dit tu !** | [ɔ̃sdity] | awng ser dee tew |
| **D'accord** | [dakɔr] | dahkor |
| **Comment vas-tu ?** | [kɔmɑ̃vaty] | kommahng vahtew |

## ■ PLEASED TO MEET YOU !

*Christian :* Dad, Mum, meet Louis, a friend of mine*.
*Mr Joffre :* Oh, hello, Louis. How are you*?
*Louis :* Very well, thank you. And you ?
...
*Mrs Joffre :* You're from Brussels, I believe ?
*Louis :* No. I'm from Namur. Do you know Namur*?
*Mrs Joffre :* Yes. I know Belgium very well.
...
*Jacques :* Louis, meet Isabelle, a friend of mine.
*Louis :* Good morning, miss!
*Isabelle :* Miss ? Call me Isabelle, we don't need to be formal*!
*Louis :* Alright. Isabelle, then. How are you ?
*Isabelle :* Very well. And you ?

## GRAMMAR

### ■ *Verbs :*

**Vous allez / tu vas** → present indicative of the verb **aller**

### ■ *The subject pronouns ... and the verb* être *:*

| person | singular | plural |
|---|---|---|
| **1st** | je suis | nous sommes |
| **2nd** | tu es | vous êtes |
| **3rd** | on/elle/il est | elles/ils sont |

Note that when addressing one or several persons, the polite form is **vous.**

**"On se dit tu"** – **On** has the same meaning as **nous** in this expression. Note that after **on** the verb is always conjugated in the third person singular.

### ■ *The indefinite articles :* un - une - des

The indefinite article is used with a noun when it is felt that the person spoken to is unfamiliar with the person or the object in question.

| | singular | plural |
|---|---|---|
| **masculine** | un ami | des amis |
| **feminine** | une amie | des amies |

Note that in French the plural is normally formed by adding an **s**.

# LES FORMES DE POLITESSE

## EXERCISES

**1. *Give the appropriate indefinite article (in the singular)***

...... ami, ...... étudiante, ...... amie, ...... Américaine, ...... commerçante, ...... Français, ...... journaliste, ...... avocat.

**2. *Put into the plural. Remember to add the* s*!***

Un avocat → des avocats
une amie → ........................................
une Allemande → ........................................
un ouvrier → ........................................
une employée → ........................................
un Anglais → ........................................

**3. *Give the appropriate subject pronoun***

...... sommes français. ...... est agricultrice. ...... êtes avocat ? ...... suis anglais. ...... sont ouvriers. ...... es commerçant.

**4. *Translate into French***

How are you ? (informal). I'm from London. Meet Paul, a friend of mine. Are you (pl.) from Bordeaux ?

## VOCABULARY

| | |
|---|---|
| d'accord : alright, okay<br>aussi : also | un frère → a brother |
| préférer → to prefer | aimer → to like, love |
| un(e) ami(e) → a friend | un collègue → a colleague |
| un père → a father | une mère → a mother |
| | une sœur → a sister |



**Key to exercises :**

1. un / une / une / une / une / un / un (une) / un
2. des amies / des Allemandes / des ouvriers / des employées / des Anglais
3. nous sommes / elle est / vous êtes / je suis / ils sont / tu es
4. Comment vas-tu ? Je suis de Londres. Je te présente Paul, un ami. Vous êtes de Bordeaux ?

## VARIATIONS

| | |
|---|---|
| **Pour vous présenter :** | ***Introducing yourself :*** |
| Je me présente.<br>Je m'appelle Louis Martin. | *I'm.*<br>*My name is Louis Martin.* |
| **Pour présenter quelqu'un :** | ***Introducing someone else :*** |
| C'est un ami.<br>Je vous/te présente Paul. | *This is a friend of mine.*<br>*Meet Paul !* |
| **Formules de politesse :** | ***Polite expressions :*** |
| Vous allez / tu vas bien ?<br>Ça va bien ? *(fam.)* | *How are you ?*<br>*How are you / How are things ?* |
| **Pour répondre :** | ***Replying :*** |
| Très bien, (merci) et vous ?<br>Très bien, et toi ? | *I'm fine, (thanks). And you ?*<br>*Very well, and you ?* |
| **Pour proposer *tu* :** | ***Suggesting the use of the more friendly* tu *form.*** |
| On se dit *tu* ?<br>On se tutoie ? | |
| **Pour accepter :** | ***Accepting :*** |
| D'accord (avec plaisir).<br>Si tu veux. | *Okay (with pleasure).*<br>*If you like.* |

## SAY IT IN FRENCH

***You are visiting some French people :***

1. Greet the person who opens the door and introduce yourself.
2. Ask this person how he/she is.
3. You are accompanied by your friend Josiane. Introduce her.
4. As a mark of friendship the use of **tu** is suggested. Agree to this.

**Possible answers :**

1. Bonjour. Je me présente / je m'appelle ... . 2. Comment allez-vous ? 3. Je vous présente Josiane. 4. D'accord, avec plaisir.

## LA FRANCE ET L'EUROPE

### PRONUNCIATION

| | | |
|---|---|---|
| **L'Allemagne** | [lalmaɲ] | lahlmahñ |
| **La Belgique** | [labɛlʒik] | lah behlzheek |
| **L'Espagne** | [lɛspaɲ] | lehspañ |
| **La Grande-Bretagne** | [lagrɑ̃dbrətaɲ] | lah grahngd brertañ |
| **La Grèce** | [lagrɛs] | lah grehss |
| **L'Italie** | [litali] | leetahlee |

## FRANCE AND EUROPE

| countries | people | currencies |
|---|---|---|
| Allemagne | Allemand(e) | mark |
| Angleterre | Anglais(e) | livre sterling |
| Belgique | Belge | franc (belge) |
| Danemark | Danois(e) | couronne (danoise) |
| Espagne | Espagnol(e) | peseta |
| France | Français(e) | franc (français) |
| Grèce | Grec(que) | drachme |
| Irlande | Irlandais(e) | livre (irlandaise) |
| Italie | Italien(ne) | lire |
| Luxembourg | Luxembourgeois(e) | franc (luxembourgeois) |
| Pays-Bas | Néerlandais(e) | florin |
| Portugal | Portugais(e) | escudo |

## EXERCISE

**Complete the following sentences:**

En France, les Français paient avec des .......
Andrés est .........il habite à Barcelone.
Malcolm est .........., il est né à Oxford.
En .........., les..........paient avec des lires.

**Key to exercise :**

francs - espagnol - anglais - Italie - Italiens.

## ■ PETITES ANNONCES

J'habite à Annecy et j'ai trente-six ans. Je suis directrice commerciale. Je suis jolie, grande, brune et j'ai les yeux marron. Je ne suis pas mariée.

Je suis de Bordeaux mais j'habite à Paris. J'aime la télévision, les voyages et l'histoire de l'art mais je n'aime pas le sport. Je parle bien anglais et espagnol. J'ai vingt-deux ans, je ne travaille pas et je suis célibataire.

## PRONUNCIATION

| | | |
|---|---|---|
| **J'ai trente-six ans** | [ʒɛtrɑ̃tsizɑ̃] | zhay trahngt seess ahng |
| **Brune** | [bryn] | brewn |
| **Les yeux marron** | [lezjømarɔ̃] | lay zyur mahrawhng |
| **Je n'aime pas** | [ʒənɛmpa] | zher nehme pah |
| **Célibataire** | [selibatɛR] | sayleebahtehr |

## CLASSIFIED ADS

I live in Annecy and I'm thirty-six years old*. I'm a sales manager. I'm pretty, tall, dark-haired and I have brown eyes. I am not married.

I'm from Bordeaux but I live in Paris. I like television, travelling and the history of art but I don't like sport. I speak good English and Spanish. I'm twenty-two, I don't work and I'm single.

## GRAMMAR

### *Verbs :*

**J'ai** → present indicative of the verb **avoir**

### *Conjugation of the present indicative of Group 1 verbs (those ending in -er in the infinitive) :*

infinitive : parler → root : parl  endings : e / es / e / ons / ez / ent

| | |
|---|---|
| je parl**e** | nous parl**ons** |
| tu parl**es** | vous parl**ez** |
| il/elle parl**e** | ils/elles parl**ent** |

Note that the verb **aller** is irregular and is not conjugated like other Group 1 (**-er**) verbs → Je vais / tu vas / il va / nous allons / vous allez / ils vont.

### *The negative form :* je ne suis pas - il ne travaille pas

The negative form is normally obtained by placing **ne** before the verb and **pas** after it. Note that before verbs beginning with a vowel or silent **h**, **ne** becomes **n'**.

### *The definite articles :* le, la, l', les

The definite article is used to designate an object which is already known or identified

| | **singular** | | **plural** |
|---|---|---|---|
| **masculine** | le théâtre | les | théâtres |
| | l'art | | arts |
| **feminine** | la télévision | | télévisions |
| | l'histoire | | histoires |

Note that in the singular the definite article always becomes **l'** before words beginning with a vowel or silent **h**.

## EXERCISES

### 1. Change the indefinite articles into definite articles

un célibataire → ....................... des sports → .......................
une directrice → ....................... une histoire → .......................

### 2. Conjugate the following Group 1 verbs

travailler → tu ................. nous ................ elles ..............
arriver → j'.................. il ..................... vous ..................
aimer → j'.............. tu ................. ils ..................

### 3. Put into the negative form

Je suis français. → je ne suis pas français.
Elle est brune. → ....................... Je parle français. → .................
Vous êtes de Toulouse. → ......... Nous aimons le théâtre. → .......

### 4. Translate into French

She lives in Lyon. I don't work in the hospital. You (pl) don't know Nice. She has brown eyes. I speak English but I don't speak French.

## VOCABULARY

| | |
|---|---|
| mais : but    bien : well | petit → small |
| une ville → a town | mince → slim |
| un département → a department | blond → fair-haired |
| un travail → a job | roux/rousse → red-haired |
| une profession → an occupation | les cheveux → hair |
| | un œil/des yeux → an eye/eyes |

**Key to exercises:**

1. le célibataire / les sports / la directrice / l'histoire
2. tu travailles, nous travaillons, elles travaillent / j'arrive, il arrive, vous arrivez / j'aime, tu aimes, ils aiment.
3. Elle n'est pas brune. Je ne parle pas français. Vous n'êtes pas de Toulouse. Nous n'aimons pas le théâtre.
4. Elle habite à Lyon. Je ne travaille pas à l'hôpital. Vous ne connaissez pas Nice. Elle a les yeux marron. Je parle anglais mais je ne parle pas français.

## VARIATIONS

| **Pour parler de quelqu'un :** | ***Talking about someone :*** |
|---|---|
| Il est grand/petit/mince/gros... | *He's tall/small/slim/fat...* |
| Elle est grande/petite/mince/grosse... | *She's tall/small/slim/fat...* |
| Il est beau/moche... | *He's handsome/ugly...* |
| Elle est belle/moche... | *She's beautiful/ugly...* |
| **Les cheveux :** | ***Hair :*** |
| Il est brun/blond/roux/chauve... | *He's dark-/fair-/red-haired/bald...* |
| Elle est brune/blonde/rousse... | *She's dark-/fair-/red-haired...* |
| **Les yeux :** | ***Eyes :*** |
| Il/elle a les yeux verts/noirs/gris/bleus/marron | *He/she has green/dark/grey/blue/brown eyes.* |
| **L'âge :** | ***Age :*** |
| Il est vieux/jeune. | *He is old/young.* |
| Elle est vieille/jeune. | *She is old/young.* |
| Il/elle a 27 ans. | *He/she is 27.* |
| **Les goûts :** | ***Tastes :*** |
| Il/elle aime la famille. | *He/she loves the family.* |
| Il/elle adore travailler. | *He/she adores working.* |
| Il/elle déteste voyager. | *He/she hates travelling.* |

## SAY IT IN FRENCH

***Read the classified ads once again before doing the following exercise :***

1. Say where the man lives and how old he is.
2. Describe the lady.
3. Say where you come from, how old you are and what your occupation is.
4. Describe yourself.



**Possible answers:**

1. Il habite à Bordeaux et il a vingt-deux ans. 2. Elle est grande, brune, jolie et elle a les yeux marron. 3. Je suis de ..., j'ai ... ans et je suis ... .4. Je suis ..., ..., ... et j'ai les yeux ... .

# BILAN 1

## ■ NOW YOU KNOW HOW TO GIVE YOUR NATIONALITY,

***1. Complete the following.***

Elle est de Berlin, elle est .... John est de Londres, il est ..... Vous êtes de Madrid, vous êtes .... Je suis de Paris, je suis .... Maria est de Rome, elle est .....

## ■ ...HOW TO SAY WHAT JOB YOU DO,

***2. Translate into French.***

a lawyer → .....
a shopkeeper → ....
a journalist → ....
a sales manager → ....

## ■ ...HOW TO USE THE INDEFINITE AND DEFINITE ARTICLES,

***3. Complete with the appropriate articles.***

Je vous présente Sylvie, .... Française. Je connais très bien ... professeur de français. J'aime .... sport. Tu adores .... voyages. Elle déteste .... famille. Tu as .... amis très sympathiques.

## ■ ...HOW TO PUT INTO THE PLURAL,

***4. Put into the plural.***

une amie → ... l'avocat → ... l'œil → .... un commerçant → ... une employée → ... l'art → ....

## ■ ...HOW TO SAY NO,

***5. Put into the negative.***

Nous aimons travailler → .... Vous êtes français → .....
Il est vieux → ... Elle déteste les roux → ....



## ■ ...HOW TO COUNT IN FRENCH,

***6. Write out the following numbers in full.***

40 → ..... 4 → ... 13 → .... 90 → ... 127 → ....

■ ...HOW TO CONJUGATE FRENCH VERBS.

*7. Complete the following sentences using appropriate verbs.*

Ils .... américains. Je .... très bien la Belgique. Comment ... -vous ? Elle te ..... Louis. Nous .... à Lyon.

*8. Complete the following sentences using appropriate pronouns.*

... avez, .... sommes, .... habites, ..... allez, .... es, .... travaillons, .... parlez, .... ont, .... adorent.

## KEY TO EXERCISES

1 - allemande - anglais - espagnol(s) ou espagnole(s) - français(e) - italienne.
2 - un avocat - un commerçant - un journaliste - un directeur commercial.
3 - une - le - le - les - la - des -
4. des amies - les avocats - les yeux - des commerçants - des employées - les arts.
5. Nous n'aimons pas travailler. Vous n'êtes pas français. Il n'est pas vieux. Elle ne déteste pas les roux.
6. quarante - quatre - treize - quatre-vingt-dix - cent vingt-sept.
7. sont - connais - allez - présente - habitons.
8. vous - nous - tu - vous - tu - nous - vous - ils ou elles - ils ou elles.

## N'OUBLIEZ PAS LE CODE POSTAL !

### PRONUNCIATION

| | | | |
|---|---|---|---|
| **Le nom** | [lənɔ̃] | nawng | **name** |
| **L'adresse** | [ladrɛs] | ahdrehss | **address** |
| **La rue** | [lary] | rew | **street** |
| **La place** | [laplas] | plahss | **place** |
| **La ville** | [lavil] | veel | **town** |
| **Le pays** | [ləpei] | pehee | **country** |

## DON'T FORGET THE POST CODE!

**Read the following text and fill in the address on the postcard.**
Corinne Papin est célibataire et elle habite à Pau dans le Sud-Ouest de la France. Elle a un appartement au n° 3 de la place de la République. Le numéro de code postal de Pau est le 64000.

| | |
|---|---|
| *Paris, le 2 novembre 19..*<br><br>*Salut Corinne !*<br>*Tu vas bien ?*<br>*Moi, ça va très bien !*<br>*Je suis en vacances à Nice.*<br>*Amitiés,*<br>*François* | (1) ........................................<br>(2) ..................................<br>(3) ........................<br>(4) ................. |

**Key to exercise :**

1. Mademoiselle Corinne Papin.
2. 3, Place de la République.
3. 64000 Pau.
4. France.

## RENDEZ-VOUS À PARIS

*Paris, le 2 juillet,*

*Chers amis,*

*Que se passe-t-il ? Nous n'avons pas de nouvelles. Quels sont vos projets ? Quand arrivez-vous à Paris ? Quel jour ? À quelle heure ?*

*Nous, nous partons en vacances le 5 août. Mais avant nous attendons votre visite. Merci de téléphoner ou d'écrire rapidement.*

*Amitiés,*

*Sylvie et Daniel*

### PRONUNCIATION

| | | |
|---|---|---|
| **Le 2 juillet** | [lədøʒɥijɛ] | ler dur zhweeyeh |
| **Chers amis** | [ʃɛRzami] | shehr zahmee |
| **Que se passe-t-il ?** | [kəspastil] | kerser pahssteel |
| **À quelle heure ?** | [akɛlœR] | ah kehl urr |
| **Le 5 août** | [ləsɛ̃kut] | ler sang koot |

## RENDEZ-VOUS IN PARIS

Paris, 2nd July,

Dear Friends,
What's happening ? We haven't heard from you*. What are your plans ? When are you arriving in Paris ? What day ? At what time ? We're going on holiday on 5th August*. But we're expecting you to visit before then*. Please 'phone or write soon.
Lots of love,
Sylvie and Daniel

## GRAMMAR

### Verbs :

**Nous partons** → present indicative of **partir**
**Nous attendons** → present indicative of **attendre**
Note that the present tense in French can be used to express future actions (as in English) : **Quand arrivez-vous ? Nous partons le 5 août.**

### Disjunctive pronouns... and the present indicative of the verb avoir :

**moi, j'ai / toi, tu as / lui, il a / elle, elle a / nous, nous avons / vous, vous avez / eux, ils ont / elles, elles ont.**
The disjunctive pronouns in these examples are used to give added emphasis to the subject.

### The negative construction :

The indefinite article changes to **de** or **d'** in the negative.

| | | | | |
|---|---|---|---|---|
| nous avons | un ami<br>une voiture<br>des nouvelles | → | nous n'avons pas | **d'**ami<br>**de** voiture<br>**de** nouvelles |

Note that **de** becomes **d'** before words beginning with a vowel or silent **h**.

***Quel*** agrees in number and gender with the noun it replaces or qualifies.

Un jour → **Quel** jour ? une heure → À **quelle** heure ? des projets → **Quels** sont vos projets ? des amies → **Quelles** amies ?

## EXERCISES

### 1. *Complete with the appropriate disjunctive pronouns*

......, je parle français. ......, vous connaissez Paris. ......, il travaille à Paris. ......, nous sommes en vacances. ......, elle est anglaise. ......, elles ont des amis.

### 2. *Put into the negative form*

Il connaît un Français → Il ne connaît pas de Français.
Nous avons une voiture. → ..........................................................
Elles ont des projets. → ..............................................................
J'ai une amie. → .......................................................................
Vous attendez des nouvelles. → ...................................................

### 3. *Complete with* quel, quels, quelle *or* quelles

...... amie ? ...... profession ? ...... vacances ? ...... amis ? ...... projet ?

### 4. *Translate into English*

Que se passe-t-il ? Nous n'avons pas d'amis. Quand partez-vous en vacances ? Nous attendons des amis. Merci de téléphoner.

## VOCABULARY

quand : when
quel : what
avant : before
tout : all
rapidement : quickly

une minute → a minute
une matinée → a morning
un après-midi → an afternoon
un jour → a day
une semaine → a week
un mois → a month
un an → a year



**Key to exercises**

1. Moi, je... / Vous, vous... / Lui, il... / Nous, nous... / Elle, elle... / Elles, elles...
2. Nous n'avons pas de voiture. / Elles n'ont pas de projets. / Je n'ai pas d'amie. / Vous n'attendez pas de nouvelles.
3. Quelle / quelle / quelles / quels / quel
4. What's happening ? We haven't any friends. When are you going on holiday? We are expecting some friends. Please 'phone.

## VARIATIONS

**Pour interroger sur le moment :**

Tu viens quand ?
Vous partez à quelle date ?
Tu arrives quel jour ?
Vous venez à quelle heure ?

***Asking when :***

*When are you coming ?*
*What date are you leaving ?*
*What day are you arriving ?*
*What time are you coming ?*

**Pour informer sur le moment :**

Je viens à huit heures.
Nous partons le 2 (mai).
J'arrive mardi.

***Saying when :***

*I'm coming at 8 o'clock.*
*We're leaving on the 2nd (May).*
*I'm arriving on Tuesday.*

**Pour demander la date :**

Nous sommes quel jour ?
On est quel jour ?

***Asking the date :***

*What day is it today ?*

**Pour donner la date :**

Nous sommes mardi (9).
On est le 1er (premier),
le 2 (deux) (décembre) (1990).

***Giving the date :***

*It's Tuesday (the 9th).*
*It's the 1st (first),*
*the 2nd (second)*
*(of December) (1990).*

**Pour demander l'heure :**

Quelle heure est-il ?
Vous avez/tu as l'heure ?

***Asking the time :***

*What time is it ?*
*Do you have the time ?*

**Pour donner l'heure :**

Il est quatorze heures trente.

***Giving the time :***

*It's 2.30 p.m.*

## SAY IT IN FRENCH

***You're in Paris and you're writing a postcard to a friend :***

1. Write today's date.
2. Begin your letter with a friendly greeting.
3. Ask him/her what date he/she is arriving.
4. Ask what time he/she is arriving at the station.

**Possible answers :**

1. Paris, le ... ... 19.. / 2. Cher/chère ... / 3. Tu viens quand ? / 4. Tu arrives à quelle heure ?

## LE TEMPS QUI PASSE...

### JANVIER

| | | | | | |
|---|---|---|---|---|---|
| D | | 6 | 13 | 20 | 27 |
| L | | 7 | 14 | 21 | 28 |
| M | **1** | 8 | 15 | 22 | 29 |
| M | 2 | 9 | 16 | 23 | 30 |
| J | 3 | 10 | 17 | 24 | 31 |
| V | 4 | 11 | 18 | 25 | |
| S | 5 | 12 | 19 | 26 | |

### FEVRIER

| | | | | | |
|---|---|---|---|---|---|
| D | | 3 | 10 | 17 | 24 |
| L | | 4 | 11 | 18 | 25 |
| M | | 5 | 12 | 19 | 26 |
| M | | 6 | 13 | 20 | 27 |
| J | | 7 | 14 | 21 | 28 |
| V | 1 | 8 | 15 | 22 | |
| S | 2 | 9 | 16 | 23 | |

### MARS

| | | | | | | |
|---|---|---|---|---|---|---|
| D | | 3 | 10 | 17 | 24 | **31** |
| L | | 4 | 11 | 18 | 25 | |
| M | | 5 | 12 | 19 | 26 | |
| M | | 6 | 13 | 20 | 27 | |
| J | | 7 | 14 | 21 | 28 | |
| V | 1 | 8 | 15 | 22 | 29 | |
| S | 2 | 9 | 16 | 23 | 30 | |

### AVRIL

| | | | | | |
|---|---|---|---|---|---|
| D | | 7 | 14 | 21 | 28 |
| L | **1** | 8 | 15 | 22 | 29 |
| M | 2 | 9 | 16 | 23 | 30 |
| M | 3 | 10 | 17 | 24 | |
| J | 4 | 11 | 18 | 25 | |
| V | 5 | 12 | 19 | 26 | |
| S | 6 | 13 | 20 | 27 | |

### MAI

| | | | | | |
|---|---|---|---|---|---|
| D | | 5 | 12 | **19** | 26 |
| L | | 6 | 13 | **20** | 27 |
| M | | 7 | 14 | 21 | 28 |
| M | **1** | **8** | 15 | 22 | 29 |
| J | 2 | **9** | 16 | 23 | 30 |
| V | 3 | 10 | 17 | 24 | 31 |
| S | 4 | 11 | 18 | 25 | |

### JUIN

| | | | | | | |
|---|---|---|---|---|---|---|
| D | | 2 | 9 | 16 | 23 | 30 |
| L | | 3 | 10 | 17 | 24 | |
| M | | 4 | 11 | 18 | 25 | |
| M | | 5 | 12 | 19 | 26 | |
| J | | 6 | 13 | 20 | 27 | |
| V | | 7 | 14 | 21 | 28 | |
| S | 1 | 8 | 15 | 22 | 29 | |

### JUILLET

| | | | | | |
|---|---|---|---|---|---|
| D | | 7 | **14** | 21 | 28 |
| L | 1 | 8 | 15 | 22 | 29 |
| M | 2 | 9 | 16 | 23 | 30 |
| M | 3 | 10 | 17 | 24 | 31 |
| J | 4 | 11 | 18 | 25 | |
| V | 5 | 12 | 19 | 26 | |
| S | 6 | 13 | 20 | 27 | |

### AOUT

| | | | | | |
|---|---|---|---|---|---|
| D | | 4 | 11 | 18 | 25 |
| L | | 5 | 12 | 19 | 26 |
| M | | 6 | 13 | 20 | 27 |
| M | | 7 | 14 | 21 | 28 |
| J | 1 | 8 | **15** | 22 | 29 |
| V | 2 | 9 | 16 | 23 | 30 |
| S | 3 | 10 | 17 | 24 | 31 |

### SEPTEMBRE

| | | | | | |
|---|---|---|---|---|---|
| D | 1 | 8 | 15 | 22 | 29 |
| L | 2 | 9 | 16 | 23 | 30 |
| M | 3 | 10 | 17 | 24 | |
| M | 4 | 11 | 18 | 25 | |
| J | 5 | 12 | 19 | 26 | |
| V | 6 | 13 | 20 | 27 | |
| S | 7 | 14 | 21 | 28 | |

### OCTOBRE

| | | | | | |
|---|---|---|---|---|---|
| D | | 6 | 13 | 20 | 27 |
| L | | 7 | 14 | 21 | 28 |
| M | 1 | 8 | 15 | 22 | 29 |
| M | 2 | 9 | 16 | 23 | 30 |
| J | 3 | 10 | 17 | 24 | 31 |
| V | 4 | 11 | 18 | 25 | |
| S | 5 | 12 | 19 | 26 | |

### NOVEMBRE

| | | | | | |
|---|---|---|---|---|---|
| D | | 3 | 10 | 17 | 24 |
| L | | 4 | **11** | 18 | 25 |
| M | | 5 | 12 | 19 | 26 |
| M | | 6 | 13 | 20 | 27 |
| J | | 7 | 14 | 21 | 28 |
| V | **1** | 8 | 15 | 22 | 29 |
| S | 2 | 9 | 16 | 23 | 30 |

### DECEMBRE

| | | | | | |
|---|---|---|---|---|---|
| D | 1 | 8 | 15 | 22 | 29 |
| L | 2 | 9 | 16 | 23 | 30 |
| M | 3 | 10 | 17 | 24 | 31 |
| M | 4 | 11 | 18 | **25** | |
| J | 5 | 12 | 19 | 26 | |
| V | 6 | 13 | 20 | 27 | |
| S | 7 | 14 | 21 | 28 | |

## TIME FLIES...

### PRONUNCIATION

| | | |
|---|---|---|
| **Lundi** | [lɛ̃di] | langdee |
| **Mardi** | [maRdi] | mahrdee |
| **Mercredi** | [mɛRkRədi] | mehrkrerdee |
| **Jeudi** | [ʒødi] | zhurdee |
| **Vendredi** | [vɑ̃dRədi] | vahngdrerdee |
| **Samedi** | [samdi] | sahmdee |
| **Dimanche** | [dimɑ̃ʃ] | deemahngsh |

### EXERCISES

***1. Look at the calendar and complete the following sentences***

Le 31 janvier est un ..................................
Le 12 mai est un ........................................
Le 8 avril est un .........................................
Le 15 juin est un .......................................
Le 25 décembre est un ..............................

***2. Write out the following dates in full***

3.5.1953 → le trois mai mille neuf cent cinquante-trois
12.8.1993 → ..........................................................................
27.9.1993 → ..........................................................................
15.12.1994 → ..........................................................................
9.4.1995 → ..........................................................................



**Key to exercises :**

1. jeudi - dimanche - lundi - samedi - mercredi.
2. le douze août mille neuf cent quatre-ving-douze - le vingt-sept septembre mille neuf cent quatre-vingt-treize - le quinze décembre mille neuf cent quatre-vingt-quatorze - le neuf avril mille neuf cent quatre-vingt-quinze.

« Jeter l'argent par les fenêtres »

*« Throwing money down the drain »*

## DID YOU KNOW?

In hotels, restaurants and virtually all shops, you can pay by *chèque* (cheque), which is the most common way of paying, by *carte de crédit* (credit card) or *en espèces* (in cash). Banknotes in circulation have the following denominations : 20, 50, 100, 200, and 500 francs and there are coins for 5, 10, 20 and 50 centimes (100 centimes = 1 franc) and for 1, 2, 5 and 10 francs.

The French are proud of their postal service. There's a *bureau de poste* (post office) in every town and village. You can go there to use the telephone, to send and receive mail (*Poste restante*) and even open a current account.

**A group of tourists come to Paris but they are all interested in different things. Help them to have a pleasant stay by advising them what to do.**

**1. A painter, interested in 19th century Impressionist paintings, should visit...**

a) Le Louvre  b) Le musée d'Orsay  c) Le Centre Pompidou

**2. A scientist would be happy to spend a day at...**

a) La Cité des Sciences et de l'Industrie de La Villette

b) La Défense  c) Le Forum des Halles

**3. A historian, interested in the French revolution, should go to...**

a) La Bastille  b) Les Invalides  c) Montmartre

**4. The ladies want to see the latest fashions. They should go to...**

a) Le Marché aux Puces  b) Les Grands Magasins

c) Le Faubourg St-Honoré

**5. If they want to have an excellent evening ou together, they should go to...**

a) Le Sénat  b) L'Arc de Triomphe  c) Le Moulin Rouge

***Answers:***

**1.b.** The musée d'Orsay houses an excellent collection of 19th century art in a converted railway station. The other two museums exhibit works of art from before (Louvre) and after (Centre Pompidou) that period.

**2.a.** The La Villette museum of science and industry is a "must" for people interested in the latest scientific developments and their industrial applications... La Défense is the business district and the Forum des Halles is a large underground shopping centre in the heart of Paris.

**3.a.** The Bastille, site of the infamous château stormed during the Revolution... The Invalides contains Napoleon's remains. Montmartre, on its hill overlooking Paris, is famous for its street artists.

**4.c, possibly b.** The Faubourg St-Honoré is home to many famous French fashion designers. For fashion at more accessible prices, try the different Grand Magasins (Department Stores). The Marché aux puces, or Flea Market, is fascinating... but hardly "haute couture"!

**5.c.** The Moulin Rouge is famous worldwide for its cabaret. The Senate is certainly much more staid! The Arc de Triomphe is beautiful lit-up at night but few people would want to spend an evening there...

## ■ ENVOI URGENT !

— Un timbre, s'il vous plaît.
— Pour une lettre ou pour une carte postale ?
— Une carte postale.
— C'est pour quel pays ?
— L'Italie.
— Alors, mettez un timbre à deux francs cinquante.

— Je voudrais envoyer un télégramme en Allemagne.
— Tenez, utilisez un imprimé, et surtout laissez une case blanche entre les mots.
— C'est combien le mot ?
— Trois francs, mademoiselle.

### PRONUNCIATION

| | | |
|---|---|---|
| **l'Italie** | [litali] | leetahlee |
| **En Allemagne** | [ɑ̃nalmaɲ] | ahng nahlmahñ |
| **C'est combien ?** | [sɛkɔ̃bjɛ̃] | seh kawnhbyang |
| **Trois francs** | [trwafrɑ̃] | trwah frahng |

## ■ URGENT PACKAGE !

— A stamp, please*.
— For a letter or a postcard ?
— A postcard.
— Where's it going ?
— To Italy.
— Put a 2.50-franc stamp on it, then.
...
— I'd like to send a telegram to Germany.
— Here, take a form but above all, leave a blank space between the words.
— How much is it per word*?
— Three francs, Miss.

## GRAMMAR

### ■ *Verbs :*

**Mettez** → imperative of the verb **mettre**

### ■ *The imperative is derived from the present indicative*

| present indicative | | imperative | negative imperative |
|---|---|---|---|
| tu utilises | → | utilise ! | n'utilise pas ! |
| nous utilisons | → | utilisons ! | n'utilisons pas ! |
| vous utilisez | → | utilisez ! | n'utilisez pas ! |

Note that for Group 1 verbs only the **s** of the first person of the imperative disappears.

### ■ En, au, aux, à *before the name of a country, city or geographical place :*

**En** is used before the names of feminine countries (or geographical places) and all names beginning with a vowel.

La Grèce → **en** Grèce L'Italie → **en** Italie

**Au** is used before the names of masculine countries (or geographical places)

Le Portugal → **au** Portugal

**Aux** is used before the names of plural countries (or geographical places)

Les États-Unis → **aux** États-Unis Les Antilles → **aux** Antilles

**À** is used before the names of cities: **à** Paris, **à** Rome,

Be careful not to confuse **ou** : or and **où** : where. → **où** indicates place or time.

## EXERCISES

### 1. *Complete the following sentences with* en, au, aux, à *(Consult the vocabulary)*

Il habite ... Berlin, ... Allemagne. Nous allons ... Rome, ... Italie. Je vais ... Nice, ... France. Elle va ... Londres, ... Angleterre. J'habite ... New York, ... États-Unis.

### 2. *Put into the negative imperative form. (If necessary, consult the present tense of the verbs at the end of the book)*

aller → ne va pas, n'allons pas, n'allez pas.
écouter → ..................., ..................., ...................
partir → ..................., ..................., ...................
venir → ..................., ..................., ...................
attendre → ..................., ..................., ...................

### 3. *Translate into French*

A form, please. I'd like to send a letter to Spain. Fill in the telegram. Above all, put a stamp.

## VOCABULARY

ou : or — où : where
encore : again — pour : for
combien : how much, how many
surtout : above all, especially
entre : between

le facteur → the postman

une enveloppe → an envelope
un mandat → a money order
international → international
le destinataire → the addressee
l'expéditeur → the sender
la signature → the signature
signer → to sign

**Key to exercises :**

1. à Berlin, en Allemagne / à Rome, en Italie / à Nice, en France / à Londres, en Angleterre / à New York, aux États-Unis.
2. n'écoute pas, n'écoutons pas, n'écoutez pas / ne pars pas, ne partons pas, ne partez pas / ne viens pas, ne venons pas, ne venez pas / n'attends pas, n'attendons pas, n'attendez pas.
3. Un imprimé, s'il vous plaît. Je voudrais envoyer une lettre en Espagne. Remplissez le télégramme. Surtout mettez un timbre.

## VARIATIONS

| | |
|---|---|
| **Pour demander une information :** | ***Asking for information :*** |
| Tu pars quand en vacances ?<br>Vous allez où ? | *When are you going on holiday ?*<br>*Where are you going ?* |
| **Pour dire que vous ne savez pas :** | ***Saying that you do not know :*** |
| Je ne sais pas (encore). | *I don't know (yet).* |
| **Pour proposer un conseil :** | ***Offering advice :*** |
| Tu veux un bon conseil ? | *Do you want some good advice ?* |
| Vous voulez mon avis ? | *Do you want my opinion ?* |
| **Pour donner un conseil :** | ***Giving advice :*** |
| Utilisez le service Chronopost !<br>Allez en Europe !<br>Pars en train/en avion/en bateau!<br>Partez en janvier/en août ! | *Use the Chronopost service!*<br>*Go to Europe!*<br>*Go by train/plane/boat!*<br>*Go in January/in August!* |
| **Pour accepter un conseil :** | ***Accepting advice :*** |
| D'accord, c'est une bonne idée.<br>Oui, c'est vrai, vous avez raison. | *Okay, that's a good idea.*<br>*Yes, that's true, you're right.* |
| **Pour refuser un conseil :** | ***Refusing advice :*** |
| Ah non, c'est cher ! / loin ! / difficile ! | *Oh no, it's expensive! / far! / difficult!* |

## SAY IT IN FRENCH

***One of your friends wants to send a parcel abroad:***

1. Offer him some advice.
2. Ask him where the parcel is going.
3. Advise him to use the Chronopost service.
4. Tell him not to forget the stamp.



**Possible answers :**

1. Tu veux mon avis ? 2. C'est pour quel pays, ce paquet ? 3. Utilise le service Chronopost. 4. Surtout n'oublie pas le timbre.

## VA FAIRE LES COURSES !

*Mon chéri,*

*S'il te plaît, va faire les courses. Moi, je n'ai pas le temps !*

*Il faut du pain, de la viande, de la charcuterie, du fromage, de l'eau et des fruits.*

*Prends :*

*À la boulangerie : 2 baguettes et un pain complet.*

*À la boucherie : 2 biftecks*

*À la charcuterie : 4 tranches de jambon et un peu de pâté*

*À l'épicerie : un camembert, 3 grandes bouteilles d'eau minérale et 1 kilo de pommes*

*N'oublie pas de prendre assez d'argent et... n'achète pas trop de bonbons !*

*Grosses bises*

***Maman***

## PRONUNCIATION

| | | |
|---|---|---|
| **À la boulangerie** | [alabulɑ̃ʒri] | ah lah boolahngzherree |
| **Deux baguettes** | [døbagɛt] | dur bahgeht |
| **Un peu de pâté** | [ɛ̃pødpate] | ang pur der pahtay |
| **N'oublie pas** | [nublipa] | nooblee pah |
| **Trop de bonbons** | [trodbɔ̃bɔ̃] | troa der bawngbawng |

## ■ GO AND DO THE SHOPPING !

Darling,

Please, go and do the shopping. I haven't got the time!
We need* some bread, some meat, something from the delicatessen, some cheese, water and fruit.
Get*:
at the baker's : two sticks of French bread and a wholemeal loaf*.
at the butcher's : 2 steaks.
at the delicatessen : 4 slices of ham and a little bit of pâté.
at the grocer's : one camembert cheese, 3 large bottles of mineral water and 1 kilo of apples.
Don't forget to take enough money and ... don't buy too many* sweets !

Big kiss,
Mummy

## GRAMMAR

### ▮ *Verbs :*

**Il faut** → present indicative of the impersonal verb **falloir**

### ▮ *Partitive articles :*

Partitive articles are used when talking of a quantity that is not defined precisely (compare with **some** in English).

| | **singular** | **plural** |
|---|---|---|
| **masculine** | du pain | des bonbons |
| | de l'argent | des aliments |
| **feminine** | de la viande | des tranches |
| | de l'eau | des oranges |

Note that the partitive article changes in the negative (**any** in English) :
Nous n'avons pas **de** pain. Il ne veut pas **de** fruits.
Il n'y a pas **d'**eau.

### ▮ *Adverbs of quantity :*

We can use the following expressions to estimate a quantity :
**assez de** : enough
**beaucoup de** : much/many/a lot of
**un peu de** : a little
**trop de** : too much/many

## EXERCISES

### 1. Complete using the appropriate partitive articles

Pour faire un bon repas il faut ...... charcuterie, ...... pain, ...... viande, ...... fromage, ...... fruits et ...... café.

### 2. Where can you buy the following food ?

*légumes, pain, jambon, viande, baguette, fruits, pâté, bifteck*

À la boucherie : de la viande et un bifteck.
À la boulangerie : ..................................................................
À la charcuterie : ..................................................................
À l'épicerie : ..................................................................

### 3. Complete the following sentences using **un peu de (–), assez de (+), beaucoup de (++), trop de (+++)**

J'achète (–) ......... viande. → J'achète un peu de viande.
Il prend (++) ......... fromage. Tu as (+) ......... argent. Elle veut (+++) ......... bonbons. Il faut (–) ......... eau.

### 4. Translate into English

Achète beaucoup de fromage ! Tu n'as pas le temps. Il faut de l'argent. Je vais faire les courses. Demande de l'eau !

## VOCABULARY

s'il te plaît : please (intimate form)

s'il vous plaît : please (polite form)

il faut : have to, be needed

les magasins → the shops
la pâtisserie → cake shop
les aliments → food
le sucre → sugar
le sel → salt
une boîte → a tin



**Key to exercises :**

1. de la charcuterie, du pain, de la viande, du fromage, des fruits et du café.
2. du pain et une baguette - du jambon et du pâté - des fruits et des légumes.
3. beaucoup de fromage / assez d'argent / trop de bonbons / peu d'eau.
4. Buy a lot of cheese! You haven't got the time. We need some money. I'm going to do the shopping. Ask for some water!

## VARIATIONS

**Dans les magasins :**

*In the shops :*

**Pour dire ce que vous voulez :**

*Saying what you want :*

Donnez-moi une boîte de sardines !
*Give me a tin of sardines !*

Je voudrais deux cents grammes de ...
*I'd like 200 grams of ...*

Il me faut un paquet de lessive.
*I need a packet of soap powder.*

**Pour demander le prix de quelque chose :**

***Asking the price of something :***

Combien coûte le kilo de ... ?
*How much does a kilo of ... cost ?*

Combien vaut le litre de ... ?
*How much is a litre of ... ?*

Ça coûte/fait combien ?
*How much does that cost / come to ?*

C'est combien ?
*How much is it ?*

**Pour exprimer votre accord :**

***Agreeing to buy something :***

C'est (très) bien.
*Very well.*

C'est bon, je le prends.
*That's fine, I'll take it.*

**Pour exprimer votre désaccord :**

***Refusing to buy something :***

Non, c'est (trop/très) cher.
*No, it's (too/very) expensive.*

## SAY IT IN FRENCH

***You are in France with three friends and you are preparing the shopping list :***

1. Say that you haven't got a lot of money.
2. Make a list of things you need at the grocer's.
3. Say that you also need to buy some bread.
4. You don't want to buy any meat : it's too expensive !

**Possible answers :**

1. Nous n'avons pas beaucoup d'argent. 2. à l'épicerie : une boîte de sardines, du fromage, des fruits et de l'eau minérale. 3. Il faut aussi prendre du pain. 4. Non, pas de viande. C'est trop cher !

## AUSSITÔT DIT, AUSSITÔT FAIT

— Allô, Paul ? Bonjour, c'est Sylvie. Dis, ça vous plairait de venir en week-end avec nous ?
— C'est gentil de penser à nous. Où est-ce que vous allez ?
— Dans les Alpes, à Chamonix.
— Super ! On part quand ?
— Demain matin. Préparez votre sac.
— Qu'est-ce qu'on prend ?
— Votre tente, vos chaussures de marche... et la caméra.
— On part comment ? Avec ma voiture ?
— Non, on tient tous dans le minibus.
— O.K. À demain.

### PRONUNCIATION

| | | |
|---|---|---|
| **Ça vous plairait ?** | [savuplɛrɛ] | sah voo plehreh |
| **C'est gentil** | [sɛʒɑ̃ti] | seh zhahngtee |
| **On part quand ?** | [ɔ̃parkɑ̃] | awng pahr kahng |
| **Qu'est-ce qu'on prend ?** | [kɛskɔ̃prɑ̃] | kehsskawng prehng |
| **On part comment ?** | [ɔ̃parkɔmɑ̃] | awng pahr kommahng |
| **À demain** | [admɛ̃] | ah dermang |

## NO SOONER SAID, THAN DONE

— Hello, Paul ? Hello, it's Sylvie. Tell me, would you like to come away with us for the weekend*?
— It's nice of you to think of us. Where are you going ?
— To the Alps. Chamonix.
— Fantastic ! When are we going ?
— Tomorrow morning. Get your bag ready.
— What shall we take*?
— Your tent, your walking shoes ... and your video camera.
— How are we going ? In my car ?
— No, we can all fit in the minibus*.
— Okay. See you tomorrow*.

## GRAMMAR

### *The interrogative forms :*

| **1. Oral** | **2. Oral and written** |
|---|---|
| On va où ? | Où est-ce qu'on va ? |
| On part quand ? | Quand est-ce qu'on part ? |
| On part comment ? | Comment est-ce qu'on part ? |
| Tu achètes quoi ? | Qu'est-ce que tu achètes ? |

### *The possessive adjective :*

Possessive adjectives tell you three things about the object(s) they qualify : the owner(s), the number and the gender of the object(s) in question.

| | | **1 possessor** | | **several possessors** | |
|---|---|---|---|---|---|
| **1 object** | **masc.** | mon | livre | notre | livre |
| | **fem.** | ma | voiture | | voiture |
| | | mon | amie | | amie |
| **several objects** | **masc.** | mes | livres | nos | livres |
| | **fem.** | | voitures | | voitures |
| | | | amies | | amies |
| **1 object** | **masc.** | ton | livre | votre | livre |
| | **fem.** | ta | voiture | | voiture |
| | | ton | amie | | amie |
| **several objects** | **masc.** | tes | livres | vos | livres |
| | **fem.** | | voitures | | voitures |
| | | | amies | | amies |

Note that before a feminine noun beginning with a vowel or silent **h**, **ma** and **ta** become **mon** and **ton** → mon amie, ton amie

## EXERCISES

### 1. Transform each question as in the example below

Vous travaillez où ? → Où est-ce que vous travaillez ?
Elle part quand ? → ..........................................................................
Tu habites où ? → ..............................................................................
Vous prenez quoi ? → ......................................................................
Je viens comment ? → ......................................................................

### 2. Complete with a possessive adjective (corresponding to the same person as the verb)

Viens avec ...... caméra. → Viens avec ta caméra.
Je prends ...... voiture. Vous téléphonez à ...... amie. Je prends ...... chaussures. Attendez ...... amis. Prenez ...... sac.

### 3. Choose a verb from the list below to complete the following sentences

*connaître, être, habiter, aimer, avoir*
Sophie ......... anglaise. Je ......... bien la France. Vous n'......... pas travailler. Vous ......... 36 ans. J'......... aux États-Unis.

### 4. Translate into French

Get your (sing.) bag ready. What shall I take ? It's kind of you to think of me. We're leaving tomorrow.

## VOCABULARY

| | |
|---|---|
| où : where<br>quand : when<br>comment : how<br><br>un pull-over → a pullover | un imperméable → a raincoat<br>un parapluie → an umbrella<br>un sac à dos → a rucksack<br>des bottes → boots<br>un appareil photo → a camera |



**Key to exercises :**
1. Quand est-ce qu'elle part ? Où est-ce que tu habites ? Qu'est-ce que vous prenez ? Comment est-ce que je viens ?
2. ma voiture / votre amie / mes chaussures / vos amis / votre sac
3. est / connais / aimez / avez / habite
4. Prépare ton sac. Qu'est-ce que je prends ? C'est gentil de penser à moi. On part demain.

## VARIATIONS

**Pour inviter :**

Ça vous plairait de dîner avec nous ?
Ça te dirait d'aller au cinéma ?

Vous voulez déjeuner avec moi ?
Je vous invite à dîner.
Je t'invite au cinéma.

***Inviting :***

*Would you like to have dinner with us ?*
*Would you like to go to the cinema ?*
*Do you want to have lunch with me ?*
*Let me invite you to dinner.*
*Let me invite you to the cinema.*

**Pour accepter :**

Bien sûr !
(D'accord) avec plaisir.
C'est super !
C'est chouette !
C'est chic !
C'est gentil de penser à moi.
C'est sympa de m'inviter.

***Accepting :***

*Of course!*
*(Alright), with pleasure.*
*That's fantastic!*
*That's great!*
*That's lovely!*
*It's nice of you to think of me.*
*It's kind of you to invite me.*

**Pour refuser une invitation :**

(Je suis) désolé(e) mais j'ai du travail.
Je regrette mais je suis occupé(e).
J'aimerais bien mais je ne peux pas.

***Refusing an invitation :***

*(I'm) sorry but I have some work to do.*
*I'm sorry but I'm busy.*
*I'd like to a lot, but I can't.*

## SAY IT IN FRENCH

***You 'phone your friend Anne to invite her to spend the Christmas holidays with you :***

1. Ask her if she'd like to go to Paris with you.
2. Tell her to get her suitcase ready.
3. Advise her to take her camera and her umbrella.
4. Tell her that you are leaving tomorrow.

**Possible answers :**

1. Ça te plairait d'aller à Paris avec moi ? 2. Prépare ta valise. 3. Prends ton appareil photo et ton parapluie. 4. On part demain.

# BILAN 2

## ■ NOW YOU KNOW HOW TO WRITE AN ADDRESS,

***1. Match.***

| | |
|---|---|
| le nom • | • Marseille |
| l'adresse • | • Paul |
| la ville • | • États-Unis |
| le pays • | • 3, rue des Victoires |
| le prénom • | • Duval |

## ■ ...HOW TO SAY 'NO' TO EVERYTHING,

***2. Put into the negative.***

Nous avons un ami → ...
Ils ont des nouvelles → ...
Je fais des projets → ...
Il y a du pain → ...
Il faut du sucre → ...

## ■ ...HOW TO MAKE *QUEL* AGREE IN NUMBER AND GENDER,

***3. Complete the following sentences with* quel, quelle, quels, quelles.**

À ..... heure ? ..... amis ! ..... vacances ! ..... nouvelles ? ..... projets ? ..... jour ?

## ■ ...HOW TO WRITE THE DATE IN FRENCH,

***4. Write out the following dates in full***

le 31.01.1940 → ...
le 2.12.1992 → ...

## ■ ...HOW TO USE THE PREPOSITIONS

***5. Complete the following sentences with* en, au, aux, à.**

J'habite ... Espagne, ... Madrid. Elle va ..... Athènes, .... Grèce. Nous partons en vacances .... Antilles. Ils sont .... Belgique, .... Bruxelles. Elle habite .... Luxembourg.

## CHECK YOUR PROGRESS

■ **...HOW TO USE PARTITIVE ARTICLES,**

***6. Complete the following sentences with* du, de la, de l' *or* des.**

Va faire les courses. Achète .... poisson, .... sucre, ..... salade, .... bière, .... café, ..... eau, ..... lait et .... tomates.

■ **...HOW TO USE POSSESSIVE ADJECTIVES,**

***7. Complete the following with the appropriate possessive adjectives.***

Attendez v... amis. Tu prends t... chaussures. Vous préparez v... sacs. Prenez v... imperméables. Téléphone à t... parents. Je te présente m... amie.

■ **...HOW TO ASK QUESTIONS.**

***8. Complete the following :***

| We say: | We write : |
|---|---|
| Vous partez quand ? | .... |
| ... | Qu'est-ce que tu aimes ? |
| Nous travaillons où ? | ... |
| ... | Comment est-ce qu'ils parlent ? |
| Elle regarde quoi ? | ... |
| ... | Quand est-ce que tu viens ? |

## KEY TO EXERCISES

1. Le nom : Duval - L'adresse : 3, rue ... - La ville : Marseille - Le pays : Les États-Unis - le prénom : Paul.
2. Nous n'avons pas d'ami - Ils n'ont pas de nouvelles - Je ne fais pas de projets - Il n'y a pas de pain - Il ne faut pas de sucre.
3. quelle - quels - quelles - quelles - quels - quel.
4. le trente et un janvier mille neuf cent quarante.
le deux décembre mille neuf cent quatre-vingt-douze.
5. en - à - à - en - aux - en - à - au.
6. du - du - de la - de la - du - de l' - du - des
7. vos - tes - vos - vos - tes - mon.
8. Quand est-ce que vous partez ? - Tu aimes quoi ? - Où est-ce que nous travaillons ? - Ils parlent comment ? - Qu'est-ce qu'elle regarde ? - Tu viens quand ?

## UNE HISTOIRE SIMPLE

Virginie est vendeuse dans un grand magasin de Paris. Elle a 35 ans et elle est mariée. Bernard, son mari, est technicien.

Comme ils habitent à Saint-Denis, dans la banlieue nord de Paris, tous les matins Virginie prend le train pour Paris. Le soir, quand ils rentrent, leurs enfants les attendent avec impatience. Mais il faut encore préparer le dîner, coucher les enfants et faire le ménage.

Toutes les semaines, Virginie et Bernard jouent au loto : ils rêvent d'abandonner leur petit appartement pour une jolie maison avec un jardin. Ils voudraient changer leur vieille voiture.

Leurs moyens sont modestes mais peut-être qu'un jour...

### PRONUNCIATION

| | | |
|---|---|---|
| **Vendeuse** | [vɑ̃døz] | vahngdurz |
| **La banlieue nord** | [labɑ̃ljønɔr] | lah bahngleeur |
| **Avec impatience** | [avɛkɛ̃pasjɑ̃s] | ahvehk angpahsyangs |
| **Mais il faut encore** | [mɛilfoɑ̃kɔr] | meh eel foa tahnkor |
| **Ils jouent au loto** | [ilʒuoloto] | eel zhoo oa loatoa |
| **Vieille voiture** | [vjɛjvwatyr] | vyehy vwahtewr |

## A SIMPLE STORY

Virginie is a sales assistant in a department store in Paris. She's 35 years old and is married. Bernard, her husband, is a technician.
As they live in Saint-Denis, in the northern suburbs of Paris, Virginie takes the train to Paris every morning. In the evening, when they arrive home, their children are happy to see them*. But they still have to get the dinner ready, put the children to bed and do the housework.
Every week, Virginie and Bernard play on the lottery. They dream of swapping their tiny flat for a lovely little house with a garden. They would also like to change their old car.
They are not very well off, but one day perhaps...

## GRAMMAR

### *Verbs :*

**Ils voudraient** → present conditional of the verb **vouloir**

### *Present conditional of* vouloir :

The present conditional of **vouloir** is used for expressing a wish or as a polite way of asking for something.

### *The possessive adjectives of the third person :*

| | | 1 possessor | several possessors |
|---|---|---|---|
| **1 object** | **masc.** | son livre | leur livre |
| | **fem.** | sa maison | leur maison |
| | | son amie | leur amie |
| **several objects** | **masc.** / **fem.** | ses livres / maisons / amies | leurs livres / maisons / amies |

Note that before a feminine word beginning with a vowel or silent **h**, **sa** becomes **son**.

## EXERCISES

### 1. Answer the questions as in the example given below

C'est la maison de Paul ? → Oui, c'est sa maison.
C'est l'amie de Virginie ? → ..........................................................
Ce sont les économies de Bernard ? → ......................................
C'est la maison de Paul et Ghislaine ? → ....................................
C'est la voiture de Paul ? → ..........................................................

### 2. Complete the following sentences using a possessive adjective

Mes amis viennent avec ...... voiture. Elle prend ...... sac. Bernard et Virginie rêvent de changer ...... appartement. Virginie couche ...... enfants. Sylvie change ...... voiture tous les ans.

### 3. Use the present conditional of the verb vouloir to express these wishes

acheter une voiture → Je voudrais acheter une voiture.
partir en voyage → ..........................................................
être riche. → ..........................................................
parler français. → ..........................................................
envoyer un télégramme. → ..........................................................

### 4. Translate into English

Nous préparons le dîner. Bernard prend le train pour Pontoise. Je suis marié et j'ai deux enfants. Virginie rêve d'avoir une maison.

## VOCABULARY

après : after
encore : still, again

le fils → son
la fille → daughter

un garçon → a boy
une fille → a girl
l'homme → man
la femme → woman



**Key to exercises :**

1. son amie / Ce sont ses économies. / leur maison / sa voiture
2. leur voiture / son sac / leur appartement / ses enfants / sa voiture
3. Je voudrais partir en voyage. Je voudrais être riche. Je voudrais parler français. Je voudrais envoyer un télégramme.
4. We're getting the dinner ready. Bernard takes the train to Pontoise. I'm married and I have two children. Virginie dreams of having a house.

## VARIATIONS

| | |
|---|---|
| **Pour parler de votre journée :** | ***Talking about your day :*** |
| Tous les matins/le matin, je vais à ... | *Every morning/in the morning, I go to ...* |
| À midi/tous les midis, je déjeune à ... | *At midday/every midday, I have lunch at ...* |
| L'après-midi/tous les après-midi, je travaille. | *In the afternoon/every afternoon, I work ...* |
| À cinq heures, je rentre. | *At five o'clock, I go home.* |
| Le soir, je dîne seul. | *In the evening, I have dinner alone.* |
| Chaque soir, je dîne en famille. | *Every evening, I have dinner with the family.* |
| **Pour parler de vos habitudes :** | ***Talking about your habits :*** |
| Tous les jours/mois/ans, je fais du sport. | *Every day/month/year, I practise sport.* |
| Toutes les semaines, je vais au théâtre. | *Every week, I go to the theatre.* |
| Tous les dimanches/week-ends, je pars. | *Every Sunday/weekend I go somewhere.* |
| **Pour exprimer un souhait :** | ***Expressing a wish :*** |
| Je voudrais changer de vie. | *I'd like to change my life*.* |
| J'aimerais partir. | *I'd like to leave.* |
| Je rêve de gagner au Loto. | *I dream of winning the lottery.* |

## SAY IT IN FRENCH

***You are talking about your life and your habits :***

1. Say that you go to the office every morning by bus.
2. Say that you always eat in the canteen at midday.
3. Say that you would like to buy a big house with a garden.
4. Say that you dream of changing your life.



**Possible answers :**

1. Tous les matins, je vais au bureau en autobus. 2. Tous les midis, je mange au restaurant. 3. J'aimerais acheter une grande maison avec un jardin. 4. Je rêve de changer de vie.

## ■ APPORTEZ-MOI L'ADDITION !

— Monsieur prendra le menu ou la carte ?

— La carte. Comme entrée vous me mettrez une salade de crudités.

— Vous devriez essayer le poisson. Il est délicieux.

— Euh... oui, c'est une bonne idée.

— Vous allez prendre du fromage ?

— Non, merci.

— Et comme dessert ?

— Aïe, je ne peux pas résister, cette tarte a l'air très appétissante.

— Alors, une tarte aux pommes... et comme boisson ?

— Je vais goûter votre vin blanc d'Alsace.

### PRONUNCIATION

| | | |
|---|---|---|
| **Vous me mettrez** | [vuməmetre] | voo mer mehtray |
| **Il est délicieux** | [ilɛdelisjø] | eel eh dayleessyur |
| **C'est une bonne idée** | [sɛtynbɔnide] | seh ewn bon eeday |
| **Et comme dessert ?** | [ekɔmdesɛR] | ay komm dehssehr |
| **Votre vin blanc** | [vɔtrəvɛ̃blɑ̃] | votr vang blahng |

## BRING ME THE BILL, PLEASE !

— Would you like the set menu or choose à la carte, sir*?
— A la carte. To start with, bring me a mixed salad*.
— You should try the fish. It's delicious.
— Oh ... yes. That's a good idea.
— Will you be having some cheese ?
— No, thank you.
— And for dessert ?
— Oh dear, I just can't resist it; this pie looks really delicious.
— One apple pie, then. And what would you like to drink ?
— I'll try some of your white Alsatian wine.

## GRAMMAR

### *Verbs :*

**Vous devriez** → present conditional of the verb **devoir**

### *Immediate future :*

The immediate future is used to refer to an action which is going to happen within a relatively short time. (*going to* in English)

### *Construction :*

Present indicative of the verb **aller** + infinitive

| | |
|---|---|
| je vais partir | nous allons goûter |
| tu vas déjeuner | vous allez parler |
| il va travailler | elles vont faire |

Note how the negative form of the immediate future is constructed : je **ne** vais **pas** partir, nous **n'**allons **pas** goûter.

### *Demonstrative adjectives :*

Demonstrative adjectives are used to designate a person or an object which we wish to identify precisely.

| | singular | | plural | |
|---|---|---|---|---|
| **masculine** | ce | restaurant | ces | restaurants |
| | cet | ami | | amis |
| **feminine** | cette | tarte | | tartes |

Note that before a masculine noun beginning with a vowel or a silent **h**, **ce** becomes **cet**.

## EXERCISES

### 1. Put into the immediate future

Elle prend du café. → Elle va prendre du café.
Je prends du poisson. Tu goûtes le vin. Christian boit du champagne. Elles aiment cette tarte. Vous mangez au restaurant.

### 2. Put into the negative

Elle va manger du fromage. Nous allons essayer le poisson. Tu vas goûter la tarte. Ils vont dîner au restaurant.

### 3. Use the appropriate demonstrative adjective to complete the following sentences

Regarde ...... enfants. Elle connaît bien ...... monsieur. Nous aimons beaucoup ...... amie. Elle travaille dans ...... restaurant. J'attends ...... ami. Vous parlez souvent à ...... personnes.

### 4. Translate into French

The fish is very good here. What do you (sing.) want for dessert ? I'm going to have some red wine. You (sing.) should try the tart.

## VOCABULARY

comme : as
tout de suite : immediately

une entrée → a starter
un plat → a main dish
une boisson → a drink
un apéritif → an aperitif
le serveur → the waiter
la serveuse → the waitress
le pourboire → the tip
une réclamation → a complaint

**Key to exercises :**

1. Je vais prendre du poisson. Tu vas goûter le vin. Christian va boire du champagne. Elles vont aimer cette tarte. Vous allez manger au restaurant.
2. Elle ne va pas manger de fromage. Nous n'allons pas essayer le poisson. Tu ne vas pas goûter la tarte. Ils ne vont pas dîner au restaurant.
3. ces enfants / ce monsieur / cette amie / ce restaurant / cet ami / ces personnes
4. Ici, le poisson est très bon. Qu'est-ce que tu veux comme dessert ? Je vais prendre du vin rouge. Tu devrais goûter la tarte.

## VARIATIONS

**Pour savoir ce que quelqu'un veut :**

Qu'est-ce que vous prenez comme entrée ?
Qu'est-ce que tu veux comme poisson ?

***Asking what someone wants :***

*What are you having as a starter ?*
*What kind of fish do you want ?*

**Pour donner votre opinion :**

Je déteste ce restaurant.
Je n'aime pas du tout ce serveur.
J'aime ce champagne.
J'aime beaucoup cette viande.
J'adore ces gâteaux.

***Giving your opinion :***

*I hate this restaurant.*
*I don't like this waiter at all.*
*I like this champagne.*
*I like this meat very much.*
*I adore these cakes.*

**Pour donner un conseil :**

Prenez/prends la soupe.
Goûtez/goûte le rôti.
Essayez/essaye le poulet.

***Giving advice :***

*Have the soup.*
*Taste the roast.*
*Try the chicken.*

**Pour accepter un conseil :**

(C'est une) bonne idée !
(D'accord) je vais essayer.

***Accepting advice :***

*(That's a) good idea.*
*(Alright), I'll try it.*

**Pour refuser un conseil :**

Non, je n'aime pas...
Non, je préfère...

***Refusing advice :***

*No, I don't like...*
*No, I prefer...*

## SAY IT IN FRENCH

***You're in a restaurant with a friend :***

1. Ask him what he's going to have as a starter.
2. Advise him to taste the fish.
3. Say that you don't like the wine at all.
4. Your friend suggests champagne. Say that he is right and add that you adore champagne.



**Possible answers :**

1. Qu'est-ce que tu vas prendre comme entrée ? 2. Tu devrais goûter le poisson. 3. Je n'aime pas du tout le vin. 4. Tu as raison. J'adore le champagne !

## HEP TAXI !

— Bonsoir, vous êtes libre ?
— Ouais.
— 7, rue de la Source à Argenteuil, s'il vous plaît.
— Oh là là, c'est en banlieue ça !
— Eh bien, prenez le périphérique, je vous indiquerai.

— Attention, vous sortirez après la Porte d'Asnières.
— Et maintenant ?
— Euh... continuez tout droit et sur la place vous tournerez à droite.

...

— Voilà, c'est ici. Je vous dois combien ?
— 150 francs au compteur... donc ça vous fait 175 francs avec le supplément bagage.

## PRONUNCIATION

| | | |
|---|---|---|
| **Je vous indiquerai.** | [ʒəvuzɛ̃dikrɛ] | zher voo zangdeekerray |
| **Et maintenant ?** | [emɛ̃tnɑ̃] | ay mangternahng |
| **Je vous dois combien ?** | [ʒəvudwakɔ̃bjɛ̃] | zher voo dway kawngbyang |
| **Le supplément** | [ləsyplemɑ̃] | ler sewplaymahng |

## HEY TAXI !

— Good evening. Are you free ?
— Yeah*.
— 7, rue de la Source in Argenteuil, please.
— Oh, dear! That's out in the suburbs!
— Take the ring road. I'll show you the way.
...
— Be careful, you'll be taking the exit after the sign "Porte d'Asnières"*!
— What now ?
— Er... go straight ahead and on the square, turn right.
...
— That's it. Here it is. How much do I owe you ?
— 150 francs on the meter ... so that comes to 175 francs with the extra charge for luggage.

## GRAMMAR

### *Verbs :*

**Vous tournerez** → future of the verb **tourner**
**Vous sortirez** → future of the verb **sortir**

### *Future of the verbs* être *and* avoir *:*

| | | | |
|---|---|---|---|
| je serai | nous serons | j'aurai | nous aurons |
| tu seras | vous serez | tu auras | vous aurez |
| il/elle/on sera | ils/elles seront | il/elle/on aura | ils/elles auront |

### *Future of Group One and Group Two verbs :*

It is easy to form the future tense of the verbs in these first two groups. Just take the infinitive and add the following endings **-ai, -as, -a, -ons, -ez, -ont** :

je parlerai, tu parleras, il parlera, nous parlerons, vous parlerez, ils parleront
je finirai, tu finiras, il finira, nous finirons, vous finirez, ils finiront

Note that the verb **aller** is irregular and does not obey this rule :
J'irai, tu iras, il ira, nous irons, vous irez, ils iront

## EXERCISES

### 1. Put the following verbs into the future

manger → nous mangerons
travailler → ils ..............
acheter → tu ..............
parler → elle ..............
habiter → j'..............
aimer → vous ..............

### 2. Complete these sentences with the verbs **avoir** or **être** in the future tense

Demain, j'.............. 27 ans. En août, nous .............. en France. Vous n'.............. pas beaucoup d'argent. Elles .............. contentes de venir. Ce .............. chouette !

### 3. Put the following sentences into the future (consult the appendix, if necessary)

Nous sommes très contents. → Nous serons très contents.
Nous avons des amis. Vous parlez français. Elle travaille dimanche. Nous n'allons pas au restaurant ce soir.

### 4. Translate into English

Sur la place, tournez à gauche. Nous habitons devant un restaurant. Il y a un supplément, vous me devez 120 F.

## VOCABULARY

voici : here is/are
avant : before
après : after
ici : here
là : there
pendant : during

la route → the road

la rue → the street
le quartier → the neighbourhood
la mairie → the town hall
la gare → the station
le pont → the bridge
1er : premier → 1st : first (masc.)



**Key to exercises :**

1. elle parlera / ils travailleront / j'habiterai / tu achèteras / vous aimerez
2. j'aurai / nous serons / vous n'aurez pas / elles seront / ce sera
3. nous aurons / vous parlerez / elle travaillera / nous n'irons pas
4. Turn left on the square. We live in front of a restaurant. There is an extra charge, you owe me 120 F.

## VARIATIONS

**Pour demander votre chemin :**

Où est la gare ?
Vous savez où est l'avenue Foch ?
Pour aller à la poste ?

**Pour dire comment faire :**

Il faut prendre à gauche.
Vous devez prendre la deuxième rue.
Tu dois prendre l'avenue.
Prenez la rue en face.
Il faut tourner à droite.
Vous devez tourner après le feu.

Tu dois tourner à gauche.
Tournez en face de ...
Il faut traverser la place.
Vous devez traverser le pont.
Traversez le parc.

C'est { tout droit. / avant l'église. / après la mairie. / devant le stade. / derrière la gare.

***Asking the way :***

*Where's the station ?*
*Do you know where avenue Foch is ?*
*How do I get to the post office?*

***Giving directions :***

*You have to go left.*
*You have to take the second street.*
*You have to take the avenue.*
*Take the street opposite.*
*You have to turn right.*
*You have to turn after the set of traffic lights.*
*You have to turn left.*
*Turn opposite the ....*
*You have to cross the square.*
*You have to cross the bridge.*
*Cross the park.*

*It's* { *straight ahead.* / *before the church.* / *after the town hall.* / *in front of the stadium.* / *behind the station.*

## SAY IT IN FRENCH

***You are giving someone directions to the station :***

1. Tell him to cross the avenue.
2. Tell him that he must turn right at the traffic lights.
3. Tell him to take boulevard de la Paix.
4. Tell him that now it's straight ahead.



**Possible answers :**

1. Traversez l'avenue. 2. Vous devez tourner au feu à droite. 3. Prenez le boulevard de la Paix. 4. Maintenant, c'est tout droit.

# On the brighter side n° 3

**« C'est pas du gâteau ! »**

***« It's not a piece of cake! »***

## *DID YOU KNOW?*



In France, most shops are open from 9 o'clock in the morning until 12 o'clock midday and from 2 to 7 in the afternoon. Banks close at about 5 o'clock p.m. Shops in the cities usually stay open at lunchtime and many food shops are open on Sunday mornings.

The French have their *petit déjeuner* (breakfast) between 7 and 10 o'clock in the morning, their *déjeuner* (lunch) between 12 and 2 o'clock p.m. and their *dîner* (dinner) between 7 and 9 o'clock p.m. ... But you can stop off in a café and have a drink and a bite to eat at any time of the day!

**The French are very proud of their food. Can you identify where the following regional specialities come from?**

| | | | |
|---|---|---|---|
| Pancakes and cider | 1 • | • A | la Provence |
| Red wines | 2 • | • B | la Bretagne |
| Foie gras and truffes | 3 • | • C | Bordeaux, le Beaujolais la Bourgogne |
| Sauerkraut and white wine | 4 • | • D | le Périgord |
| Fish soup and pastis | 5 • | • E | la Normandie |
| Camembert cheese and calvados | 6 • | • F | la Savoie |
| Cheese fondue | 7 • | • G | l'Alsace |

***Answers:*** 1.B - 2.C - 3.D - 4.G - 5.A - 6.E - 7.F

## ATTENTION AU DÉPART !

— Excusez-moi, monsieur, les guichets des grandes lignes ?
— Vous voyez les panneaux horaires au fond du hall ?
— Euh, oui, je les vois.
— Eh bien, c'est juste en dessous.

...

— Pour faire une réservation.
— Oui, combien de places ?
— Une seule, en première classe.
— C'est pour où et à quelle date ?
— Pour Marseille le 23 à 12h30.
— Compartiment fumeur ou non fumeur ?
— Non fumeur.
— 185 francs. Voilà votre billet. Vous le payez comment ? Par carte bancaire, par chèque, en espèces ?
— En espèces.

### PRONUNCIATION

| | | |
|---|---|---|
| **Excusez-moi, monsieur** | [ɛkskyzemwamøsjø] | ehxkewzay mwah mursyur |
| **Des grandes lignes** | [degrɑ̃dliɲ] | day ggrahnd leeñ |
| **Au fond du hall** | [ofɔ̃dyol] | oa fawng dew ahl |
| **Je les vois** | [ʒlɛvwa] | zher lay vwah |
| **En première classe** | [ɑ̃prəmjɛrklas] | ahng premyehr klahss |
| **En espèces ?** | [ɑ̃nɛspɛs] | ahng ehspehss |

## MIND THE DOORS, PLEASE !

— Excuse me, sir. Where's the main line ticket office*?
— Can you see the timetable display boards at the other end of the departure hall ?
— Yes, I can .
— Well, it's just underneath.
...
— I'd like to make a reservation .
— Yes. How many seats ?
— Just one, first class.
— Where are you going and on what date ?
— Marseille on the 23rd at 12.30 p.m.
— Smoking or non-smoking compartment ?
— Non-smoking.
— 185 francs. Here's your ticket. How are you paying? By banker's card, cheque or in cash ?
— In cash.

## GRAMMAR

### *Verbs :*

**Vous voyez, je vois** → present indicative of the verb **voir**
**Vous voulez** → present indicative of the verb **vouloir**

### *The direct object pronouns* le, la, les *:*

The direct object pronoun replaces an object that has already been mentioned, thus avoiding repetition.

| | singular | plural | examples |
|---|---|---|---|
| **masculine** | le | | Vous **le** payez (**le** = le billet) |
| | | les | Je **les** vois (**les** = les panneaux) |
| **feminine** | la | | Vous **la** voulez (**la** = la place) |

Note that **le** and **la** become **l'** before a verb beginning with a vowel or a silent **h**.

La radio, il **l'**écoute toute la journée.

### *Position of the pronouns* le, la, l' *and* les *in the sentence :*

a) in affirmative sentences → Je **le** prends, tu **l'**écoutes. Tu **les** écoutes.
b) in negative sentences → Je ne **le** prends pas, tu ne **l'**écoutes pas. Tu ne **les** écoutes pas.

## EXERCISES

### 1. *Complete the following sentences using* le, la, l' *or* les

La Place d'Italie ? Je ...... connais bien. / La télévision ? Je ne ...... regarde pas. / Tes amis, je ne ...... aime pas. / La radio, vous ne ...... écoutez pas. / Tes livres, je ...... prends ? / Prenez vos sacs. — Non, je ...... laisse.

### 2. *Reply in the negative*

Les livres, il les achète ? → Non, il ne les achète pas.
La musique, il l'écoute ? → ........................................................
Votre quartier, vous l'aimez beaucoup ? → ................................
Ce train, tu le prends souvent ? → ............................................
La télévision, elle la regarde ? → ..............................................

### 3. *Translate into French*

Excuse me, sir. Where are the timetable display boards ? Two first class seats, please. Here are your tickets. How are you paying ? By banker's card.

## VOCABULARY

combien : how much /how many
quand : when
pour : for
comment : how

la seconde classe → second class

le contrôleur → ticket inspector
le quai → platform
la voie → track
le départ → departure
l'arrivée → arrival
le wagon-restaurant → restaurant car
une couchette → a berth



**Key to exercises :**

1. la, la, les, l', les, les.
2. Il ne l'écoute pas. Je ne l'aime pas beaucoup. Je ne le prends pas souvent. Elle ne la regarde pas.
3. Excusez-moi, monsieur, les panneaux horaires ? Deux places en première classe, s'il vous plaît. Voilà vos billets. Vous les payez comment ? Par carte bancaire.

## VARIATIONS

**Pour attirer l'attention :**

Madame, mademoiselle, monsieur (l'agent), s'il vous plaît !
Pardon monsieur/madame/mademoiselle...

***Attracting attention :***

*Madam, Miss, Sir, (Constable), excuse me, please!*
*Excuse me, Sir, Madam, Miss ...*

**Pour demander de l'aide :**

Est-ce que vous pouvez me dire...
Vous pouvez m'indiquer le guichet...
Vous savez où est la gare ?

***Asking assistance :***

*Can you tell me ...*
*Can you show me where the ticket window is ...*
*Do you know where the station is ?*

**Pour accepter d'aider :**

Bien sûr ! C'est facile.
Mais oui ! Ce n'est pas loin.

***Agreeing to help :***

*Of course! It's easy.*
*Certainly! It's not far.*

**Pour dire que vous ne savez pas :**

Désolé, je ne suis pas d'ici.
Non, je ne sais pas.

***Saying that you don't know :***

*I'm sorry, I don't live here.*
*No, I don't know.*

**Pour acheter un billet d'avion :**

Un aller simple pour Paris, s'il vous plaît.
Un aller-retour en classe touriste/affaire.
Une place sur le vol de demain.

***Buying a plane ticket :***

*A single to Paris, please.*
*A return ticket in economy/business class.*
*A seat on tomorrow's flight.*

## SAY IT IN FRENCH

***You are telephoning Air France :***

1. You want to make a reservation for Paris,
2. You want a seat in business class, non-smoking,
3. Say that you only want a single ticket,
4. You want to take the 9.30 flight on 20th March.

**Possible answers :**

1. Je voudrais faire une réservation pour Paris. 2. Je voudrais une place en classe affaire et non fumeur. 3. Seulement un aller simple. 4. Je voudrais prendre le vol du 20 mars à 9 h 30.

## PASSEZ À LA CAISSE !

— Dépêchez-vous, on ferme.

— Ouf ! Juste à temps ! Quel est le cours du dollar ?

— Attendez, il vient juste de baisser : 5,75 F à la vente et 5,50 F à l'achat.

— Je voudrais changer 1 000 dollars.

— Ça fait 4 520 francs.

— Seulement ?

— Oui, nous prenons une commission. Vous voulez des billets de 100 ou de 500 F ?

— Donnez-moi 4 000 francs en billets de 500.

— Et le reste ?

— Deux billets de 200 et 120 F en pièces de 10 et de 5 francs, j'ai besoin de monnaie.

## PRONUNCIATION

| | | |
|---|---|---|
| **Dépêchez-vous** | [depeʃevu] | daypehshay voo |
| **Juste à temps !** | [ʒystatɑ̃] | zhewst ah tahng |
| **Seulement ?** | [sœlmɑ̃] | surlermahng |
| **Et le reste ?** | [elrɛst] | ay ler rehst |
| **J'ai besoin de monnaie** | [ʒɛbəzwɛ̃dmɔnɛ] | zhay berzwang der monneh |

## GO TO THE CASH DESK !

— Hurry up. We're closing.
— Phew ! Just in time. What's the exchange rate for the dollar ?
— Wait a minute, it's just gone down. We are selling at 5.75 and buying at 5.50.
— I would like to change 1,000 dollars.
— That comes to 4,520 francs.
— Is that all ?
— Yes. We charge a commission. Do you want 100-franc or 500-franc notes ?
— Give me 4,000 francs in 500 franc notes.
— And the rest ?
— Two two-hundred franc notes and 120 francs in ten and five franc coins. I need some loose change.

## GRAMMAR

### *Verbs :*

**Dépêchez-vous** → imperative of the verb **se dépêcher**

### *Reflexive verbs :*

Reflexive verbs are conjugated with a reflexive pronoun : **me, te, se, nous, vous**

| | | |
|---|---|---|
| Conjugation : | je **me** lave | nous **nous** lavons |
| | tu **te** laves | vous **vous** lavez |
| | il/elle/on **se** lave | ils/elles **se** lavent |

Negative construction : je ne me lave pas

| **Affirmative imperative :** | **Negative imperative :** |
|---|---|
| lave-**toi** | ne **te** lave pas |
| lavons-**nous** | ne **nous** lavons pas |
| lavez-**vous** | ne **vous** lavez pas |

### *The recent past :*

The recent past is used to express an action which has just occurred.

Il **vient de** baisser

Construction → **venir de** (in the present) + infinitive

| | |
|---|---|
| je **viens de** me laver | nous **venons de** travailler |
| tu **viens de** partir | vous **venez de** sortir |
| il/elle/on **vient de** manger | ils/elles **viennent de** parler |

**Negative construction :** nous **ne** venons **pas** de travailler

## EXERCISES

### 1. Conjugate the following reflexive verbs in the present tense

se regarder → je .............. il .............. vous ..............
se dépêcher → je .............. vous .............. ils ..............

### 2. Answer the following questions using the imperative

Je me lève ? → Oui, lève-toi.
Je me réveille ? → Oui, ........... Nous nous dépêchons ? → Oui, ................. Je me lave ? → Non, ............. Nous nous peignons ? → Non, ................

### 3. Put into the recent past

Je travaille. Nous prenons le train. Ils téléphonent à leurs enfants. Elles prennent leur petit déjeuner.

### 4. Translate into English

Paul vient de téléphoner. Je voudrais 1000 francs en billets de 100. Donnez-moi 50 francs en pièces de 10 F. Je n'ai pas de monnaie.

## VOCABULARY

| | |
|---|---|
| juste : just | un chèque de voyage → a traveller's cheque |
| la caisse → cash desk | une carte de crédit → a credit card |
| un compte → an account | un emprunt → a loan (borrowed) |
| un chèque → a cheque | un prêt → a loan (lent) |

**Key to exercises :**

1. Je me regarde, il se regarde, vous vous regardez / je me dépêche, vous vous dépêchez, ils se dépêchent.
2. Oui, réveille-toi. Oui, dépêchons-nous. Non, ne te lave pas. Non, ne vous peignez pas.
3. Je viens de travailler. Nous venons de prendre le train. Ils viennent de téléphoner à leurs enfants. Elles viennent de prendre leur petit déjeuner.
4. Paul has just telephoned. I'd like 1,000 francs in 100-franc notes. Give me 50 francs in 10 franc coins. I haven't got any change.

## VARIATIONS

**Pour faire des reproches :**
**a. sur le manque de ponctualité :**

Il est très tard.
Il est trop tôt.
Il est temps !
Regarde l'heure !
Vous êtes toujours en retard !

**b. sur le manque d'attention :**

Vous ne faites jamais attention.
Tu pourrais écouter.
Vous pourriez faire attention.
Vous oubliez toujours tout.

**Pour présenter des excuses :**

Excusez-moi.
Je suis désolé(e).
Pardonnez-moi.
Je vais faire attention.

***Reproaching someone :***
***a. for lack of punctuality :***

*It's very late.*
*It's too early.*
*It's high time!*
*Look at the time!*
*You're always late!*

***b. for lack of attention :***

*You never pay attention.*
*You might listen.*
*You might pay attention.*
*You always forget everything.*

***Apologizing :***

*Excuse me.*
*I'm sorry.*
*Forgive me.*
*I'll pay attention in future.*

## SAY IT IN FRENCH

***This evening, you're going out with a friend who's keeping you waiting :***

1. Tell him to hurry up.
2. Tell him that he is always late.
3. Say that the taxi has just arrived.
4. Ask him if he has change for the taxi.



**Possible answers :**

1. Dépêche-toi ! 2. Tu es toujours en retard ! 3. Le taxi vient d'arriver. 4. Tu as de la monnaie pour le taxi ?

## REVUE DE PRESSE

Sondage "Le Monde" :
1 Français sur 3 a regardé
l'émission *7 sur 7* dimanche dernier.

**Les auditeurs ont choisi :**
**"France Inter" est bien la station la plus écoutée.**

Télévision :
La nouvelle chaîne culturelle a séduit les téléspectateurs.

**FR3 a changé ses programmes en raison d'une grève des journalistes.**

## PRONUNCIATION



| | | |
|---|---|---|
| **L'émission** | [lemisjɔ̃] | laymeesyawng |
| **Les auditeurs** | [lezoditœr] | lay zoadeeturr |
| **La 5$^{e}$ chaîne** | [lasɛ̃kjɛmʃɛn] | lah sangkyehm shehn |
| **Ses programmes** | [seprɔgram] | say prograhm |

## PRESS REVIEW

"Le Monde" Opinion Poll : 1 out of 3 French people watched the programme "7 sur 7" last Sunday.

The listeners' have made their choice : France Inter is the most popular radio station.

Television : The new cultural channel has won over the T.V. viewers.

FR3 has changed its programmes owing to a strike by journalists.

## GRAMMAR

### *The Perfect tense :*

The Perfect tense is used to refer to a completed action carried out in the past.

**Conjugation 1.**

Present of **avoir** + past participle :

| | |
|---|---|
| j'ai fait | nous avons fait |
| tu as fait | vous avez fait |
| il/elle/on a fait | ils/elles ont fait |

**Formation of the past participle :**

a) For Group 1 verbs, the final r of the infinitive is dropped and an acute accent is added to the final **-e**

regarder → regardé

b) For Group 2 verbs the final **r** is dropped

choisir → choisi

c) For Group 3 verbs, consult the appendix !

**Negative construction :** Je **n'**ai **pas** fait

### *The Perfect tense of the verbs* avoir *and* être *:*

J'ai eu, tu as eu, il/elle/on a eu, nous avons eu, vous avez eu, ils/elles ont eu **Negative :** je **n'**ai **pas** eu

J'ai été, tu as été, il/elle/on a été, nous avons été, vous avez été, ils/elles ont été **Negative :** je **n'**ai **pas** été

## EXERCISES

### 1. *Write the past participle of the following verbs and then conjugate them in the Perfect tense, as shown in the example*

manger → mangé → elle a mangé
oublier → ......... → tu ......... / jouer → ......... → J'.........
tourner → ......... → vous ......... / laver → ......... → ils .........

### 2. *Put the following sentences into the Perfect tense using the following past participles :* **voulu, mis, pris, attendu, ouvert**

J'ouvre la porte. Tu veux un livre. Il attend toute la journée. Nous prenons du café. Ils mettent leurs chaussures.

### 3. *Reply in the negative, as in the example*

Il a regardé l'émission ? → Non, il n'a pas regardé l'émission.
Elle a acheté un livre ? → ..........................................................
Tu as écouté l'émission ? → ......................................................
Ils ont demandé un café ? → ......................................................
Vous avez changé de chaîne ? → ...............................................

### 4. *Translate into French*

I watched TV. We listened to the radio. The journalists went on strike (faire la grève).

## VOCABULARY

contre : against
définitivement : finally, definitively

un journal / des journaux → a newspaper/newspapers

un journaliste → a journalist
la presse → the press
un quotidien → a daily
un hebdomadaire → a weekly
une revue → a review

**Key to exercises :**

1. oublié → tu as oublié / joué → j'ai joué / tourné → vous avez tourné / lavé → ils ont lavé.
2. J'ai ouvert. Tu as voulu. Il a attendu. Nous avons pris. Ils ont mis.
3. Non, elle n'a pas acheté de livre. Non, je n'ai pas écouté l'émission. Non, ils n'ont pas demandé de café. Non, nous n'avons pas changé de chaîne.
4. J'ai regardé la télé. Nous avons écouté la radio. Les journalistes ont fait la grève.

## VARIATIONS

| Pour annoncer une nouvelle : | *Announcing a piece of news :* |
|---|---|
| **a. De manière officielle.** | ***a. In an official manner.*** |
| Je vous annonce que la France a … | *I declare that France has.....* |
| Nous vous informons que … | *We inform you that ...* |
| **b. Avec une certaine réserve.** | ***b. WIth some uncertainty :*** |
| Il paraît que … | *It seems that....* |
| On dit que … | *It is said that.....* |
| **c. De manière informelle.** | ***c. In an informal manner :*** |
| Vous savez que … | *You know that ..... ?* |
| Tu sais que … | *You know that ... ?* |
| Vous connaissez la nouvelle ? | *Do you know the news ?* |
| Vous ne savez pas ? | *You don't know ?* |
| Tu ne sais pas ? | *You don't know ?* |
| J'ai une bonne nouvelle à vous annoncer. | *I've got some good news to tell you.* |
| À la télévision, on dit que … | *On the television, they say that ...* |
| À la radio, ils ont annoncé que… | *On the radio, they announced that ...* |
| Dans le journal, … | *In the newspaper, ...* |

## SAY IT IN FRENCH

***You are talking about the day's news to a friend of yours :***

1. Tell him that France Inter is the most popular radio station.
2. Tell him that, on the radio, they announced that *Le Monde* has bought a magazine.
3. Tell him that that his favourite actor may be coming to France.
4. Tell him a piece of good news : you have bought a new television.



**Possible answers :**

1. France Inter est la station la plus écoutée. 2. À la radio, ils ont annoncé que *Le Monde* a acheté un magazine. 3. Il paraît que Paul Newman vient en France. 4. Tu connais la bonne nouvelle ? J'ai acheté une nouvelle télévision.

# BILAN 3

■ **NOW YOU KNOW HOW TO USE DEMONSTRATIVE ADJECTIVES,**

***1. Complete with* ce, cet, cette, ces.**

Je voudrais ... oranges. Il achète ... jolie maison. Prends ... autobus. Vous travaillez ... nuit ? Comme dessert, je voudrais ... gâteau. Tournez devant ... station-service.

■ **...HOW TO TALK ABOUT THE FUTURE,**

***2. Put into the immediate future.***

Nous travaillons cette nuit → ...
Elle part ce soir → ...
Ils parlent français → ...
Je goûte le poulet → ...
Vous buvez du champagne → ...

***3. Put into the future.***

Elle va à la montagne → ...
Nous sommes à Paris le dix → ...
Vous mangez au restaurant → ...
Ils finissent leur travail → ...
Paul tourne à gauche → ...

■ **...HOW TO USE DIRECT OBJECT PRONOUNS**

***4. Replace the words underlined with* le, la, l', les.**

Tu connais bien la France → Tu la connais bien.
Elle prend le train tous les jours → ...
Nous regardons les photos → ...
Vous goûtez l'entrée → ...
J'aime la campagne → ...
Prends la valise → ...

***5. Answer the following questions using* le, la, l' *or* les.**

Vous prenez la voiture ? → Oui, je la prends.
Il regarde la télévision ? → Oui, il ...
Vous écoutez la radio ? → Oui, nous ...
Tu veux la radio ? → Oui, je ...
Vous appelez le garagiste ? → Oui, nous ...
Il change les pneus ? Oui, il ...

■ ...HOW TO CONJUGATE REFLEXIVE VERBS,

***6. Answer the following questions.***

Qu'est-ce qu'il fait ? (se raser) → ...
Qu'est-ce qu'ils font ? (se lever) → ...
Qu'est-ce que vous faites ? (se réveiller) → ...
Qu'est-ce qu'elles font ? (se dépêcher) → ...
Qu'est-ce que tu fais ? (se doucher) → ...

■ ...HOW TO TALK ABOUT PAST EVENTS (USING THE VERB *AVOIR*).

***7. Put into the recent past.***

Elle ouvre la porte → ... Un inconnu gagne au loto → ... Ils regardent l'émission → ... Ils déjeunent à la cantine → ... Nous jouons au tennis → ...

***8. Complete the following sentences using the passé composé (or Perfect tense), in the negative.***

Aujourd'hui je travaille mais hier je n'ai pas travaillé.
Aujourd'hui elle dort mais hier elle ...
Aujourd'hui vous oubliez mais hier vous ...
Aujourd'hui ils font la fête mais hier ils ...
Aujourd'hui tu as faim mais hier tu ...
Aujourd'hui nous regardons la télévison mais hier nous ...
Aujourd'hui j'ouvre la porte mais hier je ...

## KEY TO EXERCISES

1. ces - cette - cet - cette - ce - cette.
2. Nous allons travailler cette nuit - Elle va partir ce soir - Ils vont parler français - Je vais goûter le poulet - Vous allez boire du champagne.
3. Elle ira à la montagne - Nous serons à Paris le dix - Vous mangerez au restaurant - Ils finiront leur travail - Paul tournera à gauche.
4. Elle le prend tous les jours - Nous les regardons - Vous la goûtez - Je l'aime - Prends-la.
5. il la regarde / nous l'écoutons. / je la veux. / nous l'appelons. / il les change.
6. Il se rase. Ils se lèvent. Nous nous réveillons. Elles se dépêchent. Je me douche.
7. Elle vient d'ouvrir - Un inconu vient de gagner - Ils viennent de regarder - Ils viennent de déjeuner - Nous venons de jouer -
8. Elle n'a pas dormi - Vous n'avez pas oublié - Ils n'ont pas fait la fête - Tu n'as pas eu faim - Nous n'avons pas regardé - Je n'ai pas ouvert la porte.

## FAIT DIVERS

### Un inspecteur des impôts a disparu

Comme tous les matins, Olivier Morel, jeune inspecteur des impôts, est allé au bureau, et à midi il a déjeuné avec un collègue.
Vers 18 heures, il a fait des courses dans le centre commercial à côté de chez lui. À 20 heures, une voisine a vu le jeune inspecteur dans une voiture verte. Depuis, il n'est pas rentré chez lui, on n'a pas eu de nouvelles. Sa femme et ses enfants sont très inquiets. La police a commencé son enquête.

**PRONUNCIATION**

| | | |
|---|---|---|
| **Il est allé** | [ilɛtale] | eel eg tahlay |
| **Le jeune inspecteur** | [ləʒœnɛ̃spɛktœr] | ler zhum angspehkturr |
| **On n'a pas eu** | [ɔ̃napay] | awng nah pah zew |
| **Il n'est pas rentré** | [ilnɛparɑ̃tre] | eel neh pah rahngtray |

## NEWS IN BRIEF

**A tax inspector has disappeared**

Olivier Morel, a young tax inspector, went to his office this morning as usual. At midday, he had lunch with a colleague.
At about 6 o'clock p.m., he went shopping in a shopping centre near his home. At 8 o'clock p.m., a neighbour saw the young inspector in a green car. Since then, he hasn't returned home and we have had no news about him. His wife and children are very worried. The police had begun their investigations.

## GRAMMAR

***Verbs :***

**Elle a vu** → Perfect tense of the verb **voir**

***The Perfect tense :***

**Conjugation 2** Present tense of **être** + past participle
This conjugation concerns all reflexive verbs in addition to the following verbs :
aller, venir, entrer, sortir, rester, partir, monter, descendre, arriver, passer, naître, tomber, mourir

| **Masculine subjects :** | | **Feminine subjects :** | |
|---|---|---|---|
| je suis sorti | nous sommes sortis | je suis sortie | nous sommes sorties |
| tu es sorti | vous êtes sorti(s) | tu es sortie | vous êtes sortie(s) |
| Il est sorti | ils sont sortis | elle est sortie | elles sont sorties |

Note that when the verb is conjugated with **être** in the Perfect tense, the past participle agrees in gender and number with the subject.

## EXERCISES

### 1. Put into the Perfect tense. You will require the following past participles :

*faire → fait. voir → vu. vouloir → voulu. apprendre → appris*
Elle fait de la gymnastique. Je vois un spectacle. Tu prépares le dîner. Elle apprend le français. Ils veulent travailler.

### 2. Put into the Perfect tense. Make sure that the past participle agrees in gender and in number with the subject of the verb

Elle va au cinéma. → Elle est allée au cinéma.
*(Sophie parle)* Je pars en vacances → ........................................
*(Vous parlez à Jacques)* Vous sortez ce soir ? → ..........................
Ils restent à la maison. → ..................................................................
Elles descendent. → ...........................................................................

### 3. Put into the negative

Elle est allée au théâtre. J'ai appris le français. Vous êtes rentrés lundi. Elles ont pris l'autobus. Nous sommes partis en vacances.

### 4. Translate into English

Il est rentré chez lui. Il a commencé à 13 h. Mercredi matin, j'ai fait les courses. Elle a déjeuné avec Sylvie.

## VOCABULARY

| | |
|---|---|
| ensemble : together | aujourd'hui → today |
| hier → yesterday | demain → tomorrow |
| avant-hier → the day before yesterday | après-demain → the day after tomorrow |



**Key to exercises :**

1. Elle a fait. J'ai vu. Tu as préparé. Elle a appris. Ils ont voulu.
2. Je suis partie. Vous êtes sorti. Ils sont restés. Elles sont descendues.
3. Elle n'est pas allée. Je n'ai pas appris. Vous n'êtes pas rentrés. Elles n'ont pas pris. Nous ne sommes pas partis.
4. He went home. He started at 1 o'clock p.m. I went shopping Wednesday morning. She had lunch with Sylvie.

## VARIATIONS

**Pour dire l'heure / *Telling the time* :**

8:00 → huit heures
8:05 → huit heures cinq
8:15 → huit heures quinze
ou huit heures et quart
8:30 → huit heures trente
ou huit heures et demie
8:35 → huit heures trente-cinq
ou neuf heures moins vingt-cinq
8:45 → huit heures quarante-cinq
ou neuf heures moins le quart
12:00 → douze heures ou midi
00:00 → minuit

| **Pour prendre rendez-vous :** | ***Making an appointment :*** |
|---|---|
| On peut se retrouver à midi ? | *Can we meet at midday ?* |
| Vous pouvez me recevoir à 5 h ? | *Can you see me at 5 o'clock ?* |
| **Pour fixer un rendez-vous :** | ***Arranging to meet :*** |
| Bon, alors, on se retrouve à 5 h. | *Okay, then, we'll see each other at 5 o'clock.* |
| Bon, c'est d'accord pour 5 h. | *Okay, so that's agreed for 5 o'clock.* |
| Rendez-vous à 5 h. | *We'll meet at 5 o'clock.* |
| Attends-moi à 5 h. | *Expect me at 5 o'clock.* |
| Je vous/t'attendrai à 5 h. | *I'll expect you at 5 o'clock.* |

## SAY IT IN FRENCH

***It is Monday. Say what Madame Belin did the day before yesterday:***

| | SAMEDI | Commentaires |
|---|---|---|
| **Matin** | 10 h tennis | ........................................ |
| | 12 h restaurant | ........................................ |
| **Après-midi** | 14 h courses | ........................................ |
| | 18 h voir Daniel | ........................................ |
| **Soirée** | 19 h dîner en famille | ........................................ |



**Possible answers :**

À dix heures, elle a joué au tennis. À midi, elle a déjeuné au restaurant. À quatorze heures, elle est allée faire des courses. À dix-huit heures, elle a vu Daniel. Le soir, elle a dîné en famille.

## EN PANNE

— Allô Papa, c'est moi. La voiture est encore en panne.

— Qu'est-ce qu'elle a ?

— J'en sais rien ! Elle fait un bruit bizarre et elle ne démarre pas.

— Bon, alors, ouvre le capot et regarde le delco.

— Le delco ? Qu'est-ce que c'est que ça ?

— C'est un truc rond, en plastique noir, avec plein de câbles.

— Euh... Bon... Et après, qu'est-ce que je fais ?

— Tu le remets en place. Il y a un faux contact.

— Tu vois bien que cette bagnole est trop vieille !

— Et tu as de l'argent, toi, pour acheter une voiture neuve ?

— Moi, non. Mais ta banque, c'est sûr que oui.

### PRONUNCIATION

| | | |
|---|---|---|
| **La voiture est en panne** | [lavwatyrɛtɑ̃pan] | lah vwahtewr eh tahng pahn |
| **J'en sais rien** | [ʒɑ̃sɛrjɛ̃] | zhahng say ryang |
| **Un bruit bizarre** | [ɛ̃brɥibizar] | ang brwee beezah |
| **Cette bagnole** | [sɛtbaɲɔl] | seht bahñoal |
| **C'est sûr** | [sɛsyr] | seh sewr |

## BROKEN DOWN

— Hello, dad. It's me. The car's broken down again .
— What's the matter with it ?
— I don't known. It makes a funny noise and it won't start.
— Alright then, open the bonnet and look at the distributor.
— The distributor ? What's that ?
It's a round thing, made out of black plastic, with lots of wires.
— Er, okay ... And what do I do then ?
— You put it back into position. There's a loose connection.
— You do realise that this car is past it!
— Have you got the money to buy a new one ?
— No, I haven't. But your bank certainly has!

## GRAMMAR

### *Verbs :*

**Ouvre !** → imperative of the verb **ouvrir**

### *Feminine adjectives :*

**General rule :** feminine adjectives are formed by adding an **-e** to the masculine adjective

un truc rond → une chose ronde

**Exceptions :**

a) certain adjectives double their final consonant.

| | |
|---|---|
| **on → onne** | bon – bonne |
| **ien → ienne** | ancien – ancienne |
| **s → sse** | gros – grosse |

b) certain adjectives change their final syllable.

| | |
|---|---|
| **eau → elle** | beau – belle |
| **eux → euse** | heureux – heureuse |
| **ou → olle** | fou – folle |
| **c → che** | blanc – blanche (white) |
| **f → ve** | neuf – neuve |

Note that the feminine form of many adjectives is very irregular : vieux/vieille (old), doux/douce (gentle), faux/fausse(false), frais/fraîche (fresh), gentil/gentille (nice), long/longue (long), roux/rousse (reddish-brown), sec/sèche (dry)

## EXERCISES

### 1. Put the following adjectives into the feminine

Un beau livre → une ......... maison. un gros truc → une ......... chose. un vieux pantalon → une ......... chaussure. un petit garçon → une ......... fille

### 2. Put into the masculine

Elle est très bonne. → Il est très bon.
Elle est douce → ...................... Vous êtes folle ! → .................
Tu es gentille. → ...................... Elle est neuve. → .....................

### 3. Change the sentence and put the adjective into the feminine

Le temps est agréable. (la soirée) → La soirée .............................
Il y a un beau parc. (une place) → Il y a ....................................
Je veux un pantalon blanc. (une voiture) → Je veux .....................
Paul est roux. (Sophie) → Sophie ...............................................

### 4. Translate into French

Do you (pl) have any money for a new car ? What is it ? My car's broken down again ! It doesn't start very well.

## VOCABULARY

encore : again trop : too
qu'est-ce que c'est : what is it ?

la roue → wheel
le pneu → tyre

une crevaison → a puncture
une pièce → a part
le moteur → engine
les freins → brakes
un mécanicien → a mechanic
une réparation → a repair



**Key to exercises :**

1. une belle maison, une grosse chose, une vieille chaussure, une petite fille.
2. Il est doux. Vous êtes fou ! Tu es gentil. Il est neuf.
3. La soirée est agréable. Il y a une belle place. Je veux une voiture blanche. Sophie est rousse.
4. Vous avez de l'argent pour une voiture neuve ? Qu'est-ce que c'est ? Ma voiture est encore en panne ! Elle ne démarre pas très bien.

## VARIATIONS

| | |
|---|---|
| **Pour identifier un objet :** | ***Identifying an object :*** |
| Qu'est-ce que c'est ?<br>C'est quoi, ce machin ?/<br>ce truc ?<br>Ça sert à quoi ?<br>C'est en quoi ? | *What is it ?*<br>*What is it, this thingummyjig ? /*<br>*this contraption ?*<br>*What's it for ?*<br>*What's it made of ?* |
| **Pour décrire un objet :**<br>**La forme** | ***Describing an object :***<br>***Shape :*** |
| Il/c'est carré/rond/rectangulaire/triangulaire | *It's square/round/rectangular /triangular* |
| **La couleur** | ***Colour :*** |
| Il/c'est blanc/noir/bleu /rouge /gris/vert/jaune... | *It's white/black/blue/red/grey /green/yellow.....* |
| **L'état** | ***Condition :*** |
| Il/c'est neuf/ancien/impeccable /cassé/abimé... | *It's new/old/impeccable/broken /damaged....* |
| **La matière** | ***The material :*** |
| Il/c'est en bois/plastique/verre /fer/papier/carton/cuir... | *It's made of wood/plastic/glass /iron/paper/cardboard/leather...* |
| **L'utilité** | ***Use :*** |
| Ça sert à lire.<br>On l'utilise pour travailler.<br>Avec, on peut réparer... | *It's for reading.*<br>*It's used for working.*<br>*You can repair with it.* |

## SAY IT IN FRENCH

***Your car has broken down and you're speaking with the garage mechanic :***

1. Tell him that your car has broken down again.
2. Tell him that it is making a strange noise.
3. Ask him if it is necessary to put in a new part.
4. Ask him if he can repair your car today.

**Possible answers :**

1. Ma voiture est encore en panne. 2. Elle fait un bruit bizarre. 3. Il faut mettre une pièce neuve ? 4. Vous pouvez réparer ma voiture aujourd'hui ?

## ON SORT CE SOIR

*Au théâtre*

— Je voudrais trois places pour la séance de 14 h, s'il vous plaît.

— Désolé, monsieur, mais c'est complet.

— Et pour la séance suivante ?

— Il n'y a plus rien pour aujourd'hui mais je peux vous faire une réservation pour la séance de demain.

*Au cinéma*

*Pierre :* Qu'est-ce que vous avez pensé du film ?

*Louis :* Moi, j'ai bien aimé.

*Corinne :* Eh bien, pas moi ! Je n'ai pas du tout aimé et je n'ai rien compris ! C'est nul !

### PRONUNCIATION

| | | |
|---|---|---|
| **C'est complet** | [sɛkɔ̃plɛ] | seh kompleh |
| **La séance suivante** | [laseɑ̃sɥivɑ̃t] | lay sayahngs sweevahng |
| **Qu'est-ce que vous avez pensé ?** | [kɛskəvuzave pɑ̃se] | kehsske voo ahvay pahngsay |
| **Je n'ai rien compris** | [ʒənɛrjɛ̃kɔ̃pri] | zher nay ryang kawngpree |
| **C'est nul** | [sɛnyl] | seh newl |

## ■ WE'RE GOING OUT THIS EVENING

*At the theatre*
— I would like three seats for the 2 o'clock performance, please.
— I'm sorry sir, it's sold out*.
— And for the next performance ?
— There is nothing left for today but I can make a reservation for you for tomorrow's performance.

*At the cinema*
*Pierre :* What did you think about the film* ?
*Louis :* I enjoyed it.
*Corinne :* Not me. I didn't like it at all and I didn't understand anything. It's rubbish!

## GRAMMAR

■ ***Verbs :***

**Je n'ai rien compris** → Perfect tense of the verb **comprendre**

■ ***The negative construction with* ne ... rien, ne ... jamais, ne ... plus, ne ... personne *:***

| Simple tense | Compound tense |
|---|---|
| je **ne** comprends **rien** | je **n'**ai **rien** compris |
| je **ne** reviendrai **jamais** | je **ne** suis **jamais** revenu |
| je **ne** reviendrai **plus** | je **ne** suis **plus** revenu |
| je **ne** connais **personne** | je **n'**ai connu **personne** |

With the simple tenses, the two parts of the negative are placed on either side of the verb. With the compound tenses, the two parts of the negative are placed on either side of the auxiliary, except in the case of **ne ... personne**.

■ ***The opposites of* rien, jamais, plus *and* personne *:***

Quelque chose (something) → Tu vois **quelque chose** ? — Non, je **ne** vois **rien**.
Quelquefois (sometimes) → Tu viens **quelquefois** ? — Non, je **ne** viens **jamais**.
Souvent (often) → Tu viens **souvent** ? — Non, je **ne** viens **jamais**.
Toujours/encore (still) → Il parle **encore** ? — Non, il **ne** parle **plus**.
Quelqu'un (someone) → Tu vois **quelqu'un** ? — Non, je **ne** vois **personne**.

## EXERCISES

**1. *Reply using* pas du tout (–), bien (+), beaucoup (++)**

Il aime le sport ? (++) → Oui, il ..................................................
Vous aimez la télévision ? (+) → Oui, j'........................................
Elles aiment la musique ? (–) → Non, elles ..................................
Tu aimes le cinéma ? (+) → Oui, j' ..............................................

**2. *Put into the Perfect tense. Use :* compris, venu, vu, écouté**

Il ne voit personne. Elle ne comprend rien. Vous ne venez jamais. Je n'écoute jamais de musique. Tu ne comprends plus.

**3. *Reply using* ne ... jamais, ne ... rien, ne ... personne, ne ... plus**

Tu vois quelque chose ? → Non, je ne vois rien.
Elle connaît quelqu'un ? → Non, elle ..........................................
Ils viennent souvent ? → Non, ils ................................................
Vous mangez quelque chose ? → Non, je ..................................
Vous travaillez encore ? → Non, je ...........................................

**4. *Translate into English :***

Elle n'a pas du tout aimé. Qu'est-ce que vous pensez de ce livre ? Nous n'avons rien compris.

## VOCABULARY

pas du tout : not at all
absolument pas : absolutely not

un acteur/une actrice → an actor/actress

la troupe → theatrical company
l'auteur → author
la pièce (de théâtre) → the play
le public → audience

**Key to exercises :**

1. il aime beaucoup. j'aime bien. elles n'aiment pas du tout. j'aime bien.
2. Il n'a vu personne. Elle n'a rien compris. Vous n'êtes jamais venu. Je n'ai jamais écouté de musique. Tu n'as plus compris.
3. Non, elle ne connaît personne. Non, ils ne viennent jamais. Non, je ne mange rien. Non, je ne travaille plus.
4. She didn't like it at all. What do you think about this book ? We didn't understand anything.

## VARIATIONS

**Pour demander une opinion :**

Quel est votre avis ?
Quelle est votre opinion ?
Qu'est-ce que vous pensez/tu penses de ... ?
Tu as aimé ?

**Pour exprimer votre indifférence :**

Je ne sais pas.
Bof !
Comme ci, comme ça...

**Pour exprimer une opinion :**

J'ai détesté.
Je n'ai pas du tout aimé.
J'ai bien/beaucoup aimé.
Je trouve ça { nul. / vulgaire. / très bon. / excellent. }
J'adore !
Je pense que c'est super, génial.

***Asking someone's opinion :***

*What's your view ?*
*What's your opinion ?*
*What do you think about ... ?*
*Did you like it ?*

***Expressing indifference :***

*I don't know.*
*Not really.*
*So-so.*

***Expressing an opinion :***

*I hated it.*
*I didn't like it at all.*
*I rather/really liked it.*
*I think it's { rubbish. / vulgar. / very good. / excellent. }*
*I love it.*
*I think it's super, great.*

## SAY IT IN FRENCH

***You're going to see a show with some friends :***

1. At the ticket office, you buy four seats for the 3 p.m. performance.
2. After the show you ask them their opinion.
3. Say that you found the show vulgar.
4. Say that you didn't understand anything.



**Possible answers :**

1. Je voudrais quatre places pour la séance de 15 h. 2. Alors, votre opinion ? 3. J'ai trouvé la pièce vulgaire. 4. Je n'ai rien compris.

# On the brighter side n° 4

**« Acheter un canard »**

***« Buying a duck »***

***(newspapers are frequently referred to as "canards")***

## *DID YOU KNOW?*

The most popular pastime among the French is watching television, followed by reading, going to the cinema, listening to music and going out with friends.



The main national French newspapers for sale in a *kiosque* (newsagent's stall) are *Le Monde, Le Figaro, Libération* and *France-Soir,* but there are also many regional newspapers such as *Ouest-France, Le Dauphiné libéré, Le Provençal...* If you prefer reading weekly news magazines, you can buy *L'Express, Le Point, Paris-Match* or *Le Nouvel Observateur.*

**And now for a little culture. Can you match the following works with their authors?**

| | | | |
|---|---|---|---|
| Le Penseur | 1 • | • A | Édouard Manet |
| Les Quatre Cents Coups | 2 • | • B | Charles Baudelaire |
| Le Discours de la Méthode | 3 • | • C | Édith Piaf |
| Le Déjeuner sur l'herbe | 4 • | • D | Molière |
| Astérix et Obélix | 5 • | • E | Uderzo et Goscinny |
| Le Médecin malgré lui | 6 • | • F | François Truffaut |
| La Vie en rose | 7 • | • G | Auguste Rodin |
| Les Fleurs du mal | 8 • | • H | René Descartes |

***Answers:*** 1.G - 2.F - 3.H - 4.A - 5.E - 6.D - 7.C - 8.B.

## ■ À TABLE !

— Allez, encore un peu de soupe ?

— Oh oui ! J'en reprendrai volontiers.

— Je vous ai préparé ma spécialité : le lapin à la moutarde.

— Hum ! Ça sent bon.

...

— Oh, vous m'en donnez trop !

— Mais non, vous verrez, c'est très léger.

...

— Vous n'aimez pas ?

— Si, c'est très bon, mais je n'ai plus faim.

...

— Vous prendrez bien du dessert ?

— D'habitude, je n'en prends pas.

— De la tarte au citron !

— Alors, volontiers, j'adore ça.

### PRONUNCIATION

| | | |
|---|---|---|
| **Encore un peu** | [ɑ̃kɔrɛ̃pø] | ahngkor ang pur |
| **Vous n'aimez pas ?** | [vunemepa] | voo nehmay pah |
| **Je n'ai plus faim** | [ʒnɛplyfɛ̃] | zher nay ple fang |
| **De la tarte au citron** | [dlatartositrɔ̃] | der lah tahrt oa seetrawhg |
| **J'adore ça** | [ʒadɔrsa] | zhahdor sah |

## DINNER'S READY!

— Go on, a little more soup?
— Oh, yes! I'd love some more .
— I've made you my speciality : rabbit in mustard sauce.
— Hmm! It smells good.
...
— Oh, you've given me too much.
— No, you'll see, it's very light.
...
— Don't you like it?
— Yes, I do. It's very nice, but I couldn't eat any more.
...
— You'll have some dessert, won't you?
— I don't usually have dessert.
— Some lemon pie!
— In that case, with pleasure. I love lemon pie.

## GRAMMAR

### *Verbs :*

**Ça sent** → present indicative of the verb **sentir**

### *The pronoun* **en** *:*

The pronoun **en** is used to replace a noun preceded by :

| | | |
|---|---|---|
| **du** → | Tu bois **du** vin ? | Oui, j'**en** bois. |
| **de la** → | Vous voulez **de la** viande ? | Oui, j'**en** veux bien. |
| **de l'** → | Elle prend **de l'**eau ? | Non, elle n'**en** prend pas. |
| **des** → | Tu as acheté **des** fruits ? | Oui, j'**en** ai acheté. |
| **pas de** → | Maman, il n'y a **pas d'**eau ? | Si, il y **en** a. |

Or by :

| | | |
|---|---|---|
| **peu de** → | Tu as **peu d'**argent ? | Oui j'**en** ai **peu.** |
| **assez de** → | Tu as **assez d'**argent ? | Oui j'**en** ai **assez**. |
| **beaucoup de** → | Tu veux **beaucoup de** sucre ? | Oui, j'**en** veux **beaucoup.** |
| **trop de** → | Il boit **trop de** vin ? | Oui, il **en** boit **trop.** |
| **un, deux, ...** → | Il a **cinq** enfants ? | Oui, il **en** a **cinq.** |

Position of the pronoun **en** in a sentence :
J'**en** veux. → Je n'**en** veux pas. J'**en** ai voulu. → Je n'**en** ai pas voulu.
Prenez-**en**. → N'**en** prenez pas.

### *Si :*

**Si** is used to reply in the affirmative to a negative question.
Tu as faim ? — **Oui**, j'ai faim. Tu n'as pas faim ? — **Si**, j'ai faim.

## EXERCISES

### 1. Reply to the following questions, using le, la, les, l' or en

Tu veux **le** pain ? → Oui, je **le** veux. **Du** pain ? → Oui, j'**en** veux.
Vous prenez de l'eau ? → Oui, ..................................................
Elle mange du poisson ? → Non, ..................................................
Tu achètes les fruits ? → Oui, ..................................................
Vous voulez du sucre ? → Oui, ..................................................

### 2. Reply in the affirmative, as in the example

Tu as assez de vin ? → Oui, j'en ai assez.
Vous voulez beaucoup d'argent ? → Oui, j' ..................................
Elle mange trop de pain ? → Oui, elle ..................................
Tu veux deux sucres ? → Oui, j' ..................................
Tu prends assez de pain ? → Oui, j' ..................................

### 3. Reply in the affirmative

Vous ne mangez pas ? Nous partons ce soir ? Vous ne parlez pas français ? Tu ne connais pas Paris ? Il travaille aujourd'hui?

### 4. Translate into French

It's very good but I'm not hungry. Will you (pl) have some coffee ? Don't you (pl) like it ? — Yes, I like it very much.

## VOCABULARY

| | |
|---|---|
| ça : that<br>normalement : normally<br>voilà : there you are | une assiette → a plate<br>un verre → a glass<br>un couteau → a knife |
| le poivre → pepper<br>le pain → bread | une fourchette → a fork<br>une cuiller → a spoon<br>une serviette → a napkin |

**Key to exercises :**

1. Oui, j'en prends. Non, elle n'en mange pas. Oui, je les achète. Oui, j'en veux.
2. Oui, j'en veux beaucoup. Oui, elle en mange trop. Oui, j'en veux deux. Oui, j'en prends assez.
3. Si, je mange. Oui, nous partons ce soir. Si, je parle français. Si, je connais Paris. Oui, il travaille aujourd'hui.
4. C'est très bon, mais je n'ai pas faim. Vous prendrez du café ? Vous n'aimez pas ? — Si, j'aime beaucoup.

## VARIATIONS

**Pour proposer quelque chose à table :**

Servez-vous/sers-toi
Vous préférez du thé ou du café ?
Qu'est-ce que vous buvez ?
Encore { un morceau ? / un verre ? / un peu ? }
Tenez, voilà le plateau de fromage/le sel/du gâteau.

***Offering things at the table :***

*Help yourselves/yourself!*
*Do you prefer tea or coffee ?*
*What would you like to drink ?*
*Another helping ?*
*Another glass ?*
*A little more ?*
*Here's the cheese board/the salt/some cake.*

**Pour accepter :**

Oui, s'il vous plaît.
Avec plaisir.

***Accepting :***

*Yes, please.*
*With pleasure.*

**Pour refuser :**

Non, merci, c'est beaucoup trop. / Je n'ai plus faim /soif. / Le médecin me l'interdit.

***Refusing :***

*No, thank you, It's far too much. / I'm not hungry/thirsty any more. / The doctor forbids me to have it.*

**Pour féliciter la cuisinière :**

C'est délicieux !
Quel délice !
Quel repas !

***Congratulating the cook :***

*It's delicious.*
*What a delight!*
*What a meal!*

## SAY IT IN FRENCH

***You are invited to have lunch with some friends :***

1. You are asked what you want to drink. Say that you will have a little water.
2. You are given a dish. Say that it smells good and that you love it.
3. You are offered some more of the same dish. Refuse politely and say that you are no longer hungry.
4. Congratulate the lady of the house on this delicious meal.



**Possible answers :**

1. Je prendrai un peu d'eau. 2. Hum, ça sent bon ! J'adore ça ! 3. Non, merci. Je n'ai plus faim. 4. Quel délicieux repas !

## QUEL TEMPS FAIT-IL ?

**Bulletin météo du 3 août :**

Il fera très chaud et le soleil brillera sur toute la France.

Au lever du jour, le ciel sera parfois brumeux.

Cet après-midi, on aura de 29 à 34 degrés du nord au sud.

En fin de journée, quelques coups de tonnerre et de nouveaux orages pourront se produire dans le Sud-Ouest.

**Bulletin météo du 5 janvier :**

Il fera froid et la journée sera en général très couverte avec de timides apparitions du soleil.

On observera de nombreuses zones de brouillard et de sérieux risques de verglas sur les routes du Centre et de l'Est.

Pendant la journée, au nord de la Loire et sur les Alpes, les chutes de neige seront fréquentes et abondantes.

Températures entre – 6° et – 3°.

### PRONUNCIATION

| | | |
|---|---|---|
| **Le soleil brillera** | [ləsɔlɛjbrijra] | ler solehy breeyerah |
| **Le ciel sera brumeux** | [ləsjɛlsərabrymø] | ler syehl serrah brewmur |
| **Zones de brouillard** | [zondəbrujar] | zoan der brooyahr |
| **Les chutes de neige** | [leʃytdənɛʒ] | lay shewt der nehzh |

## ■ *WHAT'S THE WEATHER LIKE ?*

**Weather forecast for 3rd August :**
It will be very hot with bright sunshine all over France.
There will be patches of mist at dawn.
This afternoon, temperatures will range between 29 and 34 degrees in northern and southern France.
Towards the end of the day, we may have some thunder and more electric storms in the South-West.

**Weather forecast for 5th January :**
It will be cold and, on the whole, the day will be overcast with occasional brighter spells .
There will be many foggy patches and a serious risk of black ice on the roads in the Center and East.
In the course of the day, we can expect frequent heavy snowfalls north of the Loire and over the Alps.
The temperature will vary between - 6° and + 3°.

## GRAMMAR

### *Verbs :*

**Des orages pourront** → future of the verb **pouvoir**

### *The plural form of adjectives :*

**General rule :** The plural of an adjective is formed by adding **-s** to the singular.

une timide apparition → de timides apparitions

Note that before an adjective **des** usually changes to **de**
When an adjective already ends in **-s** or **-x** in the singular, it does not change in the plural :

un sérieu**x** risque → de sérieu**x** risques
un gro**s** orage → de gro**s** orages

**Exceptions :**
For adjectives ending in **-eau**, the plural is formed by adding an **-x**

un nouv**eau** livre → de nouv**eaux** livres

For adjectives ending in **-al**, the plural becomes **-aux**.

un problème loc**al** → des problèmes loc**aux**

### *The feminine plural of adjectives :*

The adjective must first be put into the feminine form, and then **s** is added : grand → grand**e** → grand**es**   beau → belle → belles

## EXERCISES

### 1. Put into the plural

un vieux vêtement → .............. un beau spectacle → ..............
un examen oral → .................. un nouveau professeur → ........
un orage local → .................... un garçon sérieux → ...............

### 2. Give the correct form of the adjective (in brackets)

de (beau) ......... femmes / de (vieux) ......... amies / de (nouveau) ......... voitures / des filles (roux) .........

### 3. Study the VARIATIONS and then comment about the weather

Il fait chaud. → Quelle chaleur !
Il y a du brouillard. → ..................................................................
Il pleut. → ..............................................................................
Il y a du vent. → ......................................................................
Il fait du froid. → .....................................................................

### 4. Translate into English

Il fera très froid sur toute la France. Le matin, on aura 27 degrés dans l'Ouest. Un orage pourra se produire en fin de journée.

## VOCABULARY

parfois : sometimes
quelques : some

pleuvoir → to rain
neiger → to snow
le vent → wind

la pluie → rain
le brouillard → fog
la tempête → storm
un nuage → a cloud
nuageux → cloudy



**Key to exercises :**

1. de vieux vêtements / de beaux spectacles / des examens oraux / de nouveaux professeurs / des orages locaux / des garçons sérieux
2. de belles femmes / de vieilles amies / de nouvelles voitures / des filles rousses
3. Quel brouillard ! Quelle pluie ! Quel vent ! Quel froid !
4. It will be very cold all over France. This morning it will be 27 degrees in the West. There may be a thunder storm at the end of the day.

## VARIATIONS

**Pour parler du temps qu'il fait :**
Il fait (très) chaud/froid.
Il pleut.
Il neige.
Il gèle.
Il y a du brouillard.
Il y a du soleil.
Il y a du vent.
Quel brouillard !
Quel soleil !
Quel vent !
Quel froid !
Quelle chaleur/pluie !

***Talking about the weather :***
*It is (very) hot/cold.*
*It's raining.*
*It's snowing.*
*It's freezing.*
*It's foggy.*
*It's sunny.*
*It's windy.*
*How foggy it is!*
*How sunny it is!*
*How windy it is!*
*How cold it is!*
*How hot/rainy it is!*

**Pour exprimer des sensations liées au temps qu'il fait :**
J'ai (très) chaud/froid.
Quel froid !
Quelle chaleur !
Je meurs de froid/de chaud.
Qu'est-ce qu'il fait froid !
Qu'est-ce qu'il fait chaud !

***Expressing reactions to the weather :***
*I'm (very) hot/cold.*
*What freezing weather!*
*What heat!*
*I'm freezing/boiling.*
*How cold it is!*
*How hot it is!*

## SAY IT IN FRENCH

***You're talking to a friend about the weather :***
1. Say how cold it is.
2. Tell him it is foggy this morning.
3. Tell him that the temperature is -2°.
4. Tell him that it is going to snow this afternoon.



**Possible answers :**

1. Quel froid ! 2. Ce matin, il y a du brouillard. 3. Il fait moins deux degrés. 4. Il va neiger cet après-midi.

## NE QUITTEZ PAS...

— Allô ! Madame Serreaux ?
— Non, c'est sa secrétaire.
— Bonjour, madame, ...gnin à l'appareil.
— Allô ? Vous pouvez répéter, s'il vous plaît ? Je n'ai pas compris.
— Ici, Jules Magnin.
— Ah, bonjour, monsieur, madame Serreaux est sortie. Vous voulez lui laisser un message ?
— ... je lui téléphonerai cet après-midi...
— Vous pouvez parler plus fort et moins vite ?
— Annoncez-lui que nous avons fini les travaux.
— D'accord. Alors, je lui dis que vous avez fini les travaux. C'est bien ça ?

### PRONUNCIATION

| | | |
|---|---|---|
| **Non, c'est sa secrétaire** | [nɔ̃sɛsasəkretɛr] | nawng, seh sah serkraytehr |
| **Vous pouvez répéter ?** | [vupuverepete] | voo poovay raypaytay |
| **Vous voulez lui laisser** | [vuvulelɥilese] | voo voolay lwee lehssay |
| **Plus fort** | [plyfɔr] | plew for |
| **Les travaux** | [letravo] | lay trahvoa |
| **C'est bien ça ?** | [sɛbjɛ̃sa] | seh byang sah |

## HOLD THE LINE, PLEASE...

— Hello ? Mrs Serreaux ?
— No. It's her secretary.
— Good morning... ..gnin speaking.
— Hello ? Could you repeat that, please ? I didn't understand.
— Jules Magnin speaking.
— Oh, good morning, Mr Magnin. Mrs Serreaux is out. Do you want to leave her a message ?
— ... I'll call her this afternoon ...
— Can you speak louder and less quickly ?
— Tell her that we have finished the work.
— Very well. So, I'll tell her that you have finished the work. Is that right ?

## GRAMMAR

### *Verbs :*

**Je n'ai pas compris** → Perfect tense of the verb **comprendre**
**Dites-lui** → imperative of the verb **dire**

### *The indirect object pronouns* lui *and* leur *:*

| | singular | plural | examples |
|---|---|---|---|
| **masculine** **feminine** | **lui** | **leur** | Je lui dis (**lui** = à Mme Serreaux) Je lui téléphonerai (**lui** = à Mme Serreaux) |

These personal pronouns are used to replace the name of a person, already mentioned, in the indirect construction :

verb + **à** + name of the person

Je parle **à** Pierre. Je **lui** parle. Je parle **à** Marie. Je **lui** parle.

Some other verbs also require this indirect construction :
téléphoner, écrire, parler, donner, annoncer, dire, expliquer...
Paul téléphone **à ses amis.** → Il **leur** téléphone.
J'annonce la nouvelle **à** mes parents ? → Oui, annonce-**leur** la nouvelle.

### *Position of the pronouns in the sentence :*

See the rules given in lesson 16.

## EXERCISES

### 1. Answer the following questions using lui or leur

Tu expliques le problème à Sophie ? Oui, je lui explique le problème.
Vous téléphonez à monsieur Magnin ? Oui, je ..........................
Elle écrit à ses amies ? Oui, elle ..............................................
Ils disent l'heure à madame Serreaux ? Oui, ils ..........................

### 2. Put into the Perfect tense. You will need the following irregular past participles : écrit, dit

Nous lui racontons notre voyage. Elle lui écrit une lettre. Je lui laisse un message. Vous leur téléphonez. Vous leur dites l'heure.

### 3. Put into the negative

Elle lui parle beaucoup. Je lui ai raconté mon voyage. Il m'a expliqué la solution. Elle lui donne du lait. Je lui dis l'heure.

### 4. Translate into French

Monsieur Dupont speaking. Can you (sing.) speak louder? Can you (plur.) repeat, please ? Is that right ?

## VOCABULARY

plus : more    moins : less

| | |
|---|---|
| composer le numéro → to dial the number | la standardiste → telephone operator |
| le téléphone → telephone | la cabine téléphonique → telephone booth |
| l'indicatif → dialling code | les renseignements → directory inquiries |
| le standard → switchboard | l'annuaire → telephone directory |

**Key to exercises :**

1. Je lui téléphone / elle leur écrit / ils lui disent l'heure.
2. Nous lui avons raconté notre voyage. Elle lui a écrit une lettre. Je lui ai laissé un message. Vous leur avez téléphoné. Vous leur avez dit l'heure.
3. Elle ne lui parle pas beaucoup. Je ne lui ai pas raconté mon voyage. Il ne m'a pas expliqué la solution. Elle ne lui donne pas de lait. Je ne lui dis pas l'heure.
4. Monsieur Dupont à l'appareil. Peux-tu parler plus fort ? Pouvez-vous répéter, s'il vous plaît ? C'est bien ça ?

## VARIATIONS

| | |
|---|---|
| **Pour dire que vous n'avez pas compris ou entendu :** | ***Saying that you did not understand or hear properly :*** |
| Pardon, je n'ai pas compris.<br>Qu'est-ce que vous avez dit ?<br>Pardon, comment ?<br>La ligne est mauvaise/coupée. | *I'm sorry, I didn't understand.<br>What did you say ?<br>Sorry, what ?<br>The line is bad/cut off.* |
| **Pour demander de répéter :** | ***Asking someone to repeat :*** |
| Vous pouvez répéter, s'il vous plaît ?<br>Qu'est-ce que tu as dit ? | *Can you repeat that, please ?<br>What did you say ?* |
| **Pour demander de parler autrement :** | ***Asking someone to speak differently :*** |
| Vous pouvez parler moins vite ?<br>Vous pouvez parler plus fort ? | *Can you speak less quickly<br>Can you speak more loudly ?* |
| **Pour vérifier que vous avez bien compris :** | ***Checking that you have understood properly :*** |
| Vous avez bien dit à huit heures ?<br>C'est bien 600 francs ? | *You did say at eight o'clock ?<br>600 francs, is that right ?* |
| **Vous pouvez aussi répéter ce que l'autre personne a dit et demander :** | ***You can also repeat what the other person said and ask :*** |
| C'est bien ça ?<br>J'ai bien compris ? | *Is that right ?<br>Have I understood correctly ?* |

## SAY IT IN FRENCH

***You are holding a telephone conversation but the line is very bad :***

1. Tell the other person that you have not understood very well.
2. Tell him that the line is very bad.
3. Ask him to talk louder and less quickly.
4. Ask him to repeat.

**Possible answers :**

1. Je n'ai pas bien compris. 2. La ligne est très mauvaise. 3. Vous pouvez parler plus fort et moins vite ? 4. Vous pouvez répéter ?

# BILAN 4

## ■ Now you know how to talk about past events (using the verb *être*),

### *1. Put into the perfect tense (don't forget to make the past participle agree when necessary).*

Elle sort lundi → ... Nous n'allons pas au théâtre mercredi → ... Elles se lavent le matin → ... Il reste toute la semaine → ... Ils se réveillent à 8 h → ... Elles se retrouvent au café → ...

### *2. Put into the perfect tense.*

Vous travaillez beaucoup → ... Nous aimons bien l'opéra → ... Je n'apprécie pas du tout cet acteur → ... Tu travailles assez ? → ... Le spectacle m'intéresse beaucoup → ...

## ■ ...HOW TO PUT ADJECTIVES INTO THEIR FEMININE FORM,

### *3. Transform the following as in the example.*

Ce garçon est beau, (fille) → Cette fille aussi est belle.
Cet homme est heureux, (femme) → ...
Ce vin est bon, (eau) → ...
Ce monsieur est fou, (dame) → ...
Ce camion est vieux, (voiture) → ...
Ces gens sont gentils, (personnes) → ...
Cet appartement est grand, (maison) → ...
Ces garçons sont roux, (filles) → ...

## ■ ...HOW TO ASK QUESTIONS,

### *4. Give the right question. Use* **quelque chose, quelqu'un, encore...**

Non, je ne bois rien → Tu bois quelque chose ?
Non, elle ne connaît personne → Elle ...
Non, nous ne faisons rien → Vous ...
Non, je ne travaille plus → Tu ...
Non, ils ne viennent jamais → Ils ...
Non, nous n'avons rencontré personne → Vous ...

## ■ ...HOW TO USE THE PRONOUN *EN*,



### *5. Replace the words in bold print using the pronoun* **en.**

J'ai beaucoup d'**amis** → J'en ai beaucoup.
Elle a trop d'**argent** → ... Il a bu cinq **bières** → ... Tu manges peu de **pain** → ... Vous mettez assez de **moutarde** → ... Prenez beaucoup de **fruits** → ...

■ ...HOW TO REPLY IN THE AFFIRMATIVE,

***6. Answer in the affirmative.***

Tu ne viens pas ? → ... Vous avez compris ? → ... Vous ne parlez pas français ? → ... Tu en veux ? → ... Elles ne sont pas françaises ? → ...

■ ...HOW TO MAKE ADJECTIVES AGREE,

***7. Make the adjectives agree when necessary.***

J'ai de (nouveau) ... amis. Il passe des examens (oral) ... Vous avez de (beau) ... enfants. J'adore les (vieux) ... maisons. Ce sont de très (beau) ... photos. Voilà de (gros) ... hommes.

■ ...HOW TO USE INDIRECT OBJECT PRONOUNS

***8. Replace the words in bold print with* lui *or* leur.**

Elle prête de l'argent **à ses amis** → ... Vous écrivez **à Paul et à sa femme** → ... Explique la solution **à ton frère** → .... Ne parlez pas **à cet homme** → ... Racontez vos vacances **à vos enfants** → ... J'ai annoncé la bonne nouvelle **à mes parents** → ...

## KEY TO EXERCISES

1. Elle est sortie lundi - Nous ne sommes pas allés au théâtre mercredi - Elles se sont lavées le matin - Il est resté toute la semaine - Ils se sont réveillés à 8 h - Elles se sont retrouvées au café.
2. Vous avez beaucoup travaillé - Nous avons bien aimé l'opéra - Je n'ai pas du tout apprécié cet acteur - Tu as assez travaillé ? - Le spectacle m'a beaucoup intéressé.
3. Cette femme aussi est heureuse - Cette eau aussi est bonne - Cette dame aussi est folle - Cette voiture aussi est vieille - Ces personnes aussi sont gentilles - Cette maison aussi est grande - Ces filles aussi sont rousses.
4. Elle connaît quelqu'un ? Vous faites quelque chose ? Tu travailles encore ? Ils viennent souvent ? Vous avez rencontré quelqu'un ?
5. Elle en a trop - Il en a bu cinq - Tu en manges peu - Vous en mettez assez - Prenez-en beaucoup.
6. Si, je viens - Oui, j'ai/nous avons compris - Si, je parle/nous parlons français - Oui, j'en veux - Si, elles sont françaises.
7. nouveaux - oraux - beaux - vieilles - belles - gros.
8. Elle leur prête de l'argent - Vous leur écrivez - Explique-lui la solution - Ne lui parlez pas - Racontez-leur vos vacances - Je leur ai annoncé la bonne nouvelle.

## ■ SERVICE COMPRIS

*Le garçon :* Bonjour, monsieur, qu'est-ce que je vous sers ?

*Paul :* Un demi, s'il vous plaît... bien frais.

*Une femme :* Excusez-moi, je peux prendre cette chaise ?

*Paul :* Désolé, mais j'attends quelqu'un.

*Michel :* Salut, Paul ! Il y a longtemps que tu es là ?

*Paul :* Tu exagères, tu arrives en retard et tu ne t'excuses même pas. Tu sais que ça fait trois quarts d'heure que je t'attends !

*Michel :* Mais tu es assis, en train de boire et il fait beau... Qu'est-ce que tu veux de plus ? Allez, je paie l'addition.

*Paul :* N'oublie pas de laisser un pourboire !

### PRONUNCIATION

| | | |
|---|---|---|
| **Qu'est-ce que je vous sers ?** | [kɛskəʒvusɛr] | kehsske zher voo ser |
| **Excusez-moi** | [ɛkskyzemwa] | ehxkewzay mwah |
| **Il y a longtemps** | [iljalɔ̃tɑ̃] | eeleeah lawngtahng |
| **En train de boire** | [ɑ̃trɛ̃dbwar] | ahng trang der bwahr |

## SERVICE INCLUDED

*The waiter :* Good afternoon, sir. What can I bring you ?
*Paul :* A half, please... nice and cold.
*A lady :* Excuse me, may I take this chair ?
*Paul :* I'm sorry, but I'm waiting for somebody.
...
*Michel :* Hi, Paul ! Have you been here long ?
*Paul :* You go too far sometimes. You arrive late and you don't even apologize. You know that I've been waiting for you for three-quarters of an hour !
*Michel :* But you're sitting down, drinking a beer and the weather is fine... What more could you ask for ? Come on, I'll pay the bill.
*Paul :* Don't forget to leave a tip !

## GRAMMAR

### *Verbs :*

**Je vous sers** → present indicative of the verb **servir**

### Être en train de + *infinitive :*

This verbal construction is used to express an action which is in the process of being carried out (compare with the present continuous in English).

Tu es **en train de** boire.
**Negative form :** Tu n'es pas **en train de** boire.

### *To express duration :*

We use **il y a ... que** and **ça fait ... que** to express the duration of an action or state. Note that the present tense is used to express the notion of duration, unlike English which uses the present perfect.

**Ça fait** un quart d'heure **que** j'attends.
**Il y a** un quart d'heure **que** j'attends.

### *The length of time since an action took place :*

We can also use **il y a, il y a ... que** and **ça fait ... que** to express the length of time since an action took place.

Madame Serreaux est sortie **il y a** cinq minutes;
**Il y a** cinq minutes **que** madame Serreaux est sortie.
**Ça fait** cinq minutes **que** madame Serreaux est sortie.

## EXERCISES

### 1. Reply as shown in the example

Il vient ? (dormir) → Non, il est en train de dormir.
Elle mange ? (parler) → Non, elle ..........................................
Vous jouez au tennis ? (travailler) → Non, nous ......................
Il téléphone ? (écrire) → Non, il ..........................................

### 2. Put into the negative

Vous êtes en train de déjeuner. Ils sont en train de partir. Nous sommes en train de faire de la gymnastique. Je suis en train de prendre ma douche.

### 3. Change the sentences as shown in the example

Il a déjeuné il y a une heure. → Ça fait une heure qu'il a déjeuné. Elle est venue il y a dix minutes. Vous êtes allées au cinéma il y a trois jours. Je suis parti en vacances il y a deux semaines. Ils sont arrivés il y a un quart d'heure.

### 4. Translate into English

Ça fait une heure que je t'attends ! Qu'est-ce que je vous sers ? Je peux prendre ce journal ? Non, désolé.

## VOCABULARY

| | |
|---|---|
| maintenant : now<br>un croissant → a croissant<br>un petit déjeuner → breakfast<br>un café-crème → a white | coffee<br>une tartine → a slice of bread and butter<br>une eau minérale → a mineral water |

**Key to exercises :**

1. Elle est en train de parler. Nous sommes en train de travailler. Il est en train d'écrire.
2. Vous n'êtes pas en train de déjeuner. Ils ne sont pas en train de partir. Nous ne sommes pas en train de faire de la gymnastique. Je ne suis pas en train de prendre ma douche.
3. Ça fait dix minutes qu'elle est venue. Ça fait trois jours que vous êtes allées au cinéma. Ça fait deux semaines que je suis parti en vacances. Ça fait un quart d'heure qu'ils sont arrivés.
4. I've been waiting for an hour. What can I bring you ? May I take this newspaper ? No, I'm sorry.

## VARIATIONS

**Pour demander l'addition :**

Je vous dois combien ?
Ça fait combien ?
L'addition, s'il vous plaît.
Vous m'apportez la note ?

**Pour protester :**

Mais c'est { impossible ! / inadmissible ! / incroyable ! }

**Pour exprimer son découragement :**

J'en ai assez !
J'en ai marre !
J'en ai ras-le-bol !
Je suis découragé(e).
Je n'en peux plus.

***Asking for the bill :***

*How much do I owe you ?*
*How much is that ?*
*The bill, please.*
*Would you bring the bill ?*

***Complaining :***

*(But), it's { impossible! / unacceptable! / unbelievable! }*

***Expressing discouragement :***

*I've had enough!*
*I'm fed up!*
*I've had my fill!*
*I feel disheartened.*
*I can't go on.*

## SAY IT IN FRENCH

***You are in a restaurant :***

1. You want to sit down; ask if you may take a chair.
2. You have been waiting to be served for twenty minutes. Complain.
3. The waiter asks you what you would like to drink.
4. Ask for the bill.



**Possible answers :**

1. Je peux prendre cette chaise, s'il vous plaît ? 2. C'est incroyable, ça fait 20 minutes que j'attends ! 3. Qu'est-ce que je vous sers ? 4. Garçon ! L'addition, s'il vous plaît !

## VUE SUR LA MER

*Dans une agence de voyages*

— Quels sont les avantages de l'hôtel du Vieux Marin ?

— Il est plus luxueux et moins bruyant que l'hôtel du Grand Large.

— Et les inconvénients ?

— Il est plus éloigné de la plage et bien sûr plus cher.

— Finalement vous me conseillez lequel ?

— L'hôtel du Grand Large. Il est aussi confortable que l'hôtel du Vieux Marin et les chambres donnent sur la mer.

— Bon, d'accord. Réservez-moi une chambre double... avec salle de bains. Euh... pour la semaine du 8 au 15 août.

— Alors je vais vous demander un acompte. Le prix de la chambre est de 500 francs la nuit, petit déjeuner compris.

### PRONUNCIATION

| | | |
|---|---|---|
| **Plus luxueux** | [plylyksɥø] | plew lewxyur |
| **Moins bruyant** | [mwɛ̃brɥijɑ̃] | mwang brweeahng |
| **Et les inconvénients ?** | [elezɛ̃kɔ̃venjɑ̃] | ay lay zangkawngvayneeahng |
| **Plus éloigné** | [plyzelwaɲe] | plew aylwangyay |
| **Une chambre double** | [ynʃɑ̃brədubl] | ewn shahngbr doobler |

## ■ A SEA VIEW

*In a travel agency :*

— What are the advantages of the Vieux Marin hotel ?
— It's more luxurious and less noisy than the Grand Large hotel.
— And the disadvantages ?
— It's further from the beach and more expensive, of course !
— Which one would you advise me to take ?
— The Grand Large hotel. It's as comfortable as the Vieux Marin and the rooms look out over the sea.
— Um, alright. Book me a double room... with a bathroom. Er, for the week of the 8 to the 15 August.
— I'll have to ask you for a deposit. The price of the room is 500 francs a night, breakfast included.

## GRAMMAR

### ■ *The comparative with an adjective or an adverb :*

Structure: { **plus** / **moins** / **assis** } + adjective/adverb (+ **que**)

**With an adjective :**

To express superiority :
Le Grand Large est **plus** grand **que** le Vieux Marin.
To express equality :
Le Grand Large est **aussi** confortable **que** le Vieux Marin.
To express inferiority :
Le Grand Large est **moins** confortable **que** le Vieux Marin.

**With an adverb :**

Tu vas { **plus** / **aussi** / **moins** } vite (**que** moi).

**Note these two special cases :**

With the adjective **bon** → Cet hôtel est { **meilleur** / **aussi bon** / **pire** (ou **moins bon**) } que l'autre.

With the adverb **bien** → Cet hôtel est { **aussi bien** / **moins bien** / **mieux** } que l'autre

It is incorrect to say *plus bon* or *plus bien* !

## EXERCISES

### 1. *Form sentences expressing superiority or equality. Use the following adjectives :* cher, pauvre, vieux, gros, grand

Pierre / 31 ans et Paul / 62 ans → Paul est plus vieux que Pierre.
Sophie / 1,65 m et Marie / 1,72 m → ..........................................
Pain / 10 F le kg et viande / 95 F le kg → ..................................
Louis / 100 kg et Marc / 100 kg → ...........................................
M. Jacquet / 10000 F et M. Dax / 100 F → ................................

### 2. *Form sentences expressing inferiority or equality. Use the following adjectives :* éloigné, grand, cher, luxueux

Hôtel Renoir /200 chambres et hôtel Azur /50 chambres → ........
Hôtel Renoir /800 F et hôtel Azur /600 F → ................................
Paris /60 km et Fontainebleau /60 km. → ..................................
Hôtel Renoir /4 étoiles et Hôtel Azur /2 étoiles → ......................

### 3. *Translate into French*

The Vieux Marin is better than the Grand Large. Yes, but it's more expensive! What are the advantages of this hotel ? I have reserved a double room.

## VOCABULARY

pour : for
du ... au ... : from ... to ...

la réception → reception
le/la concierge → caretaker
la femme de ménage → cleaning lady
la clé → key
une valise → suitcase
les bagages → luggage
le bagagiste → porter
une suite → a suite of rooms

**Key to exercises :**

1. Marie est plus grande que Sophie. La viande est plus chère que le pain. Marc est aussi gros que Louis. M. Dax est plus pauvre que M. Jacquet.
2. L'hôtel Azur est moins grand que l'hôtel Renoir. L'hôtel Azur est moins cher que l'hôtel Renoir. Paris est aussi éloigné que Fontainebleau. L'hôtel Azur est moins luxueux que l'hôtel Renoir.
3. Le Vieux Marin est meilleur que le Grand Large. Oui, mais il est plus cher ! Quels sont les avantages de cet hôtel ? J'ai réservé une chambre double.

## VARIATIONS

| | |
|---|---|
| **Pour demander un conseil :** | ***Asking advice :*** |
| Qu'est-ce que vous me conseillez ? | *What do you advise me ?* |
| À votre/ton avis lequel est le mieux ? | *In your opinion, which is best ?* |
| Vous pensez que le Grand Large est mieux ? | *Do you think that the Grand Large is better ?* |
| À ma place, tu prendrais / vous prendriez lequel ? | *If you were me, which would you take ?* |
| Qu'est-ce que tu ferais / vous feriez à ma place ? | *What would you do if you were me ?* |
| **Pour donner un conseil :** | ***Giving advice :*** |
| Je te/vous conseille le Grand Large. | *I advise you to choose the Grand Large.* |
| Je pense/je crois que le Grand Large est le meilleur. | *I think that the Grand Large is the best.* |
| À mon avis, le Grand Large est bien/mieux. | *In my opinion the Grand Large is good/better.* |
| À mon avis, le Grand Large est pire. | *In my opinion the Grand Large is worse.* |
| À votre place, je prendrais le Grand Large. | *If I were you, I would take the Grand Large.* |

## SAY IT IN FRENCH

***You have to invite an important customer to lunch in a restaurant. You can't make up your mind between the Rhône and the Dauphiné. You are talking to a colleague about it.***

1. Ask him which is the better.
2. Tell him that you think that the Dauphiné is the better.
3. Tell him that it is more expensive than the Rhône.
4. Ask him what he would do if he were you.



**Possible answers :**

1. À ton avis, lequel est le mieux ? 2. Je pense/crois que le Dauphiné est meilleur. 3. Il est plus cher que le Rhône. 4. Qu'est-ce que tu ferais à ma place ?

## ■ LES SPORTS D'HIVER

*Au bureau*

— On est allés à Courchevel dans les Alpes.

— Pendant un mois ? C'est long !

— Ben... tu sais, le matin, on se levait à 8 h. Après, on prenait le petit déjeuner sur la terrasse, et puis on skiait toute la matinée jusqu'à une heure.

— Jusqu'à une heure ?

— Oui, et à trois heures et demie à peu près, on retournait sur les pistes.

— Mais alors vous faisiez tous les jours la même chose !

— Non, des fois, on faisait de la luge ou du patin à glace.

— Et vous vous couchiez à quelle heure ?

— Tôt, tu parles ! Pas question d'aller à la discothèque !

### PRONUNCIATION

| | | |
|---|---|---|
| **Pendant un mois ?** | [pɑ̃dɑ̃œ̃mwa] | pahngdahng ang mwah |
| **C'est long !** | [sɛlɔ̃] | seh lawng |
| **Jusqu'à une heure** | [ʒyskaynœr] | zhewskah ewn urr |
| **Pas question** | [pakɛstjɔ̃] | pah kehstyawng |

## WINTER SPORTS

*At the office*

— We went to Courchevel in the Alps.
— For a whole month ? That's a long time !
— Well, you know, in the morning, we got up at 8 o'clock. Then we had breakfast on the terrace and then went skiing all morning until one o'clock.
— One o'clock ?
— Yes. And at about half past three, we went back to the slopes.
— But that means you did the same thing every day ?
— No. Sometimes we went tobogganing or ice skating.
— And when did you go to bed ?
— Early, as you can imagine. No question of going to the discotheque !

## GRAMMAR

### *The Imperfect tense :*

The imperfect is used to express habitual actions carried out in the past.
In the dialogue, all the verbs in the imperfect refer to habitual actions carried out by persons during their past holidays.

**Conjugation :** To conjugate a verb in the imperfect we start from the first person plural of the present tense.

**faire** → nous **fais**ons

We thus obtain a root (**fais**) to which we add the endings of the imperfect : **ais, ais, ait, ions, iez, aient.**

| | |
|---|---|
| je fais**ais** | nous fais**ions** |
| tu fais**ais** | vous fais**iez** |
| il/elle/on fais**ait** | ils/elles fais**aient** |

Note that the verb **être** does not follow this general rule :
j'étais, tu étais, il était, nous étions, vous étiez, ils étaient

### *Agreement of the past participle :*

**on** est allés

Although the verb is in the third person singular, the past participle agrees with the subject **on** which, in this case, represents several persons as it is the equivalent of **nous**.

## EXERCISES

### 1. Describe your past habitual actions as in the example

(Faire de la gymnastique) → je faisais de la gymnastique.
(Partir seul en vacances) → ........................................................
(Écrire des poèmes) → ........................................................
(Skier toute la matinée) → ........................................................

### 2. Use the imperfect to describe Louis's past habitual actions

11 h. Lever → Il se levait à huit heures
11 h 30. petit déjeuner → ........................................................
12 h. patin à glace → ........................................................
21 h. sortir avec ses amis → ........................................................
23 h. discothèque → ........................................................

### 3. Translate into English

Deux ans, c'est long ! Je prenais le petit déjeuner sur la terrasse. Elles retournaient à l'hôtel vers 9 h. On est allés en France.

## VOCABULARY

| | |
|---|---|
| pendant : during<br>après : after<br>puis : then    vers : about<br><br>le ski → skiing<br>des skis → skis | un skieur → skier<br>une station → resort<br>un moniteur → instructor<br>un stage → training course<br>un sportif → sportsman |



**Key to exercises :**

1. Je partais. J'écrivais. Je skiais.
2. À 11 h 30, il prenait son petit déjeuner. À 12 h, il faisait du patin à glace. À 21 h, il sortait avec ses amis. À 23 h, il allait à la discothèque.
3. Two years is a long time! I used to have breakfast on the terrace. They used to return to the hotel at about 9 o'clock. We went to France.

## VARIATIONS

**Pour exprimer l'habitude au présent et au passé :**

À huit heures,
Le matin,
L'après-midi,
Le soir,
Le dimanche,
} on va se promener
on allait
se promener

Tous les jours,
Tous les mois,
Tous les ans,
Tous les vendredis,
Tous les week-ends,
} je vais à Paris.
j'allais à Paris.

Toutes les semaines, on va à la piscine.
En général, j'achète le journal.
D'habitude, j'écoutais la radio.
Normalement, il était en retard.

***Expressing habits in the present or the past :***

*At eight o'clock,*
*In the morning,*
*In the afternoon,*
*In the evening,*
*On Sundays,*
} *we go for a walk.*
*we went (used to go, would go) for a walk.*

*Every day,*
*Every month,*
*Every year,*
*Every Friday,*
*Every weekend,*
} *I go to Paris.*
*I went (used to go, would go) to Paris.*

*We go to the swimming pool every week.*
*I generally buy a newspaper.*
*I would usually listen to the radio.*
*Normally, he was late.*

## SAY IT IN FRENCH

***You are relating a childhood memory to a friend :***

1. Tell him that you usually did a lot of sport.
2. Tell him that you generally went to the winter sports.
3. Tell him that every Saturday you normally went skiing with an instructor.
4. Tell him that you bought new skis every year.



**Possible answers :**

1. D'habitude, je faisais beaucoup de sport. 2. En général, je partais aux sports d'hiver. 3. Tous les samedis, j'allais faire du ski avec un moniteur. 4. Tous les ans, j'achetais de nouveaux skis.

« C'est branché ! »

*« It's with it! »*

## DID YOU KNOW?

If you want to use a public telephone, you should first buy a phone card at a post office or *tabac* (a café where you can also buy stamps, tobacco, matches...) because it is sometimes difficult to find a telephone that accepts coins.

Many French people have a *Minitel* at home, a small computer terminal which gives them access via their telephone to a whole range of services such as the electronic telephone directory, train or theatre reservations, etc.

When travelling in France, you can take the high-speed TGV (or *Train à Grande Vitesse*) that gets you to Lyon from Paris in just two hours. The TGV also links Paris to Bordeaux, Brest and Nantes. Don't forget to book a seat — it's compulsory on the TGV!

**The French use a lot of abbreviations. Can you identify these and match them with their definitions?**

| | |
|---|---|
| SNCF • | • One of the major TV channels |
| CNRS • | • A high-speed train |
| TF1 • | • A radio station |
| RATP • | • A scientific research centre |
| TGV • | • The national railway company |
| RFI • | • The Paris underground |

***Answers:*** SNCF: Société nationale des chemins de fer français. CNRS: Centre national de la recherche scientifique. TF1: Télévision Française 1. RATP: Régie autonome des transports parisiens (métro). TGV: Train à grande vitesse. RFI: Radio France International.

## ■ À LA MODE

*Dans un magasin*

— Cette veste vous va parfaitement, madame.

— Oui… vous trouvez ? … Elle me serre un peu aux épaules.

— Mais c'est un modèle qui se porte très serré. C'est très à la mode cette année.

— Je vais quand même essayer la taille au-dessus et… vous avez la même en vert ?

*Dans une cabine d'essayage*

— Tu as essayé le pantalon blanc ?

— Oui, mais il est trop grand, c'est du 42.

— Tu as vu celui-ci ? … Il ressemble au mien.

— Non, le tien est mieux coupé.

### PRONUNCIATION

| | | |
|---|---|---|
| **Dans un magasin** | [dɑ̃zɛ̃magazɛ̃] | dahng zang mahgahzang |
| **Elle me serre** | [ɛlməsɛr] | ehl mer sehr |
| **La taille au-dessus** | [latajodsy] | lah tahy oa derssew |
| **Il ressemble au mien** | [ilrəsɑ̃blomjɛ̃] | eel rehssahngblomyang |

## IN FASHION

*In a shop*

— That jacket fits you perfectly, Madam.
— Yes... do you think so ? ...It's a little tight around the shoulders.
— It's a style that's worn very tight. It's very fashionable this year.
— Even so, I'll try the next size up and... do you have the same in green ?

*In a fitting room*

— Have you tried the white trousers ?
— Yes, but they're too big. They're size 42.
— Have you seen these ? They look like mine.
— No, yours are cut better.

## GRAMMAR

### Verbs :

**Tu as vu** → Perfect tense of the verb **voir**

### The possessive pronouns :

The possessive pronouns are used to avoid repetition :

| person | | 1 possessor | several possessors |
|---|---|---|---|
| **1st** | 1 masc. object | **le mien** | **le nôtre** |
| | fem. | **la mienne** | **la nôtre** |
| | several masc. objects | **les miens** | **les nôtres** |
| | fem. | **les miennes** | **les nôtres** |
| **2nd** | 1 masc. object | **le tien/le vôtre** | **le vôtre** |
| | fem. | **la tienne/la vôtre** | **la vôtre** |
| | several masc. objects | **les tiens/les vôtres** | **les vôtres** |
| | fem. | **les tiennes/les vôtres** | **les vôtres** |
| **3rd** | 1 masc. object | **le sien** | **le leur** |
| | fem. | **la sienne** | **la leur** |
| | several masc. objects | **les siens** | **les leurs** |
| | fem. | **les siennes** | **les leurs** |

## EXERCISES

### 1. *Avoid repetition by using the appropriate possessive pronouns*

J'écoute mes disques et toi, tu écoutes ............ . Je prends ma voiture et vous, vous prenez ............ . Elle aime ses amis et lui, il aime ............ . J'invite mes collègues et eux, ils invitent ...... ...... .

### 2. *Reply using the appropriate possessive adjectives and pronouns*

| | |
|---|---|
| C'est la voiture de Paul ? | → Oui, c'est sa voiture. |
| | → Oui, c'est la sienne. |
| C'est ton pantalon ? | → Oui, c'est .............................. |
| | → Oui, c'est .............................. |
| C'est la maison de tes parents ? | → Oui, c'est .............................. |
| | → Oui, c'est .............................. |
| Ce sont les amis de Sylvie ? | → Oui, ce sont .......................... |
| | → Oui, ce sont .......................... |

### 3. *Translate into French*

These trousers fit me well. Let's take yours (fem. sing.). I'm going to try the next size up. This jacket is a little tight.

## VOCABULARY

| | |
|---|---|
| là-bas : over there | un chemisier → blouse |
| | un pull → pullover |
| une jupe → skirt | une veste → jacket |
| une robe → dress | un costume → suit (man's) |
| une chemise → shirt | un tailleur → suit (lady's) |



**Key to exercises :**

1. les tiens / la vôtre / les siens / les leurs
2. mon pantalon / le mien / leur maison / la leur / ses amis / les siens.
3. Ce pantalon me va bien. Prenons la tienne. Je vais essayer la taille au-dessus. Cette veste me serre un peu.

## VARIATIONS

**Dans les magasins.**

*In the shops.*

**Pour exprimer l'hésitation :**

J'hésite, je ne sais pas lesquelles prendre.
Je ne sais pas quoi prendre/faire.
Qu'est-ce que je prends ?/fais ?

***Expressing hesitation :***

*I'm not sure, I don't know which ones to take.*
*I don't know what to take/to do.*
*What shall I take ? / do ?*

**Pour exprimer une décision :**

C'est décidé, je prends le bleu.
Ça y est, je vais prendre le petit.
Bon, je choisis les noires.
Finalement, je ne vais pas le prendre.

***Expressing a decision :***

*I've decided, I'll take the blue one.*
*That's it, I'll take the small one.*
*Good, I'll have the black ones.*
*I'm not going to take it, after all.*

**Pour retarder votre décision :**

Je ne suis pas convaincu.
Je vais réfléchir.
Laissez-moi réfléchir.
Je repasserai demain.
Finalement, je préfère attendre.

***Postponing your decision :***

*I'm not sure.*
*I'll think about it.*
*Let me think about it.*
*I'll come back tomorrow.*
*Actually, I'd rather wait.*

## SAY IT IN FRENCH

***You are in a department store :***

1. Tell the sales assistant that you would like to try on a blue jacket.
2. Ask where the fitting room is.
3. Say that you don't know what to do.
4. Say that you prefer to think about it.



**Possible answers :**

1. Je voudrais essayer cette veste bleue. 2. Où est la cabine d'essayage ? 3. Je ne sais pas quoi faire. 4. Finalement, je préfère réfléchir.

## ■ SOUVENIRS DE JEUNESSE

*Chez la grand-mère*

— Cette photo, où tu es avec l'oncle André, c'était où ?

— C'était chez moi, avant d'habiter ici.

— C'était petit chez toi ?

— Non, c'était grand ! Mais là, tu vois seulement la salle à manger.

...

— Ici, à gauche, qui est-ce ?

— Tu ne le reconnais pas ? C'est ton père.

— Mon père ?

— Eh oui, il était jeune !

...

— Et sur cette photo ? Derrière toi, qu'est-ce que c'est ?

— Ma première voiture ! C'était une Renault. Elle était splendide ! À l'époque, je conduisais...

### PRONUNCIATION



| | | |
|---|---|---|
| **Chez la grand-mère** | [ʃelagrɑ̃mɛr] | shay lah grahngmehr |
| **C'était chez moi** | [setɛʃemwa] | sehtay shay mwah |
| **C'était petit chez toi ?** | [setɛptiʃetwa] | sehtay pertee shay twah |
| **C'était une Renault** | [setɛynrəno] | sehtay ewn Rernoa |

## ■ MEMORIES OF ONE'S YOUTH

*At your grandmother's*
– And this photo, where you're with uncle André, where was it ?
– It was my house before living here.
– Was it a small house ?
– No, it was big ! But there, you can only see the dining room.
...
– Here, on the left, who's that ?
– Don't you recognize him ? It's your father.
– My father ?
– That's right. He was young !
...
– And on this photo ? Behind you, what is it ?
– My first car. It was a Renault. It was marvellous. I used to drive in those days ...

## GRAMMAR

### ▌*Verbs :*

**Tu ne le reconnais pas ?** → present of the verb **reconnaître**
**Je conduisais** → imperfect of the verb **conduire**

### ▌*Use of the imperfect :*

The imperfect is used to describe circumstances, places, things or people in the past.
C'était une Renault. Elle était splendide ! À l'époque, je conduisais. C'était petit chez toi ? — Non, c'était grand !

### ▌Qui est-ce ? *or* Qu'est-ce que c'est ? *:*

**Qui est-ce** is used to ask the identity of a person.
Qui est-ce ? — C'est ton père.
**Qu'est-ce que c'est** is used to ask the identity of an object.
Qu'est-ce que c'est ? — C'est ma première voiture.



### ▌Chez *:*

The preposition **chez** is used before a person's name or before a disjunctive pronoun to designate that person's home.
C'était où ? — C'était **chez** moi. — C'était petit **chez** toi ?
Où est-ce que tu vas ? — Je vais **chez** Paul.

## EXERCISES

### 1. *Put the verbs in brackets into the imperfect in order to describe persons, objects or circumstances in the past*

Quand elle (être) ......... petite, elle (être) ......... blonde. Quand j' (avoir) ......... vingt ans, je (conduire) ......... une belle voiture.

### 2. *Choose the correct question :* Qui est-ce ? *or* Qu'est-ce que c'est ?

C'est le frère de ma mère. → ..........................................................
C'est une vieille dame. → ..............................................................
C'est la bicyclette de mon cousin. → ............................................

### 3. *Reply using* chez *+ a disjunctive pronoun*

Tu vas chez Sophie ? → Oui, je vais chez elle.
Tu travailles chez Paul ? → Oui, je ................................................
Elle habite chez ses parents ? → Oui, elle .....................................
Vous venez chez moi ? → Oui, nous ...............................................
Elle part en vacances chez ses cousines ? → Oui, elle ..................

### 4. *Translate into English*

Elles sont belles, vos photos ! Vous ne les reconnaissez pas ? À l'époque, j'étais jeune ! C'est chez vous ?

## VOCABULARY

derrière : behind
là : there où : where
celle-là : that one (fem.)

les parents → parents
la mère → mother
le grand-père → grandfather
les grands-parents → grandparents
le cousin → cousin
la tante → aunt
le beau-frère → brother-in-law
la belle-sœur → sister-in-law



**Key to exercises :**

1. elle était, elle était / j'avais, je conduisais.
2. Qui est-ce ? Qui est-ce ? Qu'est-ce que c'est ?
3. Je travaille chez lui. elle habite chez eux. nous allons chez toi/vous. elle part en vacances chez elle.
4. Your photos are lovely! Don't you recognize them ? I was young then. Is this your house ?

## VARIATIONS

**Pour demander des informations.**

**Sur une personne :**

Qui est-ce ?
Je le connais ?
Je l'ai déjà vu ?

**Sur un objet :**

Qu'est-ce que c'est ? / c'était ?
C'est / c'était gros ?

**Sur un lieu :**

Où est-ce ? / était-ce ?
Où est-ce que c'était ?
Ça se passait où ?

**Sur le moment :**

C'était quand ?
C'était à quelle époque ?
C'était en quelle année ?

**Sur une action :**

Qu'est-ce que tu faisais ?
Tu conduisais ?

***Asking for information.***

***About a person :***

*Who is it ?*
*Do I know him ?*
*Have I already seen him ?*

***About an object :***

*What is it ? / was it ?*
*Is/was it big ?*

***About a place :***

*Where is/was it ?*
*Where was it ?*
*Where was it happening ?*

***About the time :***

*When was it ?*
*When was it ?*
*What year was it ?*

***About an action :***

*What were you doing ?*
*Were you driving ?*

## SAY IT IN FRENCH

***You are looking at some old films with a friend :***

1. Ask who the person you are looking at is.
2. Ask him if you know the person.
3. Ask him when it was.
4. Ask him if it was at the home of his parents.



**Possible answers :**

1. Qui est-ce ? 2. Je le/la connais ? 3. C'était à quelle époque ? 4. C'était chez tes parents ?

## RÉUNION DE TRAVAIL

**MAGOMA**
Société Anonyme
425, Sherbrooke est
Montréal Québec H3L1K7

Montréal, le 8 janvier

Cher collègue et ami,

Quelques lignes pour préparer ma prochaine visite à Paris.

À mon arrivée, je souhaiterais rencontrer M. Château. À 11 h, ce serait parfait. Nous pourrions également déjeuner ensemble si, bien sûr, vous êtes disponible.

L'après-midi, je voudrais me reposer un moment avant la conférence de presse de 17 h.

J'aimerais ensuite rencontrer toute l'équipe pour une brève réunion de travail.

Je vous serais reconnaissant de me confirmer tous ces points aussi rapidement que possible.

Merci d'avance et à bientôt.

*John Mitchum*

### PRONUNCIATION



| | | |
|---|---|---|
| **Cher collègue** | [ʃɛrkɔlɛg] | shehr kolehg |
| **Ma prochaine visite** | [maprɔʃɛnvizit] | mah proshehn veezeet |
| **Je souhaiterais** | [ʒəswɛtrɛ] | zher sooehterray |
| **Ce serait parfait** | [səsrɛparfɛ] | ser seray pahfay |

## A BUSINESS MEETING

Montreal, 8 January

Dear friend and colleague,
Just a few lines to prepare my next visit to Paris.
Upon arrival, I would like to meet Mr Château. 11 o'clock would be perfect. We could also have lunch together if, of course, you arc free.
In the afternoon, I would like to have a rest before the press conference at 5 o'clock p.m.
I would then like to meet the whole team for a short meeting.
I would be grateful if you would confirm all these points as quickly as possible. Thank you in advance and see you soon,
John Mitchum.

## GRAMMAR

### *Verbs :*

**Ce serait, je serais** → present conditional of the verb **être**
**Je voudrais** → present conditional of the verb **vouloir**
**Nous pourrions** → present conditional of the verb **pouvoir**

### *The present conditional :*

The present conditional is used to express suggestions, as a polite way of making requests or giving orders, or to convey the idea of some doubt about a situation.
**Conjugation :** The present conditional is conjugated by adding the endings of the imperfect tense (**ais, ais, ait, ions, iez, aient**) to the radical of the future tense of the verb in question.
Example : prendre → future : je prendr**ai** → radical : **prendr**

| | |
|---|---|
| je prendr**ais** | nous prendr**ions** |
| tu prendr**ais** | vous prendr**iez** |
| il/elle prendr**ait** | ils/elles prendr**aient** |

### *The infinitive of reflexive verbs :*

| | |
|---|---|
| **Je** voudrais **me** reposer. | **Nous** pourrions **nous** reposer. |
| **Tu** devrais **te** lever. | **Vous** aimeriez **vous** coucher. |
| **Elle/il** voudrait **se** laver. | **Ils/elles** souhaiteraient **se** laver |

### *Abbreviations :*

Monsieur → **M.** Messieurs → **MM.** Madame → **Mme**
Mademoiselle → **Mlle**

## EXERCISES

### 1. *Use the future of the following verbs to construct the present conditional*

Vouloir → je voudrai → vous ........... Pouvoir → je ........... → ils ........... Apprendre → j'........... → j'........... Faire → je ........... → nous ........... Avoir → j'........... → elle ...........

### 2. *Use the present conditional to express the following requests or orders politely*

Tu dois téléphoner à Luc. → Tu devrais téléphoner à Luc.
Vous devez faire ce travail rapidement. → ................................
Tu peux parler plus fort. → ................................................
Je veux partir tout de suite. → ..............................................

### 3. *Reply as in the example*

Qu'est-ce qu'ils veulent ? (se laver) → Ils voudraient se laver.
Qu'est-ce qu'elle souhaite ? (se reposer) → Elle ..........................
Qu'est-ce que vous voulez ? (se coucher) → Nous .....................
Qu'est-ce que tu aimerais faire ? (se promener) → J'....................

### 4. *Translate into French*

They could come at eight o'clock. That would be very good. I would be grateful if you (pl) would phone me.

## VOCABULARY

| | |
|---|---|
| vers : about<br>aussi que : as .... as | un homme d'affaires → business man |
| une entreprise → company | un voyage d'affaires → business trip |
| un chef d'entreprise → company manager | un directeur commercial → sales manager |



**Key to exercises :**

1. vous voudriez / je pourrai - ils pourraient / j'apprendrai - j'apprendrais / je ferai - nous ferions / j'aurai - elle aurait
2. vous devriez faire. tu pourrais parler. Je voudrais partir
3. Elle souhaiterait se reposer. Nous voudrions nous coucher. J'aimerais me promener.
4. Ils pourraient venir à huit heures. Ce serait très bien. Je vous serais reconnaissant de me téléphoner.

## VARIATIONS

**Pour suggérer :**

Ça te plairait de…
Il faudrait…
Tu pourrais…
On devrait…
Ce serait sympa /chouette de…
} l'inviter.

***Suggesting :***

*Would you like to ...*
*We ought to ...*
*You could ...*
*We should ...*
*That would be nice/great to ...*
} *invite him.*

**Pour exprimer poliment une demande ou un ordre :**

J'aimerais (bien) la connaître.
Je voudrais (bien) lui parler.
Je souhaiterais téléphoner
Je préférerais partir maintenant.
Je serais heureux/content de vous rencontrer.
Je vous serais reconnaissant de me tenir au courant.
Il faudrait/vous devriez/vous pourriez leur écrire.

***Expressing a request or order politely :***

*I'd (really) like to get to know her.*
*I'd (really) like to speak to her.*
*I'd like to phone.*
*I'd prefer to leave now.*
*I'd be happy/pleased to meet you.*
*I'd be grateful if you'd keep me informed.*
*You ought to/You should/You could write to them (perhaps).*

## SAY IT IN FRENCH

***Along with several colleagues, you are organizing a little party in your company :***

1. Suggest having the party on a Saturday.
2. Tell them that you could rest on the Sunday.
3. Tell them that you should invite some colleagues.
4. Suggest that perhaps you ought to invite the Managing Director.



**Possible answers :**

1. On pourrait/nous pourrions la faire un samedi. 2. Nous pourrions nous reposer/on pourrait se reposer le dimanche. 3. On devrait/nous devrions inviter quelques collègues. 4. On devrait peut-être inviter le P.-D.G.

# BILAN 5

■ **NOW YOU KNOW HOW TO DESCRIBE AN ACTION HAPPENING NOW,**

***1. Transform the following sentences as in the example.***

Ils étudient le français → Ils sont en train d'étudier le français. Vous ne mangez pas → ... Nous regardons des photos → ... Les clients laissent un pourboire → ... Nous payons → ...

■ **...HOW TO EXPRESS DURATION,**

***2. Answer the following questions.***

Elle est partie ? (dix minutes) → Oui, il y a/ça fait dix minutes qu'elle est partie.
Vous êtes en vacances ? (une semaine) → Oui, ...
Ils dorment ? (une heure) → Oui, ...
Elle habite en France ? (trois mois) → Oui, ...

■ **...HOW TO MAKE COMPARISONS,**

***3. Make comparisons between these three hotels. Use*** **confortable, grand, cher.**

| | **Hermitage** | **La Tour Bleue** | **Henri IV** |
|---|---|---|---|
| **étoiles** | ★★★★ | ★★ | ★ |
| **chambres** | 30 | 15 | 40 |
| **prix** | 800 F | 400 F | 120 F |

Hermitage et Henri IV : ....................................................................
La Tour et Hermitage : ....................................................................

■ **...HOW TO TALK ABOUT PAST HABITS,**

***4. Look at the list of times and actions and describe what Alan and Pauline did on holiday every day.***

10 h lever, 11 h plage, 13 h déjeuner, 16 h promenade, 20 h dîner, 22 h discothèque.
À 10 h, ils ... À 11 h, ... À 13 h, ...
À 16 h, ils ... À 20 h, ... À 22 h, ...



■ **...HOW TO EXPRESS POSSESSION,**

***5. Replace the words underlined with a possessive pronoun..***

Mes amis sont plus jeunes que tes amis → ... Notre voiture est plus grande que votre voiture → ... Mes parents sont plus gentils que ses parents → ... Tes voisins sont moins sympathiques que mes voisins → ... Notre famille est petite mais leur famille est grande → ... Ses enfants sont plus grands que nos enfants → ..

**■ ...HOW TO SUGGEST SOMETHING OR MAKE A POLITE REQUEST,**

***6. Put into the present conditional tense.***

Je veux sortir. Nous souhaitons voir le Directeur. Il faut fermer la porte. Je préfère ne pas le rencontrer. Nous pouvons téléphoner ? Tu dois écouter.

**■ ...HOW TO GIVE INFORMATION WITH A CERTAIN CIRCUMSPECTION,**

***7. Put into the present conditional tense.***

Ses enfants sont malades. Sophie part en vacances. Julie habite en France. Le Directeur est absent. Ils sont très riches.

**■ ...HOW TO CONJUGATE REFLEXIVE VERBS.**

***8. Complete the following sentences using the appropriate reflexive pronoun.***

Nous devons ... coucher. Vous voulez ... laver. Ils souhaitent ... reposer. Il est en train de ... doucher. Je ne veux pas ... lever.

## KEY TO EXERCISES

1. Vous n'êtes pas en train de manger - Nous sommes en train de regarder des photos - Les clients sont en train de laisser un pourboire - Nous sommes en train de payer.
2. Oui, il y a/ça fait une semaine que nous sommes en vacances - Oui, il y a/ça fait une heure qu'ils dorment - Oui, il y a/ça fait trois mois qu'elle habite en France.
3. L'Hermitage est plus confortable que le Henri IV - L'Hermitage est moins grand que le Henri IV - L'Hermitage est plus cher que le Henri IV - Le Henri IV est moins confortable que La Tour - Le Henri IV est plus grand que La Tour - Le Henri IV est moins cher que La Tour.
4. Ils se levaient - Ils allaient à la plage - Ils déjeunaient - Ils se promenaient - Ils dînaient - Ils allaient à la discothèque.
5. Mes amis sont plus jeunes que les tiens - la vôtre - les siens - les miens - la leur - les nôtres.
6. Je voudrais - nous souhaiterions - il faudrait - je préfèrerais - nous pourrions - tu devrais.
7. seraient - partirait - habiterait - serait - seraient.
8. nous - vous - se - se - me.

## ■ UN BON SALAIRE

*Dans le bureau du chef du personnel*

— Une augmentation, une augmentation... mais Madame Liban, vos responsabilités dans l'entreprise sont toujours les mêmes !

— Peut-être, mais je gagne moins que mon collègue Pierre Chanceux et nous faisons le même travail.

— Pierre Chanceux a plus d'ancienneté que vous dans la maison.

— Moi j'ai plus de diplômes et remarquez que mon salaire est le même depuis un an.

— Bon, bon, je vais voir ce que je peux faire... mais je ne vous promets rien !

### PRONUNCIATION

| | | |
|---|---|---|
| **Une augmentation** | [ynɔgmɑ̃tasjɔ̃] | ewn oagmahngtahssyawng |
| **Je gagne moins** | [ʒəgaɲmwɛ̃] | zher gahñ mwang |
| **J'ai plus de diplômes** | [ʒɛplysdədiplom] | zhay plew der deeploam |
| **Je ne vous promets rien** | [ʒənvuprɔmɛrjɛ̃] | zher ner voo promeh ryang |

## A GOOD SALARY

*In the personnel manager's office*

— A raise, a raise ... but Mrs Liban, your responsibilities in the company are still the same !

— Perhaps, but I earn less than my colleague Pierre Chanceux and we do the same work.

— Pierre Chanceux has been with the company longer than you .

— But I have more qualifications and I'd like to point out that my salary has been the same for the past year .

— Alright, alright. I'll see what I can do ... but I'm not promising you anything.

## GRAMMAR

### *Comparing quantities :*

Structure 1 :
verb + { **plus** / **autant** / **moins** } (+ **que** + noun or disjunctive pronoun)

Note that **que** becomes **qu'** before a noun or pronoun beginning with a vowel. → **plus qu'elle** **plus qu'eux**

Structure 2 :
verb + { **plus de** / **autant de** / **moins de** } + noun (+ **que** + noun or disjunctive pronoun)

Note that in this construction **de** is invariable and becomes **d'** when the following word begins with a vowel or silent **h**.

**Expressing superiority :**

Mme Liban gagne **plus** (que M. Chanceux).
Mme Liban gagne **plus d'**argent (**que** M. Chanceux).

**Expressing equality :**

Mme Liban gagne **autant** (que M. Chanceux).
Mme Liban gagne **autant d'**argent (**que** M. Chanceux).

**Expressing inferiority :**

Mme Liban gagne **moins** (que M. Chanceux).
Mme Liban gagne **moins d'**argent (**que** M. Chanceux).

### *Le même, la même, les mêmes :*

**Même** agrees in gender and number with the noun which it qualifies or replaces.

Nous avons **le même** ami. – C'est vrai, nous avons **le même**.
Nous avons **les mêmes** amis. – C'est vrai, nous avons **les mêmes**.

## EXERCISES

### 1. Make comparisons, as in the example

Paul travaille 8 h, Marie travaille 7 h → Paul travaille plus que Marie.
Pierre dort 10 h, Marc dort 12 h → Pierre dort...
Louis gagne 8 000 F, Paul gagne 10 000 F → Louis gagne...
Luc marche 1 h, Jean ne marche jamais → Luc marche...

### 2. Make comparisons, as in the example

Jacques a trois amies, Bernard a une amie → Jacques a plus d'amies que Bernard.
Ophélie lit trois livres, Laurent lit trois livres → Ophélie...
Daniel achète deux stylos, Sylvie achète quatre stylos → Daniel...
Pierre boit 1 litre de lait, Alain boit 1 litre de lait → Pierre...

### 3. *Complete using* le même, la même, les mêmes

Il a une superbe voiture. Mon frère a acheté... Vous lisez de beaux livres, Paul lit... Tu écoutes un disque, j'ai...

### 4. Translate into English

Vous avez le même salaire. Je travaille plus que Michel. Elle gagne moins que nous. Vous avez sans doute raison.

## VOCABULARY

pourtant : yes, but
même : same
sans doute : no doubt

un métier → profession, trade
un emploi → job
la paye → pay
un boulot → job (slang)
les congés → holidays
une fiche de paye → pay slip
toucher → to earn (salary)



**Key to exercises :**

1. moins que / moins que / plus que
2. lit autant de livres que Laurent / achète moins de stylos que Sylvie / boit autant de lait qu'Alain.
3. la même / les mêmes / le même.
4. You have the same salary. I work more than Michel. She earns less than us. You are certainly right.

## VARIATIONS

**Pour exprimer la similitude :**

Nous avons le même salaire.
J'ai le même salaire que toi.
Ils sont pareils.
Il ressemble à son père.
Ils se ressemblent.
Il est comme son père.
On dirait du pain.
Ça me rappelle des fruits exotiques.

***Expressing similarity :***

*We have the same salary.*
*I have the same salary as you.*
*They are the same.*
*He resembles his father.*
*They resemble each other.*
*He's like his father.*
*It's like bread.*
*It reminds me of tropical fruit.*

**Pour exprimer la différence :**

Ils sont différents.
Ils ne se ressemblent pas du tout.
C'est le contraire/l'inverse de...

***Expressing difference :***

*They're different.*
*They don't resemble each other at all.*
*It's the opposite of..*

**Pour exprimer le mécontentement :**

Je trouve ça injuste.
Je pense que c'est scandaleux.

***Expressing displeasure :***

*I find that unfair.*
*I think that it's outrageous.*

## SAY IT IN FRENCH

***You are comparing your pay slip with a colleague :***

1. Say that you work more than he does.
2. Tell him that you have the same responsibilities.
3. Say that you earn less than him.
4. Protest : you think that it is unacceptable and outrageous.

**Possible answers :**

1. Je travaille plus que toi. 2. Nous avons les mêmes responsabilités. 3. Et je gagne moins que toi. 4. Je pense que c'est inadmissible et scandaleux.

## JE ME SENS MAL

— Docteur, je ne me sens pas bien.
— Voyons… qu'est-ce qu'il vous arrive ?
— J'ai des frissons, je crois que j'ai de la fièvre et puis j'ai mal à la tête et je tousse.
— Bon, déshabillez-vous, je vais vous examiner.

— Eh bien, vous avez une bonne grippe ! Ce n'est pas bien grave. Je vais vous faire une ordonnance… aspirine, antibiotique et un sirop pour la toux.
— Je dois rester couché ?
— Bien sûr, je vais vous faire un arrêt de travail, et surtout, reposez-vous !

### PRONUNCIATION

| | | |
|---|---|---|
| **Je me sens mal** | [ʒəmsɑ̃mal] | zher mer sahngmahl |
| **Des frissons** | [defrisɔ̃] | day freessawng |
| **Je vais vous examiner** | [ʒəvɛvuzɛgza mine] | zher vay voo ehxahmeenay |
| **Je vais vous faire une ordonnance** | [ʒəvɛvufɛryn ɔrdɔnɑ̃s] | zher vay voo fehr ewn ordawngahngss |
| **Reposez-vous !** | [rəpozevu] | rerpozay voo |

## I FEEL ILL

— Doctor, I don't feel well.
— Let's see... what's the matter ?
— I'm shivering, I think I have a temperature, I've got a headache and a cough .
— Very well. Get undressed and I'll examine you.
...
— Well, you've got the 'flu ! But it's not very serious. I'm going to make you out a prescription ...aspirin, antibiotics and some cough mixture.
— Must I say in bed ?
— Of course. I'm going to take you off work. But, above all, get some rest !

## GRAMMAR

### *Verbs :*

**Déshabillez-vous** → present imperative of the verb **se déshabiller**

### Pourquoi ? *and* parce que *:*

**Pourquoi** is used to ask about the reason for something. The reply usually begins with **parce que**.
Je ne peux pas venir. — **Pourquoi** ? — **Parce que** j'ai de la fièvre.

### *Interrogative constructions with* pourquoi *:*

Vous achetez ce livre, **pourquoi** ?
**Pourquoi est-ce** que vous achetez ce livre ?

### Il faut *:*

**Il faut** is used to express obligation. There are two possible constructions :
**Il faut** + noun → Pour acheter une maison, il faut de l'argent.
**Il faut** + infinitive → Il faut dormir pour se reposer.

### Avoir besoin de *:*

**Avoir besoin de** is used to express the need for someone or something.
Je ne peux pas le faire seul. J'ai **besoin de** toi.
Nous avons **besoin d'**argent pour finir les travaux de la maison.
Note that **de** becomes **d'** before a noun beginning with a vowel or silent **h**.

## EXERCISES

### 1. *Answer the following questions using sentences beginning with* parce que

Pourquoi est-ce que tu pars ? (être fatigué) → Parce que je suis fatigué.
Pourquoi est-ce que vous mangez ? (avoir faim) → ......................
Pourquoi est-ce qu'elle se couche ? (avoir de la fièvre) → ............
Pourquoi n'écoutent-ils pas ? (détester cette musique) → ............

### 2. *Reply as in the example. Use* en

Tu as besoin du stylo ? → Oui, j'**en** ai besoin.
Elle a besoin d'argent ? → Oui, elle ............................................
Vous avez besoin de livres ? → Oui, nous ....................................
Ils ont besoin d'aspirine ? → Oui, ils ..........................................

### 3. *Transform the sentence as shown in the example*

Tu dois te reposer. → Il faut te reposer.
Nous devons nous lever. → ..........................................................
Vous devez vous déshabiller. → .................................................
Vous devez écouter. → ...............................................................

### 4. *Translate into French*

The doctor is going to examine you. You must go to bed. I need to sleep. I have a very high temperature. I've got the 'flu.

## VOCABULARY

| | |
|---|---|
| partout : everywhere<br>surtout : above all<br><br>un malade → a sick person, patient | la maladie → illness<br>un rhume → a cold<br>le ventre → belly<br>les médicaments → medicine |



**Key to exercises :**

1. Parce que j'ai/nous avons faim. Parce qu'elle a de la fièvre. Parce qu'ils détestent cette musique.
2. elle en a besoin. / nous en avons besoin / ils en ont besoin.
3. Il faut nous lever. / Il faut vous déshabiller. / Il faut écouter.
4. Le docteur va t'examiner. Il faut te coucher. J'ai besoin de dormir. J'ai beaucoup de fièvre. J'ai la grippe.

## VARIATIONS

| | |
|---|---|
| **Pour interroger quelqu'un sur sa santé :** | ***Inquiring about someone's health :*** |
| Ça ne va pas ? | *Is something wrong ?* |
| Qu'est-ce qui t'/vous arrive ? | *What's wrong with you ?* |
| Qu'est-ce qui ne va pas ? | *What's wrong ?* |
| Tu es malade ? | *Are you ill ?* |
| **Pour parler de votre santé :** | ***Talking about your health :*** |
| Ça va (très bien). | *I'm fine.* |
| Je suis en pleine forme. | *I'm on top form.* |
| Ça ne va pas (du tout). | *I'm not (at all) well.* |
| Ça va (très) mal. | *I'm feeling (very) bad.* |
| Je ne me sens pas (très) bien. | *I'm not feeling (very well).* |
| Je suis malade. | *I'm ill.* |
| **Pour dire où vous avez mal :** | ***Saying where it hurts :*** |
| J'ai (très) mal là/ici. | *I've got a (severe) pain there /here.* |
| Ça me fait mal là/ici. | *It hurts there/here.* |
| J'ai mal à la tête/à la gorge/à la jambe/à la main. | *I have a headache/a sore throat /a pain in my leg/a pain in my hand...* |
| J'ai mal au ventre/au dos/au pied/au bras... | *I have a pain in my belly/back /foot/arm...* |
| J'ai mal à l'estomac/l'œil... | *I have a sore stomach/eye...* |
| J'ai mal aux yeux/dents/pieds... | *My eyes/teeth/feet...hurt.* |

## SAY IT IN FRENCH

***You are ill and you are 'phoning your doctor :***

1. Tell him that you don't feel very well.
2. Tell him that you have a temperature and are shivering.
3. Explain that you have a bad headache and a sore throat.
4. Ask him if you have to take some medecine.

**Possible answers :**

1. Je ne me sens pas très bien. 2. J'ai de la fièvre et des frissons. 3. J'ai très mal à la tête et à la gorge. 4. Est-ce que je dois prendre des médicaments ?

## CONSULTEZ VOTRE MÉDECIN

*Dans une pharmacie*

— Je voudrais quelque chose pour mon mari, il a très mal à l'estomac.

— Ça fait longtemps ?

— Il y a deux ou trois jours qu'il se plaint et qu'il a envie de vomir.

— Le mieux c'est de voir un médecin.

— Vous pouvez nous recommander quelqu'un ?

— Bien sûr, ... le docteur Charlot, rue des Fleurs... si vous prenez rendez-vous maintenant, il vous recevra dans la journée.

— Vous ne pouvez rien me donner en attendant ?

— Si, ce sirop. S'il le prend tout de suite, ça va le soulager.

### PRONUNCIATION

| | | |
|---|---|---|
| **Ça fait longtemps ?** | [safɛlɔ̃tɑ̃] | sah fay lawngtahng |
| **Prenez rendez-vous** | [prənerɑ̃devu] | prernay rahngday voo |
| **Vous ne pouvez rien** | [vunpuverjɛ̃] | voo ner poovay ryang |
| **En attendant** | [ɑ̃natɑ̃dɑ̃] | ahng nahtahngdahng |
| **Ça va le soulager** | [savalsulaʒe] | sah vah ler soolahzhay |

## ■ *ASK YOUR DOCTOR*

*In a chemist's*

— I'd like something for my husband. He has a very bad stomach ache.
— Has he had it for a long time ?
- He's been feeling ill and wanting to vomit for about 2 or 3 days.
— The best thing is to see a doctor.
— Can you recommend someone ?
— Certainly... Dr Charlot, rue des Fleurs... If you make an appointment now, he'll see you today.
— Can't you give me something in the meantime ?
— Yes, this syrup. If he takes it straight away, it will ease his pain.

## GRAMMAR

### ▌*Verbs :*

**Il se plaint** → present indicative of the verb **se plaindre**
**Il vous recevra** → future of the verb **recevoir**

### ▌*Present conditional :*

**Si** + present tense of verb + (immediate) future tense of verb
**S'**il le **prend** tout de suite, ça **va le soulager.**
**Si** vous **prenez** rendez-vous maintenant, il vous **recevra** dans la journée.

## EXERCISES

### 1. Insert the correct form of the verbs given in brackets

Si tu te couches, tu (aller) ............. mieux. Si vous venez demain, nous (dîner) ............. au restaurant. Si elle est malade, nous ne (venir) ............. pas. Nous appellerons le médecin, si c'(être) ............. nécessaire.

### 2. Put the verbs in brackets into the appropriate tense

S'il (faire) ............. beau, nous (aller) ............. à la plage. Si vous (prendre) ............. rendez-vous, nous vous (recevoir) ............. S'ils (venir) ............., nous (aller) ............. au restaurant. Vous (allez) ............. mieux, si vous (se coucher) ............. maintenant.

### 3. *Reply using* il y a

Il y a combien de temps que vous êtes malade ? Il y a deux jours.
Il y a longtemps que vous avez mal ? (une semaine)
Il y a combien de temps qu'elle dort ? (trois heures)
Il y a longtemps qu'ils parlent ? (un quart d'heure)
Il y a longtemps que ça a commencé ? (cinq minutes)

### 4. Translate into French

If you (sing.) take it immediately, you'll feel better. Can you (sing.) recommend something to me ? I've had toothache for an hour. Make an appointment today.

## VOCABULARY

| | |
|---|---|
| quelque chose : something | une piqûre → an injection |
| | guérir → to cure |
| soigner → to nurse, tend | faire des analyses → to do tests |
| souffrir → to suffer | une brûlure → a burn |
| une blessure → an injury | une coupure → a cut |



**Key to exercises :**

1. tu iras / nous dînerons / nous ne viendrons pas / c'est
2. fait, irons / prenez, recevrons / viennent, irons / irez, vous vous couchez
3. il y a une semaine / il y a trois heures / il y a un quart d'heure / il y a cinq minutes.
4. Si tu le prends tout de suite, tu seras soulagé. Tu peux me recommander quelque chose. J'ai mal aux dents depuis une heure. Prenez rendez-vous aujourd'hui.

## VARIATIONS

**Pour mettre en garde :**

Il serait prudent de voir un médecin.
Il ne faut pas abuser des médicaments.
Vous ne devez pas fumer.
Attention ! C'est contre-indiqué.
Faites attention, il y a une contre-indication.
Je vous rappelle que l'alcool est déconseillé.

***Giving a warning :***

*It would be wise to see a doctor.*
*You shouldn't take too much medicine.*
*You shouldn't smoke.*
*Careful ! It's not advised.*
*Careful, there's a counter-indication.*
*I remind you that alcohol is not advised.*

**Pour parler de vos symptômes :**

Je souffre beaucoup.
J'ai mal au cœur
J'ai la tête qui tourne.
Ça saigne.
Ça brûle.
Ça pique.
Ça démange.

***Talking about your symptoms :***

*I feel very bad.*
*I feel sick.*
*I feel dizzy.*
*It's bleeding.*
*It's burning.*
*It's stinging.*
*It's itching.*

**Pour exprimer des besoins physiques :**

J'ai (très) envie de { dormir. / manger. / boire. / d'aller aux toilettes.

***Expressing physical needs :***

*I'd (really) like to { sleep. / eat. / drink. / go to the toilet.*

## SAY IT IN FRENCH

***A member of your family is not feeling very well :***

1. Ask him if he has not been feeling well for a long time.
2. Ask him is he is feeling very bad.
3. Warn him against taking too much medicine.
4. Tell him that he should see a doctor.

**Possible answers :**

1. Il y a longtemps que tu ne te sens pas bien ? 2. Tu souffres beaucoup ? 3. Il ne faut pas abuser des médicaments. 4. Tu devrais voir le médecin.

**« Avoir une santé de fer »**

***« To have an iron constitution »***

## *DID YOU KNOW?*

If French people fall ill or have an accident, a large part of their medical expenses are covered by the social security. If you are a national of an EEC member country, you can also benefit from this cover by having your medical expenses reimbursed on your return home.

For minor health problems, you can go to a *pharmacie* (chemist's) for advice. The pharmacists are well qualified to recommend the right medicine. There are also many so-called "homeopathic" pharmacists and doctors, and "phytothérapie" – remedies based on plants – is also extremely popular in France.

**How well do you know French society? Spot the odd man out in the following lists:**

1 François Mitterrand
Jacques Chirac
Valéry Giscard d'Estaing
Charles de Gaulle

2 Renault
Cartier
Rhône-Poulenc
IBM

3 École Polytechnique
Université de la Sorbonne
Sénat
ENA

4 Isabelle Adjani
Édith Cresson
Alain Delon
Gérard Depardieu

***Answers:*** 1. Jacques Chirac has never been President of the French Republic (he was Prime minister from 1974–1976 and again from 1986–88).
2. IBM is not a French company (it's American).
3. The Senate is not part of higher education (it's a political institution).
4. Édith Cresson in not a film star (she became France's first ever woman Prime minister in 1991).

## FAIS COMME CHEZ TOI !

*Michel,*

*Je suis à Bruxelles pour la journée. Installe-toi.*
*Fais comme chez toi.*
*Tu trouveras à manger dans le frigo.*
*Si tu veux prendre une douche, il y a des serviettes sur une petite étagère derrière la porte de la salle de bains.*
*Si tu as envie de travailler, le matériel est dans le placard à côté de la télévision.*
*Le téléphone est à droite de la cheminée. N'hésite pas à l'utiliser.*
*Si tu sors, n'oublie pas de fermer la porte en partant.*

*À ce soir.*

**Paul**

### PRONUNCIATION

| | | |
|---|---|---|
| **Installe-toi** | [ɛ̃staltwa] | angstahl twah |
| **Sur une étagère** | [syrynetaʒɛr] | sewr ewn aytahzhehr |
| **Derrière la porte** | [dɛrjɛrlapɔrt] | dehryehr lah port |
| **À côté** | [akote] | ah koatay |
| **À droite** | [adrwat] | ah drwaht |
| **À ce soir.** | [asəswar] | ah ser swahr |

## MAKE YOURSELF AT HOME !

Michel,
I have gone to Brussels for the day . Settle in. Make yourself at home.
You'll find something to eat in the fridge.
If you want to take a shower, there are towels on a small shelf behind the bathroom door.
If you want to work, everything you need is in the cupboard next to the television.
The telephone is to the right of the fireplace. Feel free to use it .
If you go out, don't forget to close the door behind you.
See you this evening. Paul

## GRAMMAR

### *Verbs :*

**Partant** → present participle of the verb **partir**

### *The present participle :*

The present participle is an impersonal verbal form. Its ending is always **-ant**.
**Formation :** As with the imperfect tense, we take the root of the first person plural of the present tense and add the ending **-ant**.
faire → nous faisons → **fais** → fais**ant**
Note that the following three verbs are exceptions to this rule :
être → **étant** avoir → **ayant** savoir → **sachant**

### *The gerund :*

**en** + present participle

The gerund is used to specify a circumstance.
**time :**
Ferme bien la porte **en sortant** = Ferme bien la porte **quand** tu sortiras
**simultaneity :**
Il se couche **en chantant** = Il se couche **et en même temps** il chante

### *Expressing condition :*

**si** + present + present

**Si tu veux** prendre une douche, **il y a** des serviettes.
**Si tu sors**, n'**oublie** pas de fermer la porte.

## EXERCISES

### 1. Form the present participle of the following verbs. (Check the first person plural of the present tense at the end of the book, if necessary)

écrire → nous écrivons → en écrivant
faire → nous ... → ... ; vouloir → nous ...→ ... ; connaître → nous ... → ... ; choisir → nous ... → ...

### 2. Transform the following sentences using the gerund

Tu fais des fautes quand tu écris. → Tu fais des fautes en écrivant.
Il travaille et en même temps il fait ses études.
Nous faisons toujours attention quand nous payons.
Il écoute la radio et en même temps il conduit.

### 3. Change the words underlined into their opposites

La table est à droite du meuble → La table est à gauche du meuble.
Laissez votre voiture devant la maison. La gare est en face de nous. Mets tes chaussures sur le lit. Je travaille près de chez toi.

### 4. Translate into French

You'll find something to drink in the fridge. Make yourselves comfortable. The television is beside the fireplace.

## VOCABULARY

| | |
|---|---|
| dans : in  sur : on<br>derrière: behind<br>à côté (de) : beside | le lit → bed<br>la porte → door<br>la chaise → chair |
| les meubles → furniture<br>le fauteuil → armchair | l'armoire → cupboard<br>la lampe → lamp<br>la fenêtre → window |

**Key to exercises :**

1. faisons, faisant / voulons, voulant / connaissons, connaissant / choisissons, choisissant
2. en faisant ses études / en payant / en conduisant.
3. Laissez votre voiture derrière la maison. La gare est derrière nous. Mets tes chaussures sous le lit. Je travaille loin de chez toi.
4. Vous trouverez à boire dans le frigo. Installez-vous. La télévision est à côté de la cheminée.

## VARIATIONS

**Pour localiser un objet :**
L'hôtel est :
à gauche (de l'église).
à droite (du stade).
devant (la gare).
La serviette est :
derrière (la porte).
en face (de la porte).
à côté (de la cheminée).
Le livre est sur la télévision.
Les chaussures sont sous le lit.
Pierre habite au-dessus (de nous)/au-dessous (de nous).

***Situating an object :***
*The hotel is:*
*to the left (of the church).*
*to the right (of the stadium).*
*in front (of the station).*
*The towel is:*
*behind (the door).*
*opposite (the door).*
*beside (the fireplace).*
*The book is on the television.*
*The shoes are under the bed.*
*Pierre lives above (us)/ underneath (us).*

**Pour évaluer l'éloignement :**
J'habite (très) près de la poste.
La poste, c'est (très) près d'ici.
J'habite (juste) à côté de la poste.
La poste, c'est (juste) à côté d'ici.
J'habite (très) loin de la poste.
La poste, c'est (très) loin d'ici.

***Specifying distance :***
*I live (very) near the post office.*
*The post office is (very) near here.*
*I live (just) beside the post office.*
*The post office is (just) beside here.*
*I live (very) far from the post office.*
*The post office is (very) far from here.*

## SAY IT IN FRENCH

***Some old friends come to spend a week with you. Make them feel at home :***

1. Tell them to settle in and make themselves at home.
2. Tell them that if they are hungry there are things to eat and drink in the fridge.
3. Tell them that if they want to have a shower there are towels in the small cupboard in the bathroom.
4. Tell them that the telephone is on the small shelf to the right of the television.



**Possible answers :**

1. Installez-vous. Vous êtes chez vous. 2. Si vous avez faim, il y a à manger et à boire dans le frigo. 3. Si vous voulez vous doucher, il y a des serviettes dans la petite armoire de la salle de bains. 4. Le téléphone est sur la petite étagère à droite de la télévision.

## ■ RÉPONDEUR AUTOMATIQUE

*Le répondeur :*
*Bonjour, vous êtes bien au 47 45 13 78, je ne suis pas là pour le moment mais si vous me laissez un message après le top sonore, je vous rappellerai dès mon retour.*

Salut, c'est Marie-Pierre. J'ai vu le type de l'agence immobilière pour la maison. Il dit qu'il tient à te voir absolument cette semaine. Il veut savoir si tu es d'accord pour le contrat et quand tu peux le rencontrer pour la signature. Oh... il demande aussi ce que tu veux comme crédit. Bon, je te rappelle ce soir. Salut.

## PRONUNCIATION

| | | |
|---|---|---|
| **Dès mon retour** | [dɛmɔ̃rətur] | day mawng rertoor |
| **Laisser un message** | [leseɛ̃mesaʒ] | lehssay ang mehssahzh |
| **Il tient à te voir** | [iltjɛ̃atvwar] | eel tyang ah ter vwahr |
| **Je te rappelle** | [ʒtərapɛl] | zher ter rahpehl |

## ■ *ANSWERING MACHINE*

*The answering machine:*
*Hello. This is 47 45 13 78, I'm not here at the moment but if you leave me a message after the bleep, I'll call you back as soon as I get home...*

Hello, it's Marie-Pierre. I've seen the man from the estate agent's about the house. He absolutely insisted that he should see you this week*. He wants to know if you agree with the contract and when you can meet him to sign it. Oh... he also wonders what kind of mortgage you want. Anyway, I'll call you back this evening. 'Bye.

## GRAMMAR

### ■ *Reported speech :*

Reported speech is used to convey words spoken by another person. The use of reported speech involves some changes in the original sentence.

| **Person 1 to person 2** | **Person 2 to person 3** |
|---|---|
| C'est urgent. | **Il dit que** c'est urgent. |
| Je tiens à lui parler. | **Il dit qu'**il tient à te/vous parler. |
| C'est urgent ? | Il veut savoir **si** c'est urgent. |
| Qu'est-ce qu'il veut ? | Il demande **ce que** vous voulez. |
| Quand peut-il me rencontrer ? | Il demande **quand** vous pouvez le rencontrer. |
| Où est-il ? | Il veut savoir **où** vous êtes. |
| Comment vient-il ? | Il demande **comment** vous venez. |

To convey the words of another person, you can begin the sentence with : **Il dit que... Elle dit que...**
To convey a question, you may begin the sentence with :
**Il/elle demande... Il/elle veut savoir...**

### ■ *Conveying an order :*

To convey an order, you can begin the sentence with
**Il/elle dit de** + infinitive
**Prenez** ces comprimés ! **Il** te/vous **dit de prendre** ces comprimés.
**Ne sortez pas** ! → **Il** te/vous **dit de ne pas sortir**.

## EXERCISES

### 1. *Qu'est-ce qu'ils disent ? Put their words into reported speech*

"C'est très important" → Il dit que c'est très important.
"Je travaille beaucoup" → Elle ...
"Il est tard !" → Il ...
"Il fait très froid." → Elle ...
"J'ai besoin d'argent" → Il ...

### 2. *Qu'est-ce qu'ils demandent ? Complete the sentences using si, ce que, quand, où*

"C'est grand ?" → Il demande si c'est grand.
"Qu'est-ce qu'il fait ?" → Il demande ... vous faites.
"Où est-ce qu'elle habite ?" → Elle demande ... tu habites.
"Quand est-ce qu'elle part ?" → Il demande ... vous partez.

### 3. *Convey the following orders*

Ne regardez pas la télévision ! → Il vous dit ...
Étudie ta leçon ! → Elle te dit ...
Mange ta soupe ! → Il te dit ...

### 4. *Translate into English*

Ne quitte pas ! Elle demande qui tu es. Il veut savoir quand tu viens. Elle demande où vous êtes.

## VOCABULARY

| | |
|---|---|
| qui : who ce que : what<br>si : if<br><br>la cabine téléphonique → phone box | l'annuaire → telephone directory<br><br>les renseignements → inquiries<br><br>une communication → a call |

**Key to exercises :**

1. Elle dit qu'elle travaille beaucoup. Il dit qu'il est tard. Elle dit qu'il fait très froid. Il dit qu'il a besoin d'argent.
2. Ce que / où / quand
3. Il vous dit de ne pas regarder la télévision. Elle te dit d'étudier ta leçon. Il te dit de manger ta soupe.
4. Hold on. She's asking who you are. He wants to know when you're coming. She's asking where you are.

## ■ *BONJOUR !*

**Pour prendre contact :**

Allô, M. Martin, s'il vous plaît ?
Allô, est-ce que je pourrais parler à M. Martin ?

**Pour maintenir le contact :**

Oui, ne quittez pas, je vous le passe.

**Pour identifier votre interlocuteur :**

Allô, c'est de la part de qui ?
Allô, vous êtes Mme... ?

**Pour différer la communication :**

M. Martin est occupé.
Je suis désolé, Paul est absent.
Vous pouvez rappeler dans dix minutes ?

**Pour proposer et laisser un message :**

Vous voulez lui laisser un message ?
Je peux lui transmettre un message ?
Vous pourriez lui dire que...
Dites-lui que...

***Making contact :***

*Hello, Mr. Martin, please.*
*Hello, could I speak to Mr. Martin ?*

***Maintaining contact :***

*Yes, hold on, he's coming to the 'phone.*

***Identifying the person you are speaking to :***

*Hello, who's speaking ?*
*Hello, you are Mrs... ?*

***Postponing the call :***

*Mr. Martin is busy.*
*I'm sorry, Paul's out.*
*Can you call back in ten minutes ?*

***Offering to take a message and leaving a message :***

*Do you want to leave him a message ?*
*Can I give him a message ?*
*Could you tell him that...*
*Tell him that...*

## SAY IT IN FRENCH

***You are in your brother's house and you answer the 'phone :***

1. Say that you are sorry, your brother is out.
2. Offer to take a message for him.

***Later on, you give your brother the message :***

3. Tell him that Mr Martin asks what he is doing this evening.
4. Tell him that Mr Martin also asks him to call back quickly.

**Possible answers :**

1. Je suis désolé(e) mais mon frère est absent. 2. Je peux lui transmettre un message ? 3. M. Martin demande ce que tu fais ce soir. 4. Il te demande de lui téléphoner rapidement.

## ■ TOUS MES VŒUX !

Bon anniversaire !

Je souhaite de tout cœur que pour tes vingt ans tes rêves les plus chers se réalisent.

Je penserai bien à toi aujourd'hui.

Affectueusement

Franck

Bonne année !

Chers Amis,

Tous nos vœux pour une heureuse année !

Nous souhaitons que cette année soit pour vous source de bonheur et de satisfactions.

Bien amicalement à vous.

Cyrille et Patricia

### PRONUNCIATION



| | | |
|---|---|---|
| **De tout cœur** | [dətukœr] | der too kurr |
| **Bonne année !** | [bɔnanə] | bon nahnay |
| **Tous nos vœux** | [tunovø] | too noa vur |
| **Heureuse année !** | [œrøzane] | urrurz ahnay |

## ■ BEST WISHES !

Happy birthday !
I hope with all my heart that on your twentieth birthday, your fondest dreams will come true .
I will be thinking of you today.
With love,
Franck

Happy New Year !
Dear friends,
All our best wishes for a happy new year !
We hope that this year will bring you happiness and satisfaction.
Lots of love, Cyrille and Patricia

## GRAMMAR

### *Verbs :*

**Que cette année soit** → present subjunctive of the verb **être**

### *The present subjunctive :*

**Conjugation**

| | **Present subjunctive** |
|---|---|
| **Present indicative** → ils **prenn**ent | → que je **prenne** |
| | → que tu **prennes** |
| | → qu'il **prenne** |
| **imperfect** → nous prenions | → que nous **prenions** |
| **imperfect** → vous preniez | → que vous **preniez** |
| | → qu'ils **prennent** |

The three persons singular and the third person plural are formed from the third person plural of the present indicative of the verb (ils prennent).
The first two persons plural are the same as in the imperfect tense.
Note that the verbs **être, avoir, aller, faire, vouloir, savoir** and **pouvoir** are irregular and do not follow this general rule.
**Use :** The subjunctive is introduced by a verb which indicates a particular attitude on the part of the subject, such as a wish, requirement, feeling, opinion, appreciation.

| | |
|---|---|
| je souhaite | que tu **partes** |
| je voudrais | que tu **réussisses** |
| j'aimerais | que tu **fasses** fortune |
| je désire | que tu **sois** heureux |

## EXERCISES

### 1. Find the present subjunctive of these verbs in the verb tables at the end of the book

être → que je ..., qu'elle ..., que vous... , qu'ils ...
avoir → que j'..., que tu ..., que nous ..., qu'elles ...
faire → que je ..., qu'il ..., que vous ..., qu'ils ...

### 2. Transform the following verbs into wishes, as in the following example

être heureux → je souhaite que tu sois heureux
aller bien → je souhaite que...
avoir de la chance → je souhaite que...
réussir vite → je souhaite que...
revenir bientôt → je souhaite que...

### 3. Put the verbs in brackets into the present subjunctive

Nous aimerions qu'elles (sortir) ... ce soir.
Il désire que vous (apprendre) ... le français.
Elle aimerait que vous (faire) ... ce travail.

### 4. Translate into English

Je souhaite que ce travail ne soit pas trop difficile. Nous désirons que tu réussisses. Je penserai bien à vous.

## VOCABULARY

| | |
|---|---|
| Pourvu que (+ subjonctif) : provided that | un vœu → (best) wishes |
| | Pâques → Easter |
| le jour de l'an → New Year's Day | le réveillon → Christmas or New Year's Eve |
| Noël → Christmas | un souhait → a wish, desire |



**Key to exercises :**

1. sois, soit, soyez, soient / aie, aies, ayons, aient / fasse, fasse, fassiez, fassent.
2. tu ailles bien / tu aies de la chance / tu réussisses vite / tu reviennes bientôt.
3. sortent, appreniez, fassiez.
4. I hope that this work isn't too difficult. We want you (sing.) to succeed. I'll be thinking of you.

## VARIATIONS

**Pour souhaiter quelque chose à quelqu'un...**
**À l'occasion d'une fête :**

Bonne année !
Tous mes vœux !
Joyeux Noël !
Bon/joyeux anniversaire !
Bonne fête !

***Expressing wishes, greetings, etc.***
***On holidays and feast days :***

*Happy New Year !*
*Best wishes !*
*Merry Christmas*
*Happy birthday !*
*Happy feast day !*

**Au moment de manger ou de boire :**

Bon appétit !
À votre/ta santé !
À la vôtre !/À la tienne !

***When about to eat or drink :***

*Enjoy your meal !*
*Good health !*
*Here's to you !*

**Au moment d'une épreuve difficile :**

Bon courage ! Bonne chance !

***At a time of difficulty :***

*Chin up ! Good luck !*

**À l'occasion d'un voyage :**

Bon voyage !
Bonne route !
Bonnes vacances !

***Before going on a trip :***

*Have a good journey !*
*Have a safe trip !*
*Have a good holiday !*

**À l'occasion d'une maladie :**

Soignez-vous bien ! / Soigne-toi bien !

***When someone is ill :***

*Take care of yourself !*

## SAY IT IN FRENCH

***You are invited to the home of a French family for the New Year :***

1. Wish them a happy new year.
2. When starting the aperitif, wish them good health.
3. Your host has the 'flu. Tell him to take care of himself.
4. The son of your hosts is studying for an important examination. Tell him that you hope his examination will be easy.



**Possible answers :**

1. Bonne et heureuse année ! 2. À votre santé ! 3. Soignez-vous bien ! 4. Je souhaite que votre/ton examen soit facile.

# BILAN 6

## ■ Now you know how to make comparisons,

***1. Observe and then complete using* plus que, autant que, moins que, plus de ... que, autant de ... que, moins de ... que.**

M. Rouland : 18 000 francs, 37 heures par semaine, 5 semaines de vacances, 2 enfants.
M. Foucault : 15 000 francs, 35 heures par semaine, 5 semaines de vacances, 4 enfants.
M. Rouland travaille ... M. Foucault.
M. Foucault gagne ... argent .... M. Rouland.
M. Rouland a ... enfants .... M. Foucault.
M. Rouland a ... vacances .... M. Foucault.

***2. Complete the following sentences with* le même, la même, les mêmes.**

Nous travaillons dans ... bureau. Vous habitez dans ... ville. Tu as ... chaussures que moi. Je connais ... personnes que toi. Nous étudions .....langue.

## ■ ...How to express simultaneity,

***3. Use the gerund to transform the following sentences.***

Il déjeune et il lit le journal → Il déjeune en lisant le journal.
Elle travaille et elle écoute la radio → ...
Il chante et il se douche → ...
Je pense à toi et je marche → ...
Vous faites attention et vous traversez la rue → ...

## ■ ...How to express the reason for something,

***4. Answer the following questions.***

Pourquoi pars-tu ? (minuit) → Parce qu'il est minuit.
Pourquoi est-ce qu'ils ne chantent pas ? (ne pas savoir) → ...
Pourquoi travailles-tu le dimanche ? (avoir besoin d'argent) → ...
Pourquoi est-ce que vous conduisez vite ? (être en retard) → ...
Pourquoi est-ce qu'il ne comprend pas ? (être difficile) → ...



## ■ ...How to express a condition,

***5. Conjugate the verbs in the following sentences using the appropriate tense.***

Nous (rester) ... à la maison, s'il fait froid demain. Si tu ne (comprendre) ... pas, je t'expliquerai comment faire. Vous (venir)

..., si c'est nécessaire. Si vous êtes malade, vous (aller) ... chez le médecin. Ils (téléphoner) ..., s'il y a un problème.

■ **...HOW TO CONVEY WHAT SOMEBODY ELSE HAS SAID,**

***6. Transmit the following questions.***

C'est grave ? → Il demande si c'est grave.
Où habite-t-il ? → Il veut savoir ... Qu'est-ce qu'elle fait ? → Elle demande ... Quand est-ce qu'elles partent ? → Il demande ... Comment font-ils ? → Nous voulons savoir ...

***7. Transmit the following orders***

N'écoutez pas ! Il vous dit de ne pas écouter.
Travaillez plus vite ! ... N'hésitez pas ! ... Ouvre la fenêtre ! ... Attendez cinq minutes ! ... Ferme la porte ! ...

■ **...HOW TO EXPRESS WISHES AND FEELINGS.**

***8. Put the verbs in brackets into the appropriate tense and mood.***

Je veux que tu (prendre) ... le train de 8 h. Elle souhaite que vous (venir) ... ce soir. Nous aimerions que vous (savoir) ... parler français. Il désire que vous (être) ... satisfaits de votre séjour. Nous voudrions que notre fils (avoir) ... une bonne profession.

## KEY TO EXERCISES

1. plus que - moins d'argent que - moins d'enfants que - autant de vacances que.
2. le même - la même - les mêmes - les mêmes - la même.
3. Elle travaille en écoutant la radio - Il chante en se douchant - Je pense à toi en marchant - Vous faites attention en traversant la rue -
4. Parce qu'ils ne savent pas - Parce que j'ai besoin d'argent - Parce que je suis/nous sommes en retard - Parce que c'est difficile.
5. resterons - comprends - viendrez - irez - téléphoneront.
6. Il veut savoir où il habite - Elle demande ce qu'elle fait - Il demande quand elles partent - Nous voulons savoir comment ils font.
7. Il vous dit de travailler plus vite - Il vous dit de ne pas hésiter - Il te dit d'ouvrir la fenêtre - Il vous dit d'attendre cinq minutes - Il te dit de fermer la porte.
8. prennes - veniez - sachiez - soyez - ait.

## ■ LE CODE DE LA ROUTE

— Mais Monsieur l'agent, le feu était tout juste orange !
— Non, Mademoiselle ! Vous avez vos papiers ? ...Permis de conduire, carte grise... ?
— Mais, votre assurance est périmée.
— Oui, excusez-moi, j'ai oublié d'aller chercher le nouveau certificat.
— Deux infractions, je suis obligé de vous mettre une amende.
— Monsieur l'agent, soyez gentil !
— Ah, et il faut que vous vous présentiez au commissariat avant 48 heures avec votre assurance.
— 48 heures ! Mais je dois aller la chercher à Marseille !

### PRONUNCIATION



| | | |
|---|---|---|
| **Non, Mademoiselle !** | [nɔ̃madmwazɛl] | nawng mahdmwahzehl |
| **Vous avez vos papiers ?** | [vuzavevopapje] | voo zahvay voa pahpyay |
| **Soyez gentil !** | [swajeʒɑ̃ti] | swahyay zhahngtee |

## THE HIGHWAY CODE

— But officer, the light had only just gone amber !
— No, miss ! Do you have your papers ? ...driving licence, registration papers... ?
— Look, your insurance is out of date !
— Yes, I'm sorry. I forgot to go and fetch the new certificate.
— Two offenses, I'm obliged to give you a fine.
— Please officer, be kind !
— Oh, and you must go to the police station with your insurance within 48 hours.
— 48 hours ! But I have to go and get it in Marseille !

## GRAMMAR

### *Verbs :*

**Je dois** → present indicative of the verb **devoir**

### *Obligation :*

The following are some constructions using the infinitive :

**être obligé(e) de** + infinitive → je suis obligé(e) de partir
**devoir** + infinitive → nous devons partir
It is also possible to use the following impersonal expressions :
**Il faut** + infinitive → Il faut partir
**Il est nécessaire de** + infinitive → Il est nécessaire de partir

N.B. : The last two expressions do not clearly identify the subject of the action (who must leave ?). If it is important to specify the subject, another construction is used :

**Il faut que** + present subjunctive
Il faut que je parte/vous partiez
**Il est nécessaire que** + present subjunctive
Il est nécessaire que tu partes

## EXERCISES

### 1. *Complete the questions using* être obligé de

Je dois partir → Vous êtes obligé de partir ?
Elle doit travailler → Elle ...
Je dois lui écrire → Vous ...
Ils doivent dormir → Ils ...

### 2. *Use the subjunctive in order to specify the subject*

Il faut travailler, (vous) → Il faut que vous travailliez.
Il est nécessaire de faire attention, (nous) → ...
Il faut manger vite, (nous) → ...
Il est nécessaire de comprendre. (ils) → ...

### 3. *Qu'est-ce qu'il faut faire ? Complete with the verbs se reposer, dormir, boire, manger (conjugating them where necessary)*

J'ai faim. → Il faut que tu ...
Nous avons sommeil. → Il faut ...
Elle est fatiguée. → Il est nécessaire qu'elle ...

### 4. *Translate into English*

Voilà mon permis de conduire. J'ai oublié ma carte grise. Je dois aller la chercher à Lyon. Il faut que je me présente au commissariat.

## VOCABULARY

tout juste : only just
contre : against

le stationnement → parking
interdit → forbidden

un accident → accident
un carrefour → crossroads
la ceinture → (seat) belt
obligatoire → compulsory

**Key to exercises :**

1. Elle est obligée de travailler ? Vous êtes obligé de lui écrire ? Ils sont obligés de dormir ?
2. Il est nécessaire que nous fassions attention. Il faut que nous mangions vite. Il est nécessaire qu'ils comprennent.
3. Manges / dormir / se repose.
4. Here's my driving license. I've forgotten my registration papers. I have to go and get it in Lyon. I have to report to the police station.

## VARIATIONS

| | |
|---|---|
| **Pour exprimer l'obligation :** | ***Expressing obligation :*** |
| Il faut travailler. | *You have to work.* |
| Il faut que vous travailliez. | |
| Il est nécessaire d'écouter. | *You must listen.* |
| Il est nécessaire que vous écoutiez. | |
| Il est obligatoire de tourner. | *You must turn.* |
| J'exige que vous sortiez. | *I insist that you go out.* |
| Vous devez sortir. | *You must go out.* |
| **Pour mettre en garde :** | ***Warning :*** |
| Je te/vous signale que c'est obligatoire. | *I inform you that it is compulsory.* |
| Je te/vous rappelle que c'est interdit. | *I remind you that it is forbidden.* |
| Je te/vous préviens que c'est dangereux. | *I warn you that it is dangerous.* |
| Attention ! C'est difficile ! | *Watch out ! It's difficult !* |
| **Pour vous excuser :** | ***Apologizing :*** |
| Je vous prie de m'excuser. | *Please excuse me.* |
| Oh, excusez-moi, | *Oh, excuse me,* |
| Je ne l'ai pas fait exprès. | *I didn't do it deliberately.* |
| (Je suis) désolé(e), j'ai oublié. | *(I'm) sorry, I forgot.* |
| Je regrette mais je suis obligé de ... | *I'm sorry, but I have to...* |

## SAY IT IN FRENCH

***You are in a car with a friend who is driving very carelessly :***

1. Ask him if he didn't see the red light.
2. Warn him that it's dangerous.
3. Tell him that it is a turn left only (compulsory to turn left).
4. Finally, tell him that he must be careful.

**Possible answers :**

1. Tu n'as pas vu le feu rouge ? 2. Attention, c'est dangereux ! 3. Il est obligatoire de tourner à gauche. 4. Il faut que tu fasses attention !

## LE PLEIN DE SUPER

— Du super, s'il vous plaît. Vous me faites le plein.
— Je vérifie aussi les niveaux ?
— Oui, si vous voulez.
— Dites, il faut que vous alliez au garage.
— Mais, j'en viens !
— Eh bien, retournez-y aujourd'hui ! Vous avez vu vos pneus ?
— Non, qu'est-ce qu'ils ont ?
— Ceux de droite sont beaucoup trop lisses. C'est sûrement un problème de direction.
— Ah, cette voiture, j'en ai assez !

### PRONUNCIATION

| | | |
|---|---|---|
| **Mais, j'en viens !** | [mɛʒɑ̃vjɛ̃] | meh zhahng vyang |
| **Retournez-y** | [rəturnezi] | rertoornay zee |
| **Qu'est-ce qu'ils ont ?** | [kɛskilzɔ̃] | kehss keelzawng |
| **Ceux de droite ?** | [sødədrwat] | sur der drwahht |
| **J'en ai assez !** | [ʒɑ̃nɛase] | zhahng ay ahssay |

## TANKFUL OF 5-STAR

— 5-star, please. Fill it up.
— Shall I check the oil as well ?
— Yes, if you would.
— You know something, you must go to the garage.
— But, I've just come from there !
— Well, you'd better go back today. Have you seen your tyres ?
— No, what's the matter with them ?
— The ones on the right are far too bald. It's undoubtedly a problem with the steering.
— Oh, I'm fed up with this car !

## GRAMMAR

### **En** *used to denote a place :*

**En** denotes a place which would normally be preceded by the preposition **de** or by the contraction of **de** + article : **du, des**

Tu sors **du** garage ? → Oui, j'**en** sors.
Elle vient **des** États-Unis ? → Oui, elle **en** vient.

### **Y** *used to denote a place :*

**Y** denotes a place which would normally be preceded by : **à, en, au, à la, aux, dans, chez**...

Elle va **en** France ? → Non, elle n'**y** va pas.
Vous travaillez **au** bureau ? → Oui, j'**y** travaille.
Il habite **à** Paris ? → Oui, il **y** habite.
Elle est **aux** États-Unis ? → Non, elle n'**y** est pas.

### *Position of* **En** *and* **Y** *:*

**En** and **Y** are always placed immediately before the verb except in affirmative imperative sentences :

**Simple tenses :**

| | | |
|---|---|---|
| | Allez-**y** ! | Sortez-**en** ! |
| but | N'**y** allez pas ! | N'**en** sortez pas ! |

**Compound tenses :**

J'**y** suis allé.
Je n'**y** suis pas allé.

## EXERCISES

### 1. *Reply to the following questions using* en

Tu viens de Paris ? → Oui, j'en viens. → Non, je n'en viens pas.
Vous sortez du cinéma ? → Oui, j'......... → Non, je .........
Ils viennent du Portugal ? → Oui, ils ......... → Non, ils .........
Elle sort de sa chambre ? → Oui, elle ......... → Non, elle .........

### 2. *Reply to the following questions using* y

Tu habites à Paris ? → Non, je n'y habite pas.
Elle travaille en France ? → Oui, elle .........
Tu vas chez Louis ? → Oui, j'.........
Il est à Lyon ? → Oui, il .........

### 3. *Use the imperative to agree or refuse*

Je peux aller au cinéma ? → Oui, vas-y → Non, n'y va pas.
Nous pouvons sortir de la cuisine ? → Oui, ......... → Non, ......
Je peux rester dans ma chambre ? → Oui, ......... → Non, .........

### 4. *Translate into French*

Your tyres are too old. Have you (plur.) seen your car ? You must go to the service station! But I've just come from there !

## VOCABULARY

| | |
|---|---|
| trop : too    assez : enough | |
| l'essence → petrol | station |
| l'ordinaire → three-star petrol | l'huile → oil |
| la station service → service | le super → five-star petrol |
| | la pompe (à essence) → (petrol) pump |



**Key to exercises :**

1. J'en sors, je n'en sors pas / ils en viennent, ils n'en viennent pas / elle en sort, elle n'en sort pas.
2. elle y travaille / j'y vais / il y est.
3. Sortez-en, n'en sortez pas / restes-y, n'y reste pas
4. Vos pneus sont trop vieux. Vous avez vu votre voiture ? Il faut que vous alliez à la station-service! Mais j'en viens !

## VARIATIONS

| | |
|---|---|
| **Pour interroger sur la cause :** | ***Asking about the cause :*** |
| Pourquoi ?<br>C'est à cause de quoi ?<br>Ça vient de quoi ?<br>C'est dû à quoi ? | *Why ?*<br>*Why is that ?*<br>*What's it caused by ?*<br>*What's it due to ?* |
| **Pour exprimer la causalité :** | ***Giving the reason :*** |
| C'est parce que le phare est cassé.<br>C'est à cause de la direction.<br>Ça vient de la batterie.<br>C'est dû à l'âge de votre voiture. | *It's because the headlight is broken.*<br>*It's because of the steering.*<br>*It's due to the battery.*<br>*It's due to the age of your car.* |
| **Pour conseiller de faire quelque chose :** | ***Advising an action :*** |
| Il faudrait le changer.<br>Il vaut/vaudrait mieux le changer. | *It should be changed.*<br>*It is/would be better to change it.* |

## SAY IT IN FRENCH

***You stop on the motorway to help a driver whose car has broken down :***

1. Tell him that it's a battery problem.
2. Explain that it is because the battery is too old.
3. Say it will have to be changed.
4. Advise him to go to a mechanic.



**Possible answers :**

1. C'est un problème de batterie. 2. C'est parce qu'elle est trop vieille. 3. Il faudrait la changer. 4. Il vaudrait mieux aller chez un mécanicien.

## NETTOYAGE DE PRINTEMPS !

*Mot à la femme de ménage*

**Je serai absente toute la journée : je ne rentrerai ni pour déjeuner ni pour dîner.**
**Il faudrait repasser la pile de chemises. Attention, celles de mon mari sont très délicates !**
**Pourriez-vous aussi faire un peu de ménage : nettoyer la cuisine et la salle de bains et laver tous les sols (sauf celui de notre chambre).**
**S'il vous reste du temps, mettez le linge dans la machine à laver. N'employez pas trop de lessive, la machine déborde facilement...**
**Si vous passez l'aspirateur, secouez les tapis (surtout ceux du salon).**

### PRONUNCIATION

| | | |
|---|---|---|
| **Je serai absente** | [ʒəsrɛapsɑ̃t] | zher serray ahbsahngt |
| **Notre chambre** | [nɔtrəʃɑ̃br] | noatr shahnbr |
| **Secouez les tapis** | [səkweletapi] | serkooay lay tahpee |
| **Ceux du salon** | [sødysalɔ̃] | sur dew sahlawng |

## SPRING CLEANING !

*A note for the cleaning lady*
I shall be out all day. I shan't be back for lunch or dinner.
The pile of shirts should be ironed. Be careful with my husband's; they are very delicate.
Could you also do a little housework, please : clean the kitchen and the bathroom and wash all the floors (except in our bedroom).
If you have enough time, put the dirty laundry in the washing machine. Don't use too much washing powder, the machine overflows easily...
If you do the hoovering, shake the carpets (especially the ones in the living room).

## GRAMMAR

### *Verbs :*

**Veuillez** → imperative of the verb **vouloir**
**Que vous rangiez** → present subjunctive of the verb **ranger**

### *The demonstrative pronouns :*

The demonstrative pronouns are used to designate persons or objects, or to avoid repetition

| | **singular** | **plural** | **indefinite** |
|---|---|---|---|
| **masculine** | celui (-ci, -là) | ceux (-ci, -là) | ceci, cela, ça |
| **feminine** | celle (-ci, -là) | celles (-ci, -là) | |

To designate an object **-ci** or **-là** is added after the pronoun.
Tu veux quel livre ? — Celui-**ci** ou celui-**là** ?

### Assez, pas assez, trop, pas trop *:*

Before an adjective : Il est **assez** grand. Vous n'êtes **pas assez** rapide.
Before a noun : n'employez **pas trop** de lessive. Il y a **trop** de linge.

### ne ... ni ... ni *:*

**Ni** is used as a coordinating word in negative sentences (thus avoiding the repetition of identical structures).
Je ne rentrerai **ni** pour déjeuner, **ni** pour dîner → Je ne rentrerai pas pour déjeuner et je ne rentrerai pas pour dîner.

## EXERCISES

### 1. *Use demonstrative pronouns to complete the answers*

Je prépare quel repas ? ...... des enfants.
Il prend quelle bicyclette ? ...... de Sylvie.
Vous aimez quels chocolats ? ...... de Belgique.

### 2. *Answer using a demonstrative pronoun +* -ci *or* -là

Vous prenez quel autobus ? → Celui-là (celui-ci)
Elle veut quelle robe ? → ..........................................................
Je te donne quels livres ? → ......................................................
Je mets quelles chaussures ? → ................................................
Vous achetez quel journal ? → ..................................................

### 3. *Complete the sentences using* assez (de) *or* trop (de)

C'est trop cher, je n'ai pas ...... argent.
Elle est ...... fatiguée pour travailler.
Tu as mis ...... sel dans la soupe ?

### 4. *Translate into English*

Elle sera absente toute la semaine. Nous ne rentrerons ni ce soir ni demain. Il faudrait faire un peu de ménage. Nettoyez les chambres (surtout celle des enfants).

## VOCABULARY

ni ... ni : neither...nor
trop (de) : too (much)
assez (de) : enough
ne ... plus : no longer
sauf : except
surtout : above all

faire la vaisselle → to do the washing up
ranger → to tidy up
l'évier → the sink
propre → clean
le robinet → the tap
sale → dirty



**Key to exercises :**

1. celui, celle, ceux
2. celle-ci/-là / ceux-ci /-là / celles-ci /-là / celui-ci/-là
3. assez d', trop, assez de.
4. She will be away all week. We shall not be back either this evening or tomorrow. A little housework should be done. Clean the bedrooms (especially the children's room).

## VARIATIONS

**Demander de faire quelque chose…**
**Avec politesse :**

Auriez-vous la gentillesse de …
Auriez-vous l'amabilité de …
Je voudrais que vous fassiez …
J'aimerais que vous laviez …

**Avec fermeté :**

Faites …
Veuillez faire …
Je vous prie de faire …

**En exprimant l'obligation :**

Il faut que vous fassiez …
Vous devez faire …
Je vous charge de faire …
Je veux que vous fassiez …

**En exprimant l'interdiction :**

Je vous/te défends de faire …
Je vous/t'interdis de…
Je ne veux pas que vous fassiez…

***Asking someone to do something…***
***Politely :***

*Would you be good enough to…*
*Would you have the kindness to…*
*I would like you to do…*
*I would like you to wash…*

***Firmly :***

*Do…*
*Please do…*
*I ask you to do…*

***Expressing obligation :***

*You must do…*
*You must do…*
*I instruct you to do…*
*I want you to do…*

***Forbidding :***

*I forbid you to do…*
*I forbid you to…*
*I do not want you to do…*

## SAY IT IN FRENCH

***You are leaving a message to someone who lives with you :***

1. Ask him politely to prepare the dinner.
2. Say that you would like him to put the dirty laundry in the machine.
3. Ask him firmly to do the washing up.
4. Say that you want him to tidy the kitchen.

**Possible answers :**

1. Aurais-tu la gentillesse de préparer le dîner ? 2. Je voudrais que tu mettes le linge dans la machine à laver. 3. Il faut que tu fasses la vaisselle. 4. Je veux que tu ranges la cuisine.

# On the bright side n° 7

**Are you ready for a stay in France? Test your reactions by completing the following questionnaire (at times, more than one answer is possible).**

**1. If you knock into someone in the street, what do you say to him?**
a. pardon
b. excusez-moi
c. merci

**2. You have been invited to the home of some French friends. What do you take with you?**
a. flowers
b. coffee
c. a good bottle of wine

**3. When should you arrive for dinner?**
a. at 6 o'clock
b. at 8 o'clock
c. at 10 o'clock

**4. For the aperitif, you have:**
a. a whisky
b. a pastis
c. a cognac



**5. With French people you can talk about:**
a. football
b. baseball
c. cricket

**6. You buy your bus tickets:**
a. in the underground
b. as you go on the bus
c. in newspaper stalls

**7. You leave a tip:**
a. at the police station
b. in the café
c. in the cinema

**8. In the morning, when you meet your neighbour, you say:**
a. Bonsoir
b. Bonjour
c. À demain

**9. If you want to annoy your French friends:**
a. You ask them how much they earn.
b. You tell them that the French do not know how to dress.
c. You tell them that the French language is incredibly complicated.

**10. The bus is full, you give up your seat:**
a. to an old lady
b. to a soldier
c. to a pregnant woman

**11. To show that you are a gourmet, you order:**

a. white wine with fish
b. water with a green salad
c. beer with cheese

**12. You want to insult someone, you call him:**

a. quel porc ! (what a pig!)
b. quel rat ! (what a rat!)
c. quel bœuf ! (what an ox!)

**13. You want to start a conversation with a woman you would like to know:**

a. you ask her for a light
b. you hand her your visiting card
c. you pretend to know her

**14. You want to start a conversation with a man you would like to know:**

a. you ask him the time
b. you ask him to carry your luggage
c. you ask him for some change for the telephone

*Answers:*

**1.** a and b
**2.** a and c
**3.** b
**4.** a and b
**5.** a
**6.** a and b
**7.** b and c
**8.** b
**9.** a and b
**10.** a and c
**11.** a and b
**12.** a and b
**13.** a and c
**14.** It's easy …everything works!

## LE COUP DE FOUDRE

— Ça y est ! Je suis amoureux. J'ai rencontré la femme de ma vie.

— Encore !

— Non, cette fois c'est sérieux.

— Tu as déjà dit ça la dernière fois !

— Je ne pense qu'à elle !

— Mais, qui est-ce ?

— Je l'ai rencontrée à la piscine. Le coup de foudre !

— Oh, tu sais, le coup de foudre, moi je n'y crois pas beaucoup.

### PRONUNCIATION

| | | |
|---|---|---|
| **Ça y est !** | [sajɛ] | sahyeh |
| **Encore !** | [ɑ̃kɔr] | ahngkor |
| **C'est sérieux.** | [sɛserjø] | seh sehryur |
| **Je ne pense qu'à elle !** | [ʒənəpɑ̃skaɛl] | zher ner pahngs kahehl |
| **Mais, qui est-ce ?** | [mɛkiɛs] | meh kee yehss |
| **Le coup de foudre !** | [ləkudfudr] | ler koo der foodr |

## ■ LOVE AT FIRST SIGHT

— That's it, then. I'm in love. I've met the woman of my life.
— Again !
— No, this time it's serious.
— You said that the last time !
— I can't think of anything but her !
— Who is it, then ?
— I met her at the swimming pool. Love at first sight !
— Oh, you know, love at first sight, I don't really believe in it.

## GRAMMAR

### ▮ *Verbs :*

**J'y crois** → present indicative of the verb **croire**

### ▮ Y :

**Y** replaces a thing which would normally be preceded by the preposition **à**.

Quel problème ! Plus j'**y** pense... (plus je pense **à** ce problème)
Le coup de foudre, j'**y** crois ! (je crois **au** coup de foudre)

Note, that when referring to a person, with the verbs **penser à**, **croire en**, **faire attention à** and **s'intéresser à**, the disjunctive pronouns must be used.

Je ne pense qu'à **lui**. Je pense bien à **toi**. Je ne crois pas en **lui**.
Faites attention à **eux**. Je m'intéresse à **vous**.

N.B. ! Refer back to lesson 38 for the position of **y** in the sentence.

### ▮ Ne ... que :

The construction **ne ... que** is equivalent to the use of the adverb **seulement**

Je **ne** pense **qu'**à lui. → Je pense **seulement** à lui.
Il **ne** boit **que** de l'eau. → Il boit **seulement** de l'eau.

Note that when **seulement** is used the negative particle **ne** disappears.

## EXERCISES

### 1. *Answer the questions using the word* y

Tu t'intéresses à la photo ? → Oui, je m'y intéresse. → Non, je ne m'y intéresse pas.
Vous croyez à l'astrologie ? → Oui, nous ......→ Non, ......
Vous faites attention aux feux ? → Oui, j'...... → Non, ......
Elle s'intéresse à la musique ? → Oui, elle ......→ Non, ......

### 2. *Answer the following questions using a disjunctive pronoun as appropriate*

Tu t'intéresses à Sophie ? → Oui, je m'intéresse à elle.
Vous pensez à votre mère ? → Oui, nous ..................................
Ils font attention aux enfants ? → Oui, ils ..................................
Elle croit en son ami ? → Oui, elle ..........................................

### 3. *Use* ne...que *to express the following restrictions*

J'aime seulement la viande. → Je n'aime que la viande.
Il boit seulement de l'eau. → ..................................................
Je pense seulement à toi. → ......................................................
J'ai seulement 100 F. → ..........................................................

### 4. *Translate into French*

I've met the woman of my life. I don't believe in love at first sight. We are thinking of you (plur.). I'm thinking only of him/her.

## VOCABULARY

ça y est : that's it
ne ... que : only

tomber amoureux → to fall in love
se fiancer → to get engaged
se marier → to get married
le divorce → divorce
le/la fiancé/e → the fiancé(e)
le mariage → marriage
divorcer → to get divorced



**Key to exercises :**

1. Nous y croyons/nous n'y croyons pas / j'y fais attention/je n'y fais pas attention / elle s'y intéresse/elle ne s'y intéresse pas.
2. nous pensons à elle / ils font attention à eux / elle croit en lui.
3. Il ne boit que de l'eau. Elle ne travaille que le matin. Je ne pense qu'à toi. Je n'ai que 100 F.
4. J'ai rencontré la femme de ma vie. Je ne crois pas au coup de foudre. Nous pensons bien à vous. Je ne pense qu'à lui.

## VARIATIONS

**Pour exprimer des sentiments :**
**L'amour :**

Tu me plais.
Je t'aime mon chéri/ma chérie.
Je t'adore, mon amour.
Je suis fou/folle de toi/lui/elle.
Je ne peux plus vivre sans toi.

**La haine :**

Je ne peux pas te sentir.
Je ne peux pas le voir.
Je ne peux pas la supporter.
Je te/le/la méprise.
Tu me dégoûtes.

**L'indifférence :**

Ça m'est égal.
Ça ne me fait ni chaud ni froid.
Je n'en ai rien à faire.
Je m'en moque.
Je m'en fous (fam.).
Qu'est-ce que tu veux que ça me fasse ?

***Expressing feelings :***
***Love :***

*I like you.*
*I love you, darling !*
*I adore you, my love !*
*I'm mad about you/him/her.*
*I can't live without you.*

***Hate :***

*I can't bear you.*
*I can't stand him.*
*I can't stand her.*
*I despise you/him/her.*
*You disgust me.*

***Indifference :***

*It's all one to me.*
*I'm not interested.*
*It's nothing to do with me.*
*I don't care.*
*I don't care.*
*What do you expect me to say ?*

## SAY IT IN FRENCH

***You are writing a love letter to the woman/man of your life :***

1. Say that you love him/her and that you are thinking only of him/her.
2. Say that you are mad about him/her.
3. Say that you believe in love at first sight.
4. Say that you can no longer live without him/her.

**Possible answers :**

1. Mon amour, je t'aime et je ne pense qu'à toi. 2. Je suis fou/folle de toi. 3. Je crois au coup de foudre. 4. Je ne peux plus vivre sans toi.

## DU JOUR AU LENDEMAIN

*Dimanche*

— Je suis en pleine forme ce matin.

— Et tu as vu le temps qu'il fait ? Génial !

— Si j'avais une voiture, j'irais à la mer.

*Lundi*

— Ben, qu'est-ce qui t'arrive ?

— Je suis déprimé. J'ai le cafard et je suis crevé.

— Eh bien, repose-toi.

— Impossible ! Si je ne faisais rien, je me sentirais coupable.

— De quoi ?

— De ne rien faire, tiens !

### PRONUNCIATION

| | | |
|---|---|---|
| **Qu'est-ce qui t'arrive ?** | [kɛskitariv] | kehss kee tahreev |
| **J'ai le cafard.** | [ʒɛlkafar] | zhay ler kahfahr |
| **Impossible !** | [ɛ̃pɔsibl] | angposseebl |

## FROM ONE DAY TO THE NEXT

*Sunday*
— I feel great this morning.
— Have you seen the weather ? Fantastic !
— If I had a car, I'd go the seaside*.

*Monday*
— Well then, what's the matter with you ?
— I'm depressed. I'm fed up and completely worn out.
— Well, get some rest.
— Impossible ! If I did nothing, I'd feel guilty.
— About what ?
— About doing nothing, of course !

## GRAMMAR

### *Verbs :*

**Je me sentirais** → present conditional of the verb **se sentir**
**J'irais** → present conditional of the verb **aller**

### *Making suppositions :*

The following structure can be used to make suppositions :

**Si** + imperfect + present conditional

**Si** tu ne **faisais** rien, je me **sentirais** coupable.
**Si** j'**avais** une voiture, j'**irais** à la mer.

Note that before **il** or **ils**, **si** becomes **s'il** or **s'ils**, but it does not change before **elle** or **elles**.

**S'il** était content, il chanterait.
**Si elle** était contente, elle chanterait.

N.B. ! For the conjugation of the present conditional refer back to lesson 30.

## EXERCISES

### 1. Put the verbs in brackets into the appropriate form

Si j'(être) ...... plus jeune, je t'(accompagner) ......
Si vous (parler) ...... français, ce (être) ...... plus facile.
Elle (venir) ......, si vous l'(inviter) ......
Nous (partir) ......, si nous le (pouvoir) ......

### 2. Make suppositions as in the example

Que feriez-vous si vous aviez de l'argent ? (aller au cinéma)
→ Si j'avais de l'argent, j'irais au cinéma.
Que ferait Paul s'il était jeune ? (danser toute la nuit) → S'il .......
Que feraient-ils s'ils gagnaient au loto ? (acheter une maison)
→ S'ils ..........................................................................................
Que ferions-nous s'il pleuvait ? (rester à la maison) → S'il ..........
Que ferait Virginie si elle était amoureuse ? (écrire à son amie)
→ Si elle ..........................................................................................

### 3. Translate into English

Qu'est-ce qui vous arrive ? Vous avez le cafard ? Si je partais, je me sentirais mal. Elle est en pleine forme aujourd'hui !

## VOCABULARY

pas question : out of the question !

tant mieux : so much the better, good (for you)

le bonheur → happiness

la joie → joy

l'espoir → hope

la tristesse → sadness

la dépression → depression

le désespoir → despair

**Key to exercises :**

1. étais/accompagnerais — parliez/serait — viendrait/invitiez — partirions/pouvions.
2. S'il était jeune, il danserait toute la nuit. S'ils gagnaient au loto, ils achèteraient une maison. S'il pleuvait, nous resterions à la maison. Si elle était amoureuse, elle écrirait à son amie.
3. What's the matter with you ? Are you feeling down ? If I went away, I would feel bad. She's on top form today !

## VARIATIONS

| **Pour exprimer des états d'âme :** | ***Expressing feelings :*** |
|---|---|
| **L'optimisme :** | ***Optimism :*** |
| Je suis en pleine forme. | *I'm on top form.* |
| C'est la grande forme ! | *I'm in fine form.* |
| Je me sens bien. | *I feel good.* |
| C'est le pied ! | *It's great (fam.).* |
| **Le pessimisme :** | ***Pessimism :*** |
| Ça (ne) va pas (bien/fort). | *Things aren't too good.* |
| J'ai le cafard. | *I'm feeling down.* |
| Je suis déprimé. | *I'm depressed.* |
| Ça me déprime. | *It's making me feel depressed.* |
| J'ai pas le moral. | *I'm feeling low.* |
| J'ai le moral à zéro. | *I'm down in the dumps.* |
| Je (ne) me sens pas bien. | *I don't feel very good.* |
| Je (n') ai envie de rien. | *Nothing interests me.* |
| Je me sens tout(e) triste. | *I feel (very) sad.* |
| Je me sens malheureux. | *I feel unhappy.* |
| Ce n'est pas mon jour ! | *It's not my day !* |

## SAY IT IN FRENCH

***You are depressed and are confiding in a friend :***

1. Say that you feel down in the dumps.
2. Say that you feel very sad.
3. Say that you are very unhappy.
4. Say that you have sentimental problems and that it's making you feel depressed.



**Possible answers :**

1. J'ai le moral à zéro, j'ai le cafard ! 2. Je me sens tout(e) triste. 3. Je suis très malheureux. 4. J'ai des problèmes sentimentaux et ça me déprime.

## LE BON VIEUX TEMPS...

— Alors, qui viendra à cette soirée ?
— Qu'est-ce que tu ferais à ma place ?
— J'inviterais uniquement les vieux copains.
— À qui est-ce que tu penses ?
— À qui ? Ben... les Langlois et Cyrille Gohin, par exemple.
— J'espère qu'on dansera toute la nuit ...
— Comme au bon vieux temps quoi !
— Mais, qui est-ce qui va s'occuper de la musique ?
— Demande à Jean-François d'apporter ses disques.
*(rire)*
— De quoi est-ce que tu ris ?
— Ça m'étonnerait que tu puisses encore danser le twist !

## PRONUNCIATION

| | | |
|---|---|---|
| **Qu'est-ce que tu ferais ?** | [kɛskətyfrɛ] | kehss ker tew ferreh |
| **À qui est-ce que tu penses ?** | [akiɛskətypɑ̃s] | ah keeyehssker tew pahngs |
| **De quoi est-ce que tu ris ?** | [dəkwaɛskətyri] | der kwah ehssker tew ree |
| **Ça m'étonnerait !** | [sametɔnrɛ] | sah maytawngnerreh |

## THE GOOD OLD DAYS...

— So, who'll be coming to the party ?
— What would you do, if you were me ?
— I'd only invite my old friends.
— Who are you thinking of ?
— Who ? Well, the Langlois' and Cyrille Gohin, for instance.
— We'll be dancing all night long, I hope.
— Like in the good old days, eh ?
— But who's going to take care of the music ?
— Ask Jean-François to bring his records.
*(laughter)*
— What are you laughing about ?
— I'd be surprised if you're still able to do the twist ?

## GRAMMAR

### *Verbs :*

**On pourrait** → present conditional of the verb **pouvoir**

### *The interrogative pronouns :*

When the question relates to a person, the following are used to inquire about the subject or the direct object :

**Qui est-ce qui** for the subject
**Qui est-ce que** for the direct object

**Qui est-ce qui** s'occupera de la musique ?
**Qui est-ce que** tu inviteras ?

To inquire about the indirect object, the following are used :

**À qui est-ce que** ou **De qui est-ce que**

**À qui est-ce que** tu penses ? **De qui est-ce que** tu parles ?

When the question relates to a thing, the following is used to inquire about the subject :

**Qu'est-ce qui**

**Qu'est-ce qui** ne va pas ?

To inquire about the direct object, the following is used :

**Qu'est-ce que**

**Qu'est-ce que** tu ferais à ma place ?

To inquire about the indirect object, the following are used :

**À quoi est-ce que** or **De quoi est-ce que**

**À quoi est-ce que** tu as pensé ? **De quoi est-ce que** nous parlons ?

## EXERCISES

### 1. *Match the appropriate answer to each question*

a. À qui est-ce qu'elle pense ?
b. De quoi est-ce que vous parlez ?
c. Qu'est-ce qui t'inquiète ?
d. Qui est-ce qui parle ?

1. Le mauvais temps.
2. Le nouveau directeur.
3. À ses amies.
4. De notre travail

### 2. *Use interrogative pronouns to complete these questions relating to persons*

— Je connais Paul → Qui est-ce que tu connais ?
— Ma mère viendra → ..........................................................
— François apportera des disques → .......................................
— J'inviterai mes copains → ...................................................

### 3. *Use interrogative pronouns to complete these questions relating to things*

Je fais mon travail. → Qu'est-ce que tu fais ?
Ce problème m'inquiète. → ...... t'inquiète ?
Il apporte ses disques. → ...... il apporte ?
Nous pensons à notre pays. → ...... vous pensez ?

### 4. *Translate into French*

Who will take care of the buffet ? We'll only invite old friends. You (plur.) could dance all night long.

## VOCABULARY

| | |
|---|---|
| uniquement : only, solely<br>jusqu'à : until<br>l'amitié → friendship<br>une boum → party<br>draguer → to chat up | une surprise-partie → a surprise party<br>un bal → a ball<br>un dragueur → a man who's always after the girls |



**Key to exercises :**

1. a-3, b-4, c-1, d-2
2. Qui est-ce qui viendra ? Qui est-ce qui apportera des disques ? Qui est-ce que tu inviteras ?
3. Qu'est-ce qui / qu'est-ce qu' / à quoi est-ce que.
4. Qui s'occupera du buffet ? Nous n'inviterons que les vieux copains. Vous pourriez danser toute la nuit.

## VARIATIONS

**Pour suggérer :**

Tu as pensé à inviter les Magnin ?
Je te conseille d'appeler un traiteur.
Tu ne veux pas que je m'en occupe ?
Pourquoi ne pas danser toute la nuit ?
Si tu veux, je les invite.

***Suggesting :***

*Have you thought of inviting the Magnin's ?*
*I advise you to call a caterer.*
*Don't you want me to see to that ?*
*Why not dance all night long ?*
*If you like, I'll invite them.*

**Pour approuver une suggestion ou une idée :**

Bravo !
Pourquoi pas ?
C'est pas bête !
C'est pas idiot !
C'est pas mal !
C'est bien pensé !
C'est super !
C'est génial !
C'est une bonne/excellente idée !

***Approving of a suggestion or idea :***

*Bravo !*
*Why not ?*
*That's not a bad idea !*
*That's not a stupid idea !*
*That's not bad !*
*That's a good idea !*
*That's great !*
*That's brilliant !*
*That's a good/excellent idea !*

## SAY IT IN FRENCH

***Along with some friends, you are trying to think of something to do to amuse yourselves :***

1. Ask them what they are thinking about.
2. Say that you could have a party.
3. Suggest having it at the weekend.
4. Ask who is going to see to the invitations.



**Possible answers :**

1. À quoi est-ce que vous pensez ? 2. On pourrait faire une boum. 3. Je propose de la faire le week-end. 4. Qui est-ce qui va s'occuper des invitations ?

# BILAN 7

■ **NOW YOU KNOW HOW TO EXPRESS OBLIGATION,**

***1. Transform the following sentences to highlight the subject of the verb.***

Il faut partir (vous) → Il faut que vous partiez.
Il est nécessaire de comprendre (ils) → ...
Il faut faire vite (elle) → ...
Il est nécessaire d'écrire (nous) → ...
Il faut respecter le code de la route (tu) → ...
Il est nécessaire d'aller à la poste (elle) → ...

■ **...HOW TO REPLACE THE NAME OF A PLACE WITH *EN* OR *Y*,**

***2. Replace the words underlined in the following sentences with* en *or* y.**

Tu viens de France ? → ...
Elle travaille à Paris → ...
Nous descendons de l'avion → ...
Pierre habite aux États-Unis depuis longtemps → ...
Elle va souvent chez ses parents → ...
Vous êtes dans la salle de bains ? → ...

***3. Complete the following sentences using* en *or* y.**

Je connais bien la France parce que j'... habite depuis dix ans. Le train arrive à Bordeaux à 8 h et il ... repart à 8 h 10. J'aime bien la Suisse et j'... passe toutes mes vacances. L'autobus est plein ; n'... montez pas. L'hiver je reste chez moi et je n'... sors presque pas.

■ **...WHERE TO PLACE *EN* OR *Y* IN THE SENTENCE,**

***4. Put into the negative,***

Allez-y ! → ... Prenez-en ! → ... Restons-y ! → ... Achetons-en ! → ... Pensez-y ! → ...

■ **...HOW TO USE DEMONSTRATIVE PRONOUNS,**



***5. Complete with* celui, celle, ceux, celles.**

Je ne prends pas ma voiture ; ... de mon père est plus rapide. Prends tes disques ; ... de Sylvie sont trop vieux. Donne-moi ton stylo ; ... que j'ai n'écrit pas bien. Viens avec tes amies ; ... de Pierre ne sont pas très sympathiques.

## ■ ...HOW TO EXPRESS A RESTRICTION,

***6. Transform as in the following example.***

Il a seulement dix ans → Il n'a que dix ans.
Elle est seulement une employée → ...
Il travaille seulement le samedi → ...
J'écoute seulement de la musique classique → ...
Nous voulons seulement danser → ...
J'ai seulement 200 francs → ...

## ■ ...HOW TO MAKE SUPPOSITIONS,

***7. Put the verbs in brackets in the appropriate tense and moods***

Si vous (avoir) .... envie, vous pourriez nous accompagner. Si ta femme venait, tu (être) ... très heureux. Si j'(être) ... malade, j'appellerais le médecin. Si le train arrivait en retard, nous (prendre) ... un taxi. Si vous le (connaître) ..., vous l'inviteriez.

## ■ ...HOW TO ASK QUESTIONS.

***8. Complete the following sentences using :* qu'est-ce que, qui est-ce qui, de quoi est-ce que, qui est-ce que, à qui est-ce que.**

J'ai invité mon frère → ... tu as invité ?
Elle parle à ses parents → ... elle parle ?
Je pense que c'est excellent → ... vous pensez ?
Ils veulent de l'argent → ... ils veulent ?
Jean vient ce soir → ... vient ce soir ?
Je me souviens de mes vacances → ... tu te souviens ?

## KEY TO EXERCISES

1. Il est nécessaire qu'ils comprennent - Il faut qu'elle fasse vite - Il est nécessaire que nous écrivions - Il faut que tu respectes le code de la route - Il est nécessaire qu'elle aille à la poste.
2. Tu en viens ? - Elle y travaille - Nous en descendons - Pierre y habite depuis longtemps - Elle y va souvent - Vous y êtes ?
3. y - en - y - y - en.
4. N'y allez pas ! N'en prenez pas ! N'y restons pas ! N'en achetons pas ! N'y pensez pas !
5. celle - ceux - celui - celles.
6. Elle n'est qu'une employée - Il ne travaille que le samedi - Je n'écoute que de la musique classique - Nous ne voulons que danser - Je n'ai que 200 francs.
7. aviez - serais - étais - prendrions - connaissiez.
8. qui est-ce que - à qui est-ce qu' - qu'est-ce que - qu'est-ce qu' - qui est-ce qui - de quoi est-ce que.

## DES NOUVELLES FRAÎCHES

*Chez le marchand de journaux*

— Je voudrais *Libération* et *Le Nouvel Observateur*, s'il vous plaît.

— Voilà mademoiselle, c'est tout ?

— Non, donnez-moi aussi la revue que mon père prend d'habitude.

— *Bricolage* ?

— Oui, c'est ça. Euh... je cherche un magazine qui parle de santé.

— *Santé Magazine* ? *Votre Santé* ?

— *Santé Magazine*. Merci, je vous dois combien ?

— Ça fait 58 F, mademoiselle.

— Excusez-moi, monsieur, je crois qu'il y a une erreur, ça doit faire 55 F.

— Vous avez raison. Je me suis trompé. Excusez-moi, mademoiselle.

— Ce n'est pas grave.

## PRONUNCIATION

| | | |
|---|---|---|
| **C'est tout ?** | [sɛtu] | seh too |
| **Oui, c'est ça.** | [wisɛsa] | wee seh sah |
| **Je vous dois combien ?** | [ʒəvudwakɔ̃bjɛ̃] | zher voo dwah kawngbyang |
| **Vous avez raison.** | [vuzaverɛzɔ̃] | voo zahvay rayzawng |

## ■ RECENT NEWS

*At the newsagent's*

— I'd like *Libération* and *Le Nouvel Observateur*, please .
— There you are, miss. Is that all ?
— No. Would you also give me the magazine that my father usually buys ?
— *Bricolage* ?
— Yes, that right. Er... I'm looking for a magazine about health.
— *Santé Magazine* ? *Votre Santé* ?
— *Santé Magazine*. Thanks. How much do I owe you ?
— That will be 58 francs, miss.
— I'm sorry, but I think there's some mistake. It should be 55 francs.
— You're right. I made a mistake. I'm sorry, miss.
— It doesn't matter*.

## GRAMMAR

### ■ *The relative pronouns* qui *and* que :

The relative pronouns are used to link together in one sentence two separate sentences relating to the same person or object.

**Qui** is used whenever the word replaced would be the subject of sentence.
Donnez-moi une revue. + Cette revue parle de santé.
= Donnez-moi une revue **qui** parle de santé.

**Que** is used whenever the word replaced would be the indirect object of the second sentence.
Donnez-moi la revue. + Mon père prend cette revue d'habitude.
= Donnez-moi la revue **que** mon père prend d'habitude.

Note that after **qui** the verb must agree with the original subject
Donnez-moi cette revue **qui** est neuve.
Donnez-moi ces revues **qui** sont neuves.
Note that **que** becomes **qu'** before a pronoun or noun beginning with a vowel. **Qui** never changes.

## EXERCISES

### 1. *Combine each pair of sentences using* qui

Regarde cet homme. Il dort → Regarde cet homme qui dort.
J'achète un livre. Il est intéressant. → ........................................
Vous connaissez Bernard. Il habite en France. → ......................
Il faut laver le linge. Il est sale. → ............................................

### 2. *Combine each pair of sentences using* que

Je vous donne le livre. Vous avez demandé ce livre. → .............
Je te présente Louis. Je le rencontre tous les jours ici. → ............
Voici une lettre. Tu attends cette lettre. → ...................................

### 3. *Complete the sentences using* qui *or* que

Tu as une amie ...... j'aime bien. Regarde la carte de vœux ...... je vais envoyer. Vous n'avez pas vu le feu ...... est rouge ! Je te présente Sylvie ...... travaille avec moi.

### 4. *Translate into English*

Donnez-moi aussi le journal que ma mère achète d'habitude. Je vais prendre la revue que mon père achète tous les jours. Je crois qu'il s'est trompé.

## VOCABULARY

d'habitude : usually
avoir raison : to be right
avoir tort : to be wrong

une information → news item
une nouvelle → piece of news
un entretien → conversation

un éditeur → editor
informer → to inform
un présentateur → presenter
une interview → interview
les petites annonces → small ads



**Key to exercises**

1. J'achète un livre qui est intéressant. Vous connaissez Bernard qui habite en France. Il faut laver le linge qui est sale.
2. Je vous donne le livre que vous avez demandé. Je te présente Louis que je rencontre tous les jours ici. Voici une lettre que tu attends.
3. que, que, qui, qui.
4. Also, give me the newspaper which my mother usually buys. I'll take the magazine which my father buys every day. I think he's made a mistake.

## VARIATIONS

**Pour dire à quelqu'un qu'il se trompe :**

Excusez-moi,
mais ce n'est pas ça.
Vous vous trompez.
C'est une erreur.
Vous devriez vérifier.

***Telling someone he has made a mistake :***

*Excuse me,*
*but that's not right.*
*You're mistaken.*
*It's a mistake.*
*You should check.*

**Pour reconnaître une erreur :**

Excusez-moi.
Oui, c'est vrai.
C'est exact.
Je suis désolé(e).
Effectivement.
*Followed by*
Je me suis trompé(e)
Il y a une erreur.
Ce n'est pas ça.
J'ai mal compté.

***Recognising a mistake :***

*Excuse me.*
*Yes, that's true.*
*That's right.*
*I'm sorry.*
*Quite true.*
*Followed by*
*I made a mistake.*
*There's a mistake.*
*That's not right.*
*I counted wrongly.*

**Pour donner tort :**

Non, je ne me suis pas trompé(e).
C'est vous qui vous trompez.
Non, c'est bien ce que je dis.
Non, vous pouvez vérifier.

***Denying an error :***

*No, I'm not mistaken.*
*No, It's you who are mistaken.*
*No, that's just what I'm saying.*
*No, you can check.*

## SAY IT IN FRENCH

***You ask a friend to buy you a newspaper or magazine :***

1. Ask him to bring you the newspaper which you take every day.
2. Ask him to bring you a newspaper which talks about sport.
3. You also want a magazine which talks about music.
4. Your friend makes a mistake when he gives you the change. Tell him.

**Possibles answers :**

1. Apporte-moi le journal que je prends tous les jours. 2. Achète-moi un journal qui parle de sports. 3. Je voudrais aussi une revue qui parle de musique. 4. Je crois que tu te trompes.

## VIVEMENT LA RETRAITE !

— Alors grand-père, comment ça va la retraite ?
— Ne m'en parle pas ! Je m'ennuie à mourir !
— Tu devrais trouver une occupation.
— Oui, mais laquelle ? Il n'y a rien qui m'intéresse !
— Eh, bien occupe-toi du jardin, sors un peu ; va au cinéma, visite un musée...
— Tu sais tout seul, ce n'est pas très drôle. Et puis, depuis la mort de ta grand-mère...
— Bon, écoute. Fais-toi beau. Ce soir, je t'emmène au restaurant avec ma copine.
— Dis, euh ... ta fiancée, elle n'a pas une amie qui pourrait nous accompagner ?
— Eh bien voilà, grand-père ! Tu vois, tu rajeunis !

### PRONUNCIATION

| | | |
|---|---|---|
| **Comment ça va ?** | [kɔmɑ̃sava] | kommahng sah vah |
| **Ne m'en parle pas !** | [nəmɑ̃parlpa] | ner mahng pahrl pah |
| **Oui, mais laquelle ?** | [wimɛlakɛl] | wee meh lahkehl |
| **Sors un peu.** | [sɔrɛ̃pø] | soar ang pur |
| **Eh bien voilà !** | [ebjɛ̃vwala] | eh byang vwahlah |

## ROLL ON RETIREMFNT!

— Well then, grandad, how are you enjoying your retirement ?
— Don't speak to me about it ! I'm bored stiff !
— You should find a hobby.
— Yes, but which one ? Nothing interests me.
— Well then, take care of the garden, go out a little, go to the cinema, visit a museum...
— You know, it's not much fun all alone. And since your grandmother died...
— Okay, listen. Make yourself smart. Tonight, I'm taking you to the restaurant with my girlfriend.
— I say, er ... your fiancée, hasn't she got a friend who could come with us ?
— There you are, grandad ! You see, you're feeling younger already !

## GRAMMAR

### *Verbs :*

**Tu rajeunis** → present indicative of the verb **rajeunir** (Group two)

### *The interrogative pronouns :*

When the question implies a choice regarding a person or object, the following pronouns are used

| | **singular** | **plural** |
|---|---|---|
| **masculine** | lequel | lesquels |
| **feminine** | laquelle | lesquelles |

The question can relate to the subject of a verb :

Un de mes amis viendra ce soir. — **Lequel** viendra ?
Les voisins sont partis. — **Lesquels** ?

or it can relate to the object :

Donne-moi une revue. — Tu veux **laquelle** ?
J'ai invité deux amies. — **Lesquelles** ?

## EXERCISES

### 1. *Complete the sentences using* lequel, laquelle, lesquels

Voilà deux disques. ......................... voulez-vous ?
Écoute une chanson. ................. me conseilles-tu ?
Un de tes amis a téléphoné. .................. a appelé ?

### 2. *Use interrogative pronouns to request explicit information*

Tu as une amie que j'aime beaucoup. → Laquelle ?
J'ai bu un excellent champagne. .......................... ?
Prends des fleurs. ................................................ ?
Sa tante est venue. .............................................. ?
J'ai vu tes voisines. ............................................ ?

### 3. *Complete the sentences using* sur, avec, pour, dans, chez

Prends le sac qui est ...... la table. Regarde si le dictionnaire est ...... mon bureau. J'ai apporté des fleurs ...... Sylvie. Je m'en vais ...... des amis.

### 4. *Translate into French*

Don't talk to me about it ! I'll take you (plur.) to the cinema. Don't you (sing.) have a girlfriend who could come ? I should do some sport.

## VOCABULARY

| | |
|---|---|
| depuis (que) : since | le sport → sport |
| le football → football | la marche → walking |
| la natation → swimming | nager → to swim |
| le tennis → tennis | la gymnastique → gymnastics |



**Key to exercises :**

1. lequel, laquelle, lequel
2. lequel ? lesquelles ? laquelle ? lesquelles ?
3. sur, dans/sur, pour, chez/avec.
4. Ne m'en parlez pas ! Je vous emmène au cinéma. Tu n'as pas une amie qui pourrait venir ? Je devrais faire du sport.

## VARIATIONS

**Pour exprimer l'indécision :**

Je ne sais pas quoi faire/dire.
Je ne sais pas ce que je dois penser.
Oui, mais lequel ?
D'accord, mais lesquelles ?

***Expressing indecision :***

*I don't know what to say/do.*
*I don't know what I should think.*
*Yes, but which one ?*
*Okay, but which ones ?*

**Pour parler de vos loisirs :**

**1. Ce que vous aimez :**

J'aime la lecture.
J'adore le cinéma.
Je suis un passionné de jazz.
Je suis fou de sport.
La musique, c'est génial !
Le vélo c'est super !
Le bricolage, c'est formidable !
La nature, c'est merveilleux !
L'opéra, ça me plaît (beaucoup).

**2. Ce que vous n'aimez pas :**

Le sport, je trouve que c'est ennuyeux.
Le foot, ça ne m'intéresse pas.

***Speaking about your leisure activities :***

***1. What you like :***

*I like reading.*
*I love the cinema.*
*I'm mad about jazz.*
*I'm crazy about sport.*
*Music's great !*
*Cycling's super !*
*Do-it-yourself is fantastic.*
*Nature's wonderful.*
*I like opera (very much).*

***2. What you don't like :***

*I find sport is boring.*

*Football doesn't interest me.*

## SAY IT IN FRENCH

***A couple of friends invite you out for the evening :***

1. You are not very keen. Express your indecision.
2. They suggest going to see a tennis match. Say that you're not mad about tennis.
3. They suggest going to see a film. Ask them which one.
4. They want to go dancing after the cinema. You think that, on your own, it's not much fun.



**Possible answers :**

1. Je ne sais pas quoi faire. 2. Je ne suis pas un passionné de tennis. 3. D'accord, mais lequel ? 4. Tout seul, ce n'est pas très drôle.

## VOYAGE ORGANISÉ

M. Pierre Truchy
Office du Tourisme
Place Royale
64000 Pau

Monsieur,

Je vous prie de bien vouloir me faire parvenir des informations sur votre ville afin d'y organiser un voyage l'été prochain.

Une brochure nous a déjà été envoyée par le Service culturel de l'Ambassade de France mais nous avons besoin de renseignements complémentaires sur Pau et sa région.

Quelle est la période la plus active du point de vue culturel ? Quelles sont les possibilités de logement, de préférence en pension complète, pour un groupe de 45 personnes ?

Je vous serais reconnaissant de me répondre aussi rapidement que possible.

Je vous prie d'accepter, Monsieur, l'expression de mes salutations les plus distinguées.

François Marteau

### PRONUNCIATION



| | | |
|---|---|---|
| **J'ai l'honneur** | [ʒɛlɔnœr] | zhay lawnurr |
| **L'été prochain** | [leteprɔʃɛ̃] | laytay proshang |
| **Nous avons besoin** | [nuzavɔ̃bəzwɛ̃] | noo zavawng berzwang |
| **L'office du tourisme** | [lɔfisdyturism] | loffeessdew tooreezm |

## ■ A PACKAGE TOUR

Dear Sir,
Would you be so kind as to send me information about your city to help me organize a trip there next summer*.
We have already been sent a brochure by the Cultural Department of the French Embassy but we need some further information about Pau and its region.
What is the busiest period from a cultural point of view ? What are the possibilities for accommodation, preferably with full board, for a group of 45 people ?
I would appeciate it if you would answer as quickly as possible.
Yours sincerely*,
François Marteau

## GRAMMAR

***The passive voice :***

The passive voice is used when the spealer wants to give prominence to the passive participant in an action.

Le directeur **invite** Sylvie.
Sylvie **est invitée** par le directeur.

The meaning of the sentence does not change but the direct object of the first sentence is given prominence by becoming the subjet of the second sentence.

**Formation :** the passive form is obtained as follows :
the verb **être** + the past participle (of the active form of the verb).

Louis XIV **a construit** Versailles.
Versailles **a été** construit **par** Louis XIV.

Note that in the passive form, the tense of the sentence is given by the conjugation of the verb **être**.
The past participle agrees in gender and number with the subject:

Sylvie est invité**e** par le directeur.

**par le ...** only appears when this information is required.

Le voleur a été arrêté (par la police).

## EXERCISES

### 1. Put the following sentences into the passive. Don't forget the agreement of the past participle

Jacques fait ce travail. → Ce travail ...........................................
En 1492 Christophe Colomb découvre l'Amérique. → ...............
Le Président reçoit les journalistes. → .......................................
En 1909 Blériot traverse la Manche. → .....................................

### 2. Answer the questions using the passive form as in the example

Qui a chanté "La vie en rose" ? (Édith Piaf) → "La vie en rose" a été chantée par Édith Piaf.
Qui a composé la "Symphonie fantastique" ? (Berlioz) → ..........
Qui a découvert les vaccins ? (Pasteur) → .................................
Qui a inventé le cinéma ? (Louis Lumière) → .............................
Qui a écrit *L'Étranger* ? (Albert Camus) → .................................

### 3. Translate into English

Quelle est la période la plus intéressante du point de vue sportif ? J'ai besoin de renseignements complémentaires. Une réponse m'a été envoyée par le directeur de l'office du tourisme.

## VOCABULARY

| | |
|---|---|
| afin de : in order to<br>(et) enfin : (and) finally<br>aussi ... que : as...as | un séjour → a stay |
| | la saison touristique → the tourist season |
| | un guide (livre) → a guide book |
| un touriste → a tourist | un circuit → a tour |
| un guide → a guide | la gastronomie → gastronomy |

**Key to exercises :**

1. Ce travail est fait par Jacques. L'Amérique est découverte par Christophe Colomb. Les journalistes sont reçus par le Président. La Manche est traversée par Blériot.
2. La "Symphonie fantastique" a été composée par Berlioz. Les vaccins ont été découverts par Pasteur. Le cinéma a été inventé par Louis Lumière. *L'Étranger* a été écrit par Camus.
3. What's the best period from the sports point of view ? I need further information. A reply was sent to me by the director of the tourist office.

## VARIATIONS

**Écrire une lettre**
**1. Officielle**

Monsieur,
Madame/Mademoiselle,
J'ai le plaisir de vous faire savoir que...
J'ai le regret de vous informer que...
Je vous prie d'agréer, Madame, l'expression de mes salutations distinguées.

**2. À une connaissance**

Cher(ère) Monsieur/Madame /Mademoiselle,
Croyez, chère Mademoiselle, en l'assurance de mes meilleurs sentiments.

**3. À un(e) ami(e)**

(Mon) Cher Georges,
(Ma) Chère Hélène,
Amitiés/Amicalement/Bien à toi/vous/Je t'embrasse/(Grosses) bises.

***Writing a letter***
***1. An official letter***

*Dear Sir,*
*Dear Madam,*
*I have the pleasure of informing you that...*
*I regret to inform you that...*

*Yours faithfully.*

***2. To a person you know***

*Dear Mr.../Mrs.../Miss...*

*Yours sincerely.*

***3. To a friend***

*Dear Georges,*
*Dear Hélène,*
*Best wishes/with love from, etc.*

## SAY IT IN FRENCH

***You are writing to Dominique, a very good French friend:***

1. Begin your letter with a friendly opening.
2. Say that you would like to receive some information about Dijon.
3. Say that a tourist brochure has already been sent to you by the tourist office.
4. Ask what the gastronomic specialities of his city are.

**Possible answers :**

1. Mon cher Dominique. 2. J'aimerais recevoir des renseignements sur Dijon. 3. Une brochure touristique m'a été envoyée par l'office du tourisme. 4. Quelles sont les spécialités gastronomiques de Dijon/ta ville ?

# BILAN 8

■ **NOW YOU KNOW HOW TO EMPHASIZE THE SUBJECT OR OBJECT OF SENTENCE,**

***1. Use c'est/ce sont ... qui, c'est/ce sont ... que.***

Le directeur l'a dit → C'est le directeur qui l'a dit.
Tes amis s'en vont → ... Elle écoute du Mozart → ...
Ils viennent demain → ... Mes parents ont des problèmes → ...
Il chante bien → ... Je connais bien les Gohin → ...

■ **...HOW TO PUT ALL THE INFORMATION TOGETHER IN A SINGLE SENTENCE,**

***2. Use qui or que to join the two sentences together***

Il reçoit un paquet. Le paquet est grand → ...
Tu m'offres un livre. J'ai déjà ce livre → ...
J'attends Paul. Paul viendra à 18 h → ...
Il a acheté une maison. Cette maison est très belle → ...
Vous invitez des voisins. Je connais bien ces voisins → ...

***3. Complete the following sentences with* qui *or* que.**

Je te présente Paul ... est médecin. Présente-moi cette jeune fille ... Je ne connais pas et ... me regarde. Donnez-moi ces oranges ... coûtent douze francs le kilo. Montrez-moi le projet ... vous avez préparé.

***4. Complete the following sentences with* qui *or* que.**

| | |
|---|---|
| Je suis dans un hôtel | ... est calme. |
| | ... vous connaissez bien. |
| Va à cette piscine | ... je te conseille. |
| | ... est nouvelle. |

■ **...HOW TO ASK FOR MORE PRECISE INFORMATIONS,**

***5. Ask which ? using* lequel, laquelle, lesquels, lesquelles.**

J'ai une nouvelle moto → laquelle ?
Achète des cigarettes → ...
Montre-moi tes photos de vacances → ...
Je t'ai apporté les journaux → ...
Je connais un de tes frères → ...

■ ...HOW TO USE THE PASSIVE VOICE.

***6. Put into the passive voice .***

Sophie raconte une longue histoire → ...
Jean a trouvé mes lunettes → ...
Un Anglais a gagné la compétition → ...
Mes amis m'inviteront → ...
Les spécialistes ont étudié toutes les solutions → ...

## KEY TO EXERCISES

1. Ce sont tes amis qui s'en vont. C'est du Mozart qu'elle écoute. C'est demain qu'ils viennent. Ce sont mes parents qui ont des problèmes. C'est lui qui chante bien. Ce sont les Gohin que je connais bien.
2. Il reçoit un paquet qui est grand. Tu m'offres un livre que j'ai déjà. J'attends Paul qui viendra à 18 h. Il a acheté une maison qui est très belle. Vous invitez des voisins que je connais bien.
3. qui - que, qui - qui - que.
4. qui, que - que, qui.
5. Lesquelles ? Lesquelles ? Lesquels ? Lequel ?
6. Une longue histoire est racontée par Sophie - Mes lunettes ont été trouvées par Jean - La compétition a été gagnée par un Anglais - Je serai invité(e) par mes amis - Toutes les solutions ont été étudiées par les spécialistes.

# Grammar Summary

## THE GENDER OF THE NOUNS

• **Gender**

Nouns have two genders in French : masculine and feminine.

□ ***General rule :***

The feminine of nouns is usually obtained by adding an **-e** to the masculine form of the noun.

*un ami → une amie*

□ ***Exceptions :***

– When a noun already ends with the letter **-e** in the masculine, the masculine and feminine forms are the same.

*un élève → une élève*

– Some nouns change their final syllable.

| | | |
|---|---|---|
| *le directeur* | → *la direc**trice*** | ***teur** → **trice*** |
| *le chanteur* | → *la chan**teuse*** | ***teur** → **teuse*** |
| *l'infirmier* | → *l'infirm**ière*** | ***er** → **ère*** |

– Other nouns double their final consonant.

| | | |
|---|---|---|
| *un technicien* | → *un technicie**nne*** | ***n** → **nne*** |

## THE PLURAL OF THE NOUNS

□ ***General rule :***

The **-s** usually marks the plural of a noun.

*la maison → les maisons*

□ ***Exceptions :***

– Nouns ending in **-s**, **-z** or **-x** do not change in the plural.

| | |
|---|---|
| *le bras* | → *les bras* |
| *le nez* | → *les nez* |
| *un choix* | → *des choix* |

– Nouns ending in **-eau** and **-eu** normally take an **-x** in the plural

*un bureau → des bureau**x*** *un feu → des feu**x***

– Some nouns ending in **-al** change their endings to **-aux** in the plural.

*un journal → des journaux*

– Proper nouns are invariable and do not take an **-s** in the plural.

*les Magnin et les Dupont*

## THE DEFINITE ARTICLE

The definite article is used to designate an object that has already been identified.

| | Singular | Plural |
|---|---|---|
| Masculine | *le garçon*<br>*l'ami* | *les garçons*<br>*les amis* |
| Feminine | *la fille*<br>*l'amie* | *les filles*<br>*les amies* |

▲ *l' is always used before words beginning with a vowel or a silent **h**.*

## THE INDEFINITE ARTICLE

The indefinite article is used to designate an object that has not been identified precisely.

| | Singular | Plural |
|---|---|---|
| Masculine | *un ami* | *des amis* |
| Feminine | *une amie* | *des amies* |



- **The negative**

The indefinite article changes when used with a verb in the negative.

| | | | |
|---|---|---|---|
| *nous avons* | *un ami*<br>*une voiture*<br>*des nouvelles* | → *nous n'avons pas* | *d'ami*<br>*de voiture*<br>*de nouvelles* |

▲ ***de*** *becomes* ***d'*** *before words beginning with a vowel or silent* ***h****.*

### • *à* + definite article

The use of the preposition **à** before the definite article can result in a number of changes.
You must say the following :

| | | |
|---|---|---|
| *à + le →* | ***au*** | *Je vais* ***au*** *cinéma* |
| *à + la →* | ***à la*** | *Je vais* ***à la*** *piscine* |
| *à + l' →* | ***à l'*** | *Tu vas* ***à l'****école ou* ***à l'****hôtel ?* |
| *à + les →* | ***aux*** | *Je vais* ***aux*** *toilettes.* |

Remember that you cannot say **à le** or **à les**. You must say **au** or **aux** !

*Aux États-Unis nous irons* ***au*** *théâtre.*

### • *de* + definite article

The presence of the preposition **de** before the definite article can result in a number of changes.
You must say the following:

| | | |
|---|---|---|
| *de + le →* | ***du*** | *Je viens* ***du*** *cinéma* |
| *de + la →* | ***de la*** | *Je viens* ***de la*** *piscine* |
| *de l' →* | ***de l'*** | *Tu viens* ***de l'****école ou* ***de l'****hôtel ?* |
| *de + les →* | ***des*** | *Je viens* ***des*** *toilettes.* |

Remember that you cannot say **de le** or **de les**. You must say **du** or **des** !

*Il sort* ***des*** *toilettes ou* ***du*** *bureau ?*



### • *en, au, aux, à* before the name of a country, town or city

**en** is used before feminine geographical names (names of countries, regions...) and before masculine geographical names beginning with a vowel.

*la Grèce* → ***en*** *Grèce* *l'Italie* → ***en*** *Italie*

**au** is used before masculine geographical names beginning with a consonant.

*le Portugal* → ***au*** *Portugal*

**aux** is used before geographical names in the plural.

*les États-Unis* → **aux** États-Unis

*les Antilles* → ***aux*** *Antilles*

**à** is used before the names of cities.

*à Paris , à Rome , à New York*

## PARTITIVE ARTICLES

The partitive article is used when referring to an indefinite quantity – like *some* and *any* in English.

| | Singular | Plural | Negative |
|---|---|---|---|
| Masculine | ***du*** *vin*<br>***de l'*** *argent* | ***des*** *vins* | ***pas de*** *vin*<br>***pas d'*** *argent* |
| Feminine | ***de la*** *viande*<br>***de l'*** *eau* | ***des*** *eaux* | ***pas de*** *viande*<br>***pas d'*** *eau* |

▲ ***de l'*** *is used before masculine and feminine nouns beginning with a vowel or silent* ***h****.*

*–* ***pas de*** *or* ***pas d'*** *are used to express the absence of quantity (English: any).*

## QUANTIFIERS

The following expressions are used to express a quantity : **un peu de, assez de, peu de, beaucoup de, trop de**.

| | | | | | |
|---|---|---|---|---|---|
| *Il prend* | ***un peu de***<br>***assez de***<br>***peu de***<br>***beaucoup***<br>***trop de*** | *sucre* | *He takes* | *a little*<br>*enough*<br>*little*<br>*a lot of*<br>*too much* | *sugar* |

## CARDINALS NUMBERS

Cardinal numbers are used to count people, animals or objects.
Cardinal numbers are invariable with the exception of **un**, which becomes **une** before a feminine noun.

*J'ai un frère et une sœur. (I have one brother and one sister).*

| From 0 to 10 | From 11 to 20 | From 21 to 30 |
|---|---|---|
| *0 – zéro* | *11 – onze* | *21 – vingt et un* |
| *1 – un* | *12 – douze* | *22 – vingt-deux* |
| *2 – deux* | *13 – treize* | *23 – vingt-trois* |
| *3 – trois* | *14 – quatorze* | *24 – vingt-quatre* |
| *4 – quatre* | *15 – quinze* | *25 – vingt-cinq* |
| *5 – cinq* | *16 – seize* | *26 – vingt-six* |
| *6 – six* | *17 – dix-sept* | *27 – vingt-sept* |
| *7 – sept* | *18 – dix-huit* | *28 – vingt-huit* |
| *8 – huit* | *19 – dix-neuf* | *29 – vingt-neuf* |
| *9 – neuf* | *20 – vingt* | *30 – trente* |
| *10 – dix* | | |

**Multiples of ten**

| | |
|---|---|
| *10 – dix* | *60 – soixante* |
| *20 – vingt* | *70 – soixante-dix ( 60 + 10 )* |
| *30 – trente* | *80 – quatre-vingts (4 x 20)* |
| *40 – quarante* | *90 – quatre-vingt-dix (4 x 20 + 10)* |
| *50 – cinquante* | *100 – cent* |

How to form cardinal numbers :
– after 20, 30, 40, 50, 60, 80, form the numbers in the same way as in column "from 21 to 30".

□ ***Exceptions***

*81 → quatre-vingt-un*

*101 → cent un*

*111 → (the **et** disappears) cent onze*

– after 70 and 90, the numbers are formed as follows :

| | |
|---|---|
| *70 - soixante-dix* | *90 - quatre-vingt-dix (4 x 20 + 10)* |
| *71 - soixante et onze* | *91 - quatre-vingt-onze (4 x 20 + 11)* |
| *72 - soixante-douze* | *92 - quatre-vingt-douze (4 x 20 + 12* |
| *73 - soixante-treize* | *93 - quatre-vingt-treize (4 x 20 + 13)* |
| *74 - soixante-quatorze* | *94 - quatre-vingt-quatorze (4 x 20 + 14)* |
| *75 - soixante-quinze* | *95 - quatre-vingt-quinze (4 x 20 + 15)* |
| *76 - soixante-seize* | *96 - quatre-vingt-seize (4 x 20 + 16)* |
| *77 - soixante-dix-sept* | *97 - quatre-vingt-dix-sept (4 x 20 + 17)* |
| *78 - soixante-dix-huit* | *98 - quatre-vingt-dix-huit (4 x 20 + 18)* |
| *79 - soixante-dix-neuf* | *99 - quatre-vingt-dix-neuf (4 x 20 + 19)* |

## ORDINAL NUMBERS

Ordinals are used to rank things in a certain order and are obtained by adding **-ième** to the cardinal numbers.

*deux → deuxième   dix → dixième   cent → centième*

The abbreviations are written as follows: $2^e$, $10^e$, $100^e$

□ ***Exception:*** *un → premier*   *une → première*

Abbreviation: $1^{er}$, $1^{re}$.

## DEMONSTRATIVE ADJECTIVES

Demonstrative adjectives are used to designate a person, animal or object that we want to identify precisely, and distinguish from others.

| | Singular | Plural |
|---|---|---|
| Masculine | *ce garçon*<br>*cet homme* | *ces garçons*<br>*ces hommes* |
| Feminine | *cette femme* | *ces femmes* |

**cet** is used before a singular masculine noun beginning with a vowel or silent **h**.

*cet homme, cet ami.*

# POSSESSIVE ADJECTIVES

The form of the possessive adjective in French changes according to the number of possessors (one or several) and the number of objects possessed (one or several).

| | 1 possessor | Several possessors |
|---|---|---|
| 1 masculine object<br>1 feminine object | **mon** *livre*<br>**ma** *voiture*<br>**mon** *amie* | **notre** *livre*<br>*voiture*<br>*amie* |
| Several masculine objects<br>Several feminine objects | **mes** *livres*<br>*voitures*<br>*amies* | **nos** *livres*<br>*voitures*<br>*amies* |
| 1 masculine object<br>1 feminine object | **ton** *livre*<br>**ta** *voiture*<br>**ton** *amie* | **votre** *livres*<br>*voiture*<br>*amie* |
| Several masculine objects<br>Several feminine objects | **tes** *livres*<br>*voitures*<br>*amies* | **vos** *livres*<br>*voitures*<br>*amies* |
| 1 masculine object<br>1 feminine object | **son** *livre*<br>**sa** *voiture*<br>**son** *amie* | **leur** *livre*<br>*voiture*<br>*amie* |
| Several masculine objets<br>Several feminine objects | **ses** *livres*<br>*voitures*<br>*amies* | **leurs** *livres*<br>*voitures*<br>*amies* |

▲ ***ma, ta, sa*** *become* ***mon, ton, son*** *before a feminine noun beginning with a vowel or a silent* ***h****.*



# ADJECTIVES OF QUALITY

**• Position :**

The usual position of the adjective of quality is after the noun.

Some common adjectives, however, are used before the noun they describe :

***beau (bel)/belle*** *(handsome/beautiful)* — ***joli/e*** *(pretty )*

***bon/ne*** *(good )* — ***mauvais/e*** *(bad)*

***petit/e*** *(small)* — ***grand/e*** *(big)*

***vieux (vieil)/vieille*** *(old)* — ***jeune*** *(young)*

***nouveau (nouvel)/nouvelle*** *(new)* — ***vrai/e*** *(true)*

***faux/fausse*** *(false)* — ***long/longue*** *(long)*

***premier/première*** *(first)* — ***deuxième*** *(second)*

***dernier/dernière*** *(last)*

## • Agreement

Adjectives of quality always agrees in gender (masculine or feminine) and in number (singular or plural) with the noun it describes.

## • Formation of the feminine

### □ *General rule*

The feminine of adjectives of quality is formed by adding an **-e** to the masculine form of the adjective (the same as for the noun)

*grand → grande*     *petit → petite*

### □ *Exceptions :*

**a)** Some adjectives double their final consonant before the **-e**

| | |
|---|---|
| *un bon dîner → une **bonne** soirée* | ***on → onne*** |
| *un livre ancien → une voiture **ancienne*** | ***ien → ienne*** |
| *un gros livre → une **grosse** voiture* | ***s → sse*** |

**b)** Some adjectives modify their final syllable.

| | |
|---|---|
| *un beau garçon → une **belle** fille* | ***eau → elle*** |
| *un garçon heureux → une fille **heureuse*** | ***eux → euse*** |
| *un livre blanc → une page **blanche*** | ***anc → anche*** |
| *un vélo neuf → une voiture **neuve*** | ***f → ve*** |
| *le premier jour → la **première** heure* | ***er → ère*** |

A large number of adjectives do not obey the general rule mentioned above and are irregular in the feminine:

***faux*** → ***fausse*** *(false)* ; ***frais*** → ***fraîche*** *(fresh)*

***gentil*** → ***gentille*** *(kind)* ; ***long*** → ***longue*** *(long)* ;
***roux*** → ***rousse*** *(red-haired)* ; ***sec*** → ***sèche*** *(dry).*

## • Formation of the plural

□ ***General rule:***

The plural of adjectives is obtained by adding an **-s** to the singular form

*le grand livre* → *les grand**s** livre**s***

□ ***Exceptions:***

**a)** When an adjective ends in an **-s** or an **-x** in the singular, it does not change in the plural.

*un sérieux risque* → *de sérieux risques*

*un gros homme* → *de gros hommes*

**b)** When an adjective ends in **-eau**, it takes an **-x** in the plural.

*un nouveau livre* → *de nouvea**ux** livres*

**c)** Adjectives ending in **-al** change their endings to **-aux** in the plural.

*un problème local* → *des problèmes loc**aux***

## • The feminine plural of adjectives

An **-s** is added to the feminine form of the adjective.

*grand* → *grande* → ***grandes*** *beau* → *belle* → ***belles***

## THE INTERROGATIVE ADJECTIVE *QUEL*

**Quel** agrees in gender and in number with the noun that it replaces or qualifies

***Un*** *jour* → ***Quel*** *jour ?*

***Une*** *heure* → *À* ***quelle*** *heure ?*

***Des*** *projets* → ***Quels*** *projets ?*

***Des*** *amies* → ***Quelles*** *amies ?*

## THE SUBJECT PRONOUN

In French, the verb is always accompanied by a subject, except in the imperative. This subject is frequently a subject pronoun.

| person | 1st | 2nd | 3rd | | |
|---|---|---|---|---|---|
| | | | Masculine | Feminine | Neutral |
| Singular : | *je* | *tu* | *il* | *elle* | *on* |
| Plural : | *nous* | *vous* | *ils* | *elles* | |

**Vous** may be used when addressing one person. This is the polite form of address, used when talking to someone one doesn't know, the elderly or one's superiors, as opposed to the more familiar **tu** form, used among friends or when addressing young children. Although the same distinction is made in German, Italian and Spanish, there is no real equivalent in modern English (cf. *thou/you*). When in doubt, use **vous** and wait for the French person to take the lead in using the **tu** form.

*Pardon Monsieur , vous parlez français ?*

**On** is frequently used as the equivalent of **nous** or impersonally, when referring to an indefinite group of people, but the verb is always conjugated in the 3rd person singular. Although similar to the English *one* (**Est-ce qu'on est censé porter une cravate ?** – Is one expected to wear a tie?), it is used much more widely than in English, translating *we*, the indefinite *you, they,* or the passive :

*On va être en retard.* (We're going to be late)

*On ne doit pas fumer ici.* (You mustn't smoke here)

*On dit qu'il est très sympathique.* (They say he's very friendly)

*Ici, on parle Anglais.* (English is spoken here)

## THE DISJUNCTIVE PRONOUN

The disjunctive pronoun is used :

– emphatically, to stress the subject of the sentence (where intonation would be used to convey the same emphasis in English):

*Moi, je suis français :* (As for me), I'm French.
– after verbs in the imperative :

*Lève-toi ! Ecoute-moi ! :* Get up ! Listen to me !

– after conjonctions and prepositions :

*Moi, je suis Français. Et toi ? :* I'm French. And you?

– to replace a noun when used with verbs such as **penser à**, **croire en**, **faire attention à** and **s'intéresser à**.

*Je pense à **toi**.* *Fais attention à **eux**.*

*Nous croyons en **lui**.* *Il s'intéresse à **elle**.*

## THE OBJECT PRONOUN

Object pronouns are used to avoid repetition. There are two sets of object pronoun – direct and indirect – corresponding to the two kinds of object they replace:
– direct object

*Tu regardes Paul ?* *– Oui, je le regarde.*

– indirect object

*Tu parles à Paul ?* *– Oui, je lui parle.*

The table below lists the object pronouns that can be used to refer to people and animate objects.

| | Direct object | | | | Indirect object | | |
|---|---|---|---|---|---|---|---|
| Person | 1st | 2nd | 3rd masc. | 3rd fem. | 1st | 2nd | 3rd |
| Singular | *me* | *te* | *le* | *la* | *me* | *te* | *lui* |
| Plural | *nous* | *vous* | *les* | | *nous* | *vous* | *leur* |

▲ ***me, te, le, la** become **m', t', l'** before verbs beginning with a vowel or a silent **h**.*



## THE PRONOUNS *EN* AND *Y*

• **en** is used to replace the name of an object in expressions of quantity where we would say *some, any, of it* in English – or nothing at all! It is used to replace nouns preceded by :

**du** → *Tu bois* ***du*** *vin ? Oui , j'****en*** *bois.*

**de la** → *Vous voulez* ***de la*** *viande ? Oui , j'****en*** *veux bien.*

**de l'** → *Elle prend* ***de l'****eau ? Non , elle n'****en*** *prend pas.*

**des** → *Tu as acheté* ***des*** *fruits ? Oui , j'****en*** *ai acheté.*

or by quantifiers such as :

**peu de** → *Tu as peu d'argent ? Oui, j'en ai peu.*

**assez de** → *Tu as assez d'argent ? Oui, j'en ai assez.*

**beaucoup de** → *Tu veux beaucoup de sucre ? Oui, j'en veux beaucoup.*

**trop de** → *Il boit trop de vin ? Oui, il en boit trop.*

**un , deux...** → *Il a cinq enfants ? Oui , c'est vrai , il en a cinq*

• **y** is used to replace an inanimate object normally preceded by the preposition **à**.

*Quel problème ! Plus j'****y*** *pense... (plus je pense* ***à ce*** *problème).*

*Le coup de foudre , j'****y*** *crois ! (Je crois* ***au*** *coup de foudre).*

*Ta santé , il faut que tu* ***y*** *fasses attention ( Il faut que tu fasses attention* ***à*** *ta santé).*

▲ *Disjunctive pronouns (see above p. 225) are used to replace the name of a person in constructions with verbs such as* ***penser à, croire en, faire attention à*** *and* ***s'intéresser à****...*

*Je ne pense qu'à elle. Je pense bien à toi. Je ne crois pas en lui. Faites attention à eux. Je m'intéresse à vous.*

## • Position of the object pronouns in the sentence

**en** replaces the name of a place normally preceded by the preposition **de** or the contractions **de +** the definite article : **du** or **des**.

*Je viens de chez le garagiste → J'en viens.*

*Tu descends du 1$^{er}$ étage ? → Oui , j'en descends.*

*Elle vient des États-Unis ? → Oui , elle en vient.*

**y** is similar to **en** except it replaces the name of a place normally preceded by the propositions **à, en, au, à la, aux, dans, chez**...

*Elle va en France ? → Non , elle n'y va pas.*

*Vous travaillez au bureau ? → Oui , j'y travaille.*

*Il habite à Paris ? → Oui , il y habite.*

*Elle est aux États-Unis ? → Non , elle n'y est pas.*

□ ***General rule***

The normal position of object pronouns is immediately before their governing verb :

**a)** In affirmative or interrogative sentences: *Je le prends. Tu en as ?*

**b)** In negative sentences: *Il ne les connaît pas. Elle n'en a pas.*

**c)** In negative imperative sentences: *Ne la regarde pas.*

The object pronoun comes **after** the verb in imperatives :

*Regarde-la !  Pensez-y !*

## POSSESSIVE PRONOUNS

Possessive pronouns are used like the corresponding English forms : *mine, yours, his,* etc., to avoid a repetition. The form of the possessive pronoun depends upon the number of owners (singular or plural), the gendre (masculine or feminine) and the number (singular or plural) of the object(s) in question.

**A single owner :**

| Person | 1st | | 2nd | | 3rd | |
|---|---|---|---|---|---|---|
| | masc. | fem. | masc. | fem. | masc. | fem. |
| 1 object | *le mien* | *la mienne* | *le tien* | *la tienne* | *le sien* | *la sienne* |
| > 1 object | *les miens* | *les miennes* | *les tiens* | *les tiennes* | *les siens* | *les siennes* |

**Several owners :**

| Person | 1st masc. | 1st fem. | 2nd masc. | 2nd fem. | 3rd masc. | 3rd fem. |
|---|---|---|---|---|---|---|
| 1 object | *le nôtre* | *la nôtre* | *le vôtre* | *la vôtre* | *le leur* | *la leur* |
| >1 object | *les nôtres* | | *les vôtres* | | *les leurs* | |

## DEMONSTRATIVE PRONOUNS

Demonstrative pronouns are used to represent people or things, or to avoid repetition.

| | Singular | Plural | Indefinite |
|---|---|---|---|
| Masculine | *celui (-ci, -là)* | *ceux (-ci, -là)* | *ceci, cela, ça* |
| Feminine | *celle (-ci, -là)* | *celles (-ci, -là)* | |

– **ça** is the contracted form of **cela**, widely used in spoken French.

– In order to distinguish between *this* and *that*, **-ci** and **-là** are respectively added to the pronoun :

*Tu veux quel livre ? **Celui-ci** , il est moins cher que **celui-là**.*

– The demonstrative pronoun is frequently used with **de**.

***Celui** de Paul est plus grand que **ceux** de Pierre.*

*Donne-moi **celle** de gauche.*

## INTERROGATIVE PHRASES

• When the question concerns a person, the following interrogative phrases are used to ask about the subject or the direct object of the sentence :

**Qui est-ce qui** for the subject and **Qui est-ce que** for the direct object

The following interrogative phrases are used when asking about the indirect object :

**À qui est-ce que** and **de qui est-ce que**

*À qui est-ce que tu penses ?*

*De qui est-ce que tu parles ?*

• When the question concerns **a thing**, the following interrogative phrase is used to ask about the subject of the sentence : **Qu'est-ce qui**

*Qu'est-ce qui ne va pas ?*

Use the following interrogative phrase when asking about the direct object of an action : **Qu'est-ce que**

*Qu'est-ce que tu ferais à ma place ?*

When asking about the indirect object, use :
**À quoi est-ce que** or **de quoi est-ce que**

*À quoi est-ce que tu penses ?*

*De quoi est-ce que tu parles ?*

## LEQUEL

This interrogative pronoun is used in questions concerning choice, to distinguish between different persons or things.

*Tu connais mon voisin ? – Lequel ? – Celui du 32.*

| | Singular | Plural |
|---|---|---|
| Masculine | *lequel* | *lesquels* |
| Feminine | *laquelle* | *lesquelles* |

The pronoun agrees in gender and in number with the thing or the person to which the question refers.
The question may concern the subject :

*Un de mes amis viendra ce soir. – Lequel viendra ?*

The question may concern the object :

*Donne-moi une revue ! – Laquelle veux-tu ?*

## RELATIVE PRONOUNS

Relative pronouns are used to connect in a single sentence two pieces of information about the same noun.
**Qui** is used whenever the noun (or phrase) it replaces would have been the subject of the 2nd sentence.

| Sentence n°1 | Sentence n°2 |
| --- | --- |
| *Donnez-moi une revue.* + | *Cettre revue parle de santé.* |

=

*Donnez-moi une revue* ***qui*** *parle de santé.*

**Que** is used whenever the noun (or phrase) it replaces would have been the direct object of the 2nd sentence.

| Sentence n°1 | Sentence n°2 |
| --- | --- |
| *Donnez-moi une revue.* + | *Mon père prend cette revue d'habitude.* |

=

*Donnez-moi une revue* ***que*** *mon père prend d'habitude.*

• Note the agreement of the verb after **qui** !

*Donnez-moi cette revue* ***qui est neuve.***

*Donnez-moi ces revues* ***qui sont neuves.***

• **Que** becomes **qu'** before a pronoun or noun beginning with a vowel. **Qui** is invariable and never changes.

## NEGATIVE SENTENCES

The usual negative form is obtained by placing **ne** before the verb and **pas** after it.

*Elle* ***ne*** *parle* ***pas.*** *Il* ***n'****habite* ***pas.*** *Il* ***n'****aime* ***pas.***

• Note that **ne** becomes **n'** before verbs beginning with a vowel or a silent **h**.
When used with an infinitive, both parts of the negative, **ne** and **pas**, are placed before it : *Pardon de ne pas écrire.*

### • Ne... Ni... ni

**ni** is used as a conjunction in negative sentences, thus avoiding the repetition of identical structures :

*Je ne rentrerai* ***ni*** *pour déjeuner ,* ***ni*** *pour dîner. → Je ne rentrerai pas pour déjeuner et je ne rentrerai pas pour dîner.*

- **Ne... que**

The **ne... que** construction conveys the same meaning as **seulement** used after the verb.

*Je **ne** pense **qu'**à lui. → Je pense **seulement** à lui.*

*Il **ne** boit **que** de l'eau → Il boit **seulement** de l'eau.*

▲ *Note that the negative **ne** is not used with **seulement** !*

- **The negative with *ne... rien, ne... jamais, ne... plus, ne... personne***

| Simple tenses | Compound tenses |
|---|---|
| *je **ne** comprends **rien*** | *je **n'ai rien** compris* |
| *je **ne** reviendrai **jamais*** | *je **ne** suis **jamais** revenu(e)* |
| *je **ne** reviendrai **plus*** | *je **ne** suis **plus** revenu(e)* |
| *je **ne** connais **personne*** | *je **n'**ai connu **personne*** |

As shown in the examples above, the **ne** (or **n'**) stands before the verb in simple tenses with the second half of the negative coming immediately after.

In compound tenses, the two parts of the negative respectively stand before and after the auxiliary, with the exception of **ne... personne**.

The opposites of **rien, personne, jamais** and **plus**.

*Quelque chose (something) → Tu vois quelque chose ? – Non, je ne vois rien.*

*Quelqu'un (someone) → Tu vois quelqu'un ? – Non, je ne vois personne.*

*Quelquefois (sometimes) → Tu viens quelquefois ? – Non, je ne viens jamais.*

*Souvent (often) → Tu viens souvent ? – Non, je ne viens jamais.*

*Toujours /encore (still / again) → Tu parles encore ? – Non, il ne parle plus.*



## INTERROGATIVE SENTENCES

- The simplest way of expressing a question is by adding a **?** to the sentence when writing, and by using a rising intonation when speaking.

written : *Vous êtes français.* *Vous êtes français ?*
oral :

- Interrogative constructions :

| Oral | Oral and written | Mainly written |
|---|---|---|
| *On va où ?* | *Où est-ce qu'on va ?* | *Où va-t-on ?* |
| *On part quand ?* | *Quand est-ce qu'on part ?* | *Quand part-on ?* |
| *On part comment ?* | *Comment est-ce qu'on part ?* | *Comment part-on ?* |
| *Tu achètes quoi ?* | *Qu'est-ce que tu achètes ?* | *Qu'achètes-tu ?* |

▲ *When constructing questions in the 3rd category, the subject must come immediately after the verb. When the verb ends in a vowel, the letter **-t-** is written (and pronounced) between the verb and the pronouns **il, elle** and **on**.*

## CONDITIONAL SENTENCES

### • To express a condition

**Si** + verb in the present tense + verb in the future

*Et **si** vous lui téléphonez , il **viendra**.*

***Si** vous prenez rendez-vous maintenant , il vous **recevra** aujourd'hui.*

### • To express a supposition

The following structure may be used to express a supposition :

**Si** + imperfect + present conditional

***Si** je ne **faisais** rien , je me **sentirais** coupable.*

***Si** tu **allais** au cinéma , ça **irait** peut-être mieux.*

## COMPARISONS

**plus**
**aussi** + adjective/adverb (+ **que**)
**moins**

• **With an adjective :**

To express superiority → *Pierre est **plus** grand (**que** Paul)*
To express equality → *Pierre est **aussi** grand (**que** Paul)*
To express inferiority → *Pierre est **moins** grand (**que** Paul)*

• **With an adverb :**

▲ *Make a careful note of these two exceptions !*

With the adjective bon → *Cet hôtel est* { ***meilleur*** / ***aussi bon*** / ***pire** (ou **moins bon**)* }

With the adverb bien → Cet hôtel est { **mieux** / **aussi bien** / **moins bien** }

Never say **plus bon** or **plus bien** !

## COMPARISON OF QUANTITIES

Structure n°1 : Verb + { **plus** / **autant** / **moins** } (+ **que** + noun or disjunctive pronoun)

To express superiority → *Tu gagnes **plus que** moi ?*
*– Oui, je gagne **plus**.*
To express equality → *Tu gagnes **autant que** moi ?*
*– Oui, je gagne **autant**.*
To express inferiority → *Tu gagnes **moins que** moi ?*
*– Oui, je gagne **moins**.*

**Que** becomes **qu'** when the following word or pronouns begins with a vowel.

Structure n°2 : Verb + { **plus de** / **autant de** / **moins de** } + nom (+ **que** + noun or disjunctive pronoun)



To express superiority → *Tu as plus d'amis que moi ?*
*– Oui , j'en ai plus.*
To express equality → *Tu as autant d'amis que moi ?*
*– Oui , j'en ai autant.*

To express inferiority → *Tu as moins d'amis que moi ?*
*– Oui , j'en ai moins.*

**De** in these examples is invariable but it becomes **d'** when the following word begins with a vowel or a silent **h** → **plus d'amis**

## THE SUPERLATIVE ABSOLUTE

The superlative absolute is obtained by using adverbs of degree such as **très**, **fort**, **bien**, **tout**, **extrêmement**,... to modify the adjective :

*Vous êtes très aimable. (You are very kind.)*

*Je vous serais fort reconnaissant de... (I would be most grateful...)*

- **With an adjective :**

| | | | |
|---|---|---|---|
| + | **le**<br>**la**<br>**les** | **plus**<br>**moins** | + adjective + (**des/de** ...) |

*Je te présente* ***le plus*** *grand (****de*** *mes enfants). (Meet my eldest child.)*

*J'ai rencontré* ***le plus*** *célèbre (****des*** *acteurs). (I met the most famous actor.)*

The superlative of **bon** is **le meilleur**, **la meilleure**, **les meilleur(e)s**.

- **With an adverb :**

| | | | |
|---|---|---|---|
| + | **le**<br>**la**<br>**les** | **plus**<br>**moins** | + adverb |

*C'est lui qui travaille* ***le plus*** *rapidement. (He works the quickest.)*

▲ *The superlative of* ***bien*** *is* ***le mieux****.*

## REPORTED SPEECH

Reported speech is used to relate what another person has said. When direct speech (what the person actually said) is turned into reported speech, some changes are usually necessary.

| Person A to person B | Person B to person C (reported speech) |
|---|---|
| *Quand peut-il me rencontrer ?* | *Il demande* ***quand*** *tu peux le rencontrer.* |
| *Où est-il ?* | *Il veut savoir* ***où*** *vous êtes.* |
| *Comment vient-il ?* | *Il demande* ***comment*** *vous venez.* |
| *C'est urgent ?* | *Il demande* ***si*** *c'est urgent.* |
| *Qu'est-ce qu'il veut ?* | *Il demande* ***ce que*** *vous voulez.* |

If you want to report statements made by another person, you can start your sentence with : **Il dit que... Elle dit que...**
If you want to report a question, you can start your sentence with expressions such as: **Il/elle demande... Il/elle veut savoir...**

- **Reporting an order :**

If you want to report an order, you can start your sentence with **Il/elle dit de** + the infinitive

*Prenez ces comprimés !* → ***Il te/vous dit de*** *prendre ces comprimés.*

*Ne sortez pas !* → ***Il te/vous dit de*** *ne pas sortir.*

## OBLIGATION

There are several ways of expressing obligation in French. Here are a few examples of constructions with the infinitive :
**être obligé(e) de** + infinitive → *Je suis obligée de partir.*
**devoir** + infinitive → *Nous devons partir.*
**Il faut** + infinitive → *Il faut partir*
**Il est nécessaire de** + infinitive → *Il est nécessaire de partir.*

The last two examples are impersonal expressions that do not clearly identify the subject of the action (*who* must leave?). If you want to use these expressions and specify the subject of the action, you must modify the construction and use the subjunctive.

**Il faut que** + present subjunctive → *Il faut que je parte/vous partiez.*

**Il est nécessaire que** + present subjunctive → *Il est nécessaire que tu partes.*

## EXPRESSING DURATION

**Il y a... que** and **ça fait... que** are used to express a period of time extending up to the moment of speaking. Note that French uses a present tense where we would expect the present perfect tense in English.

*Ça fait un quart d'heure que j'attends. (I've been waiting for a quarter of an hour.)*

*Il y a une semaine que je suis seul. (I've been alone for a week.)*

### • Expressing the length of time since an action took place

We can also use **il y a**, **il y a... que** and **ça fait... que** to express the length of time since an action took place.

*Madame Serreaux est sortie il y a cinq minutes.*

*Il y a cinq minutes que Madame Serreaux est sortie.*

*Ça fait cinq minutes que Madame Serreaux est sortie.*

(Mrs Serreaux went out five minutes ago.)

### • Expressing the length of an on-going action

The expressions **ça fait... (que)**, **il y a... (que)** and **depuis** are used to express how long an action has been going on.

| Asking for information | Giving information |
|---|---|
| *Ça fait longtemps (qu'il a mal) ?* | *Ça fait deux heures (qu'il a mal).* |
| *Il y a longtemps (qu'il a mal) ?* | *Il y a deux heures (qu'il a mal)* |
| *(Il a mal) depuis longtemps ?* | *(Il a mal) depuis deux heures.* |

# THE GERUND

The gerund is used to express the circumstances of an action

| |
|---|
| **en** + the present participle |

- *The moment :* Ferme la porte **en sortant** = Ferme la porte **quand** tu sortiras.
- *Simultaneity :* Il se douche en chantant = Il se douche et **en même temps** il chante.

# Verb Tables

# THE FRENCH VERB

French verbs can be divided into three groups or conjugations :

- **First group**

Verbs whose infinitives end in **-er**. With the exception of **aller**, they are all regular.

- **Second group**

Verbs whose infinitives end in **-ir** and the first person plural of the present indicative ends in **-issons**.
finir → **Nous finissons**, choisir → **Nous choisissons**...

- **Third group**

The so-called irregular verbs, such as **partir, voir, comprendre**... Refer to the verb tables to see how to conjugate these verbs correctly.
All the verbs with infinitives not ending in **-er** or **-ir** belong to the third group.
Some verbs ending in **-ir**, such as **partir**, **sortir** and **venir** belong to the 3rd group.

# THE PRESENT TENSE

## The present indicative

- **Conjugation of verbs in the 1st group**

| infinitive : parler → radical : **parl-** |
|---|

endings: **-e -es -e -ons -ez -ent**

| | |
|---|---|
| *Je parle* | *Nous parlons* |
| *Tu parles* | *Vous parlez* |
| *Il/elle parle* | *Ils/elles parlent* |

Note that **aller** does not obey the general rule:

| | |
|---|---|
| *Je vais* | *Nous allons* |
| *Tu vas* | *Vous allez* |
| *Il/elle va* | *Ils/elles vont* |

- **Conjugation of verbs in the 2nd group**

| infinitive : finir → radical : **fin-** |
|---|

endings : **-is -is -it -issons -issez -issent**

| | |
|---|---|
| *Je finis* | *Nous finissons* |
| *Tu finis* | *Vous finissez* |
| *Il/elle finit* | *Ils/elles finissent* |

## The imperative

The imperative is based upon the present indicative form of the verb :

| present indicative | imperative | negative imperative |
|---|---|---|
| *Tu **finis*** | ***Finis** !* | *Ne **finis** pas !* |
| *Nous **finissons*** | ***Finissons** !* | *Ne **finissons** pas !* |
| *Vous **finissez*** | ***Finissez** !* | *Ne **finissez** pas !* |

▲ *Note a slight irregularity for verbs in the 1st group only : the **s** on the second person singular is dropped in the corresponding imperative → **parle !***

## Reflexive verbs

Reflexive verbs are conjugated along with a reflexive pronoun : **me, te, se, nous, vous.**

| | |
|---|---|
| *Je **me** lave* | *Nous **nous** lavons* |
| *Tu **te** laves* | *Vous **vous** lavez* |
| *Il/Elle **se** lave* | *Ils/Elles **se** lavent* |

*Negative construction: Je ne **me** lave pas*

| Imperative : | Negative imperative : |
|---|---|
| *Lave-**toi** !* | *Ne **te** lave pas !* |
| *Lavons-**nous** !* | *Ne **nous** lavons pas !* |
| *Lavez-**vous** !* | *Ne **vous** lavez pas !* |

## The present continuous

This construction is used to describe an action happening at the time of speaking (like the present continuous in English):

| **être en train de** + the infinitive |
|---|

*Le patron est **en train de** jouer aux cartes. (The boss is playing cards)*

*Il ne peut pas répondre, il est **en train de** dormir. (He can't answer, he's sleeping)*

Negative form : *Le patron n'est pas **en train de** jouer.*
*Il n'est pas **en train de** dormir.*

# THE PERFECT TENSE

## The passé composé

The passé composé (perfect tense) is used to describe a past event : **J'ai vu ce film la semaine dernière** *(I saw that film last week)* – or to describe an action that happened at some indefinite time in the past but which is still true : **J'ai déjà vu ce film** *(I have already seen that film)*. French does not make the same distinction as English between the present perfect and the preterite.

### •Conjugation n° 1

| Present of **avoir** + the past participle |
|---|

| | |
|---|---|
| *J'**ai** fait* | *Nous **avons** fait* |
| *Tu **as** fait* | *Vous **avez** fait* |
| *Il/Elle **a** fait* | *Ils/Elles **ont** fait* |

Negative construction : *Je **n'**ai **pas** fait*

□ ***Formation of the past participle :***

**a)** For verbs belonging to the 1st group

The final **-r** is dropped from the infinitive and the final **-e** becomes **-é**.

parl**er** → parl**é**

**b)** For verbs belonging to the 2nd group

The final **-r** is dropped.

fin**ir** → fin**i** grand**ir** → grand**i**

- **Conjugation n° 2**

Present of **être** + the past participle

This conjugation concerns reflexive verbs and the following verbs : **aller, venir, sortir, rester, partir, monter, descendre, arriver, passer, naître, tomber, mourir.**
Note that all these verbs are verbs of motion, with the exception of **naître** and **mourir**.

**Masculine subjects :**

| | |
|---|---|
| *Je **suis** sorti* | *Nous **sommes** sortis* |
| *Tu **es** sorti* | *Vous **êtes** sorti(s)* |
| *Il **est** sorti* | *Ils **sont** sortis* |

**Feminine subjects :**

| | |
|---|---|
| *Je **suis** sortie* | *Nous **sommes** sorties* |
| *Tu **es** sortie* | *Vous **êtes** sortie(s)* |
| *Elle **est** sortie* | *Elles **sont** sorties* |

Negative construction : *Je **ne** suis **pas** sorti, elle **n'**est **pas** sortie.*

- **Agreement of the past participle**

Note that when a verb is conjugated with the auxiliary **être**, the past participle agrees in gender and in number with the subject of the verb.
Note the special case : ***on** est allés*
Although the verb is in the third person singular, the past participle agrees with the subject **on** which in this case is the equivalent of **nous** and refers to several people.

## The passé composé of reflexive verbs

**Masculine subjects :**

| | |
|---|---|
| *Je me **suis** lavé* | *Nous nous **sommes** lavés* |
| *Tu t'**es** lavé* | *Vous vous **êtes** lavé(s)* |
| *Il s'**est** lavé* | *Ils se **sont** lavés* |

**Feminine subjects :**

| | |
|---|---|
| *Je me **suis** lavée* | *Nous nous **sommes** lavées* |
| *Tu t'**es** lavée* | *Vous vous **êtes** lavée(s)* |
| *Elle s'**est** lavée* | *Elles se **sont** lavées* |

Negative construction : *Elle **ne** s'est **pas** lavée.*

## The recent past

The recent past is used to express an action that has just taken place.

| **venir de** (in the present) + the infinitive |
|---|

| | |
|---|---|
| *Je **viens de** me laver* | *Nous **venons de** travailler* |
| *Tu **viens de** partir* | *Vous **venez de** sortir* |
| *Il/elle **vient de** parler* | *Ils/Elles **viennent de** se lever* |

Negative construction: *Nous **ne** venons **pas** de travailler.*

## The imperfect tense

The imperfect tense is used to describe circumstances, people or places in the past, or to describe past habits, what used to happen.

To conjugate a verb in the imperfect tense, take the first person plural of the present and remove the ending **-ons** :
faire → nous faisons → **fais**

This gives us the radical (fais) which forms the stem for the endings of the imperfect tense : **-ais, -ais, -ait, -ions, -iez, -aient**

# THE FUTURE TENSE

## The future tense of verbs belonging to the 1st and 2nd groups

It is easy to form the future of these verbs – just add the following endings to their infinitives : **-ai, -as, -a, -ons, -ez,-ont**

| | |
|---|---|
| *Je parler**ai*** | *Je finir**ai*** |
| *Tu parler**as*** | *Tu finir**as*** |
| *Il/Elle parler**a*** | *Il-Elle finir**a*** |
| *Nous parler**ons*** | *Nous finir**ons*** |
| *Vous parler**ez*** | *Vous finir**ez*** |
| *Ils/Elles parler**ont*** | *Ils/Elles finir**ont*** |

▲ *Note that the verb **aller** is irregular and does not obey this rule :*

*J'**irai***

*Tu **iras***

*Il/Elle **ira***

*Nous **irons***

*Vous **irez***

*Ils/Elles **iront***

▲ *For the future of group 3 verbs, consult the verb tables.*

### Immediate future

The immediate future is used to express an intention, or to speak about a state or an action which is going to happen within a relatively short time.

| present indicative of the verb **aller** + the infinitive |
|---|

*Je vais partir*

*Tu vas déjeuner*

*Il va travailler*

*Noux allons goûter*

*Vous allez parler*

*Elles vont faire*

*Negative construction:* *Je **ne** vais **pas** partir*

*Nous **n'**allons **pas** goûter*

## THE CONDITIONAL TENSE

### The present conditional

The conjugation of the present conditional is obtained by adding the endings of the imperfect tense (**-ais, -ais, -ait, -ions, -iez, -aient**) to the stem of the verb used to form the future tense.

For example : prendre → future : Je prendrai (stem : **prendr**-)

*Je prendr**ais***

*Tu prendr**ais***

*Il/elle prendr**ait***

*Nous prendr**ions***

*Vous prendr**iez***

*Ils/elles prendr**aient***

## THE SUBJUNCTIVE MOOD

### The present subjunctive

The subjunctive mood is used after verbs expressing wishes, obligations, doubts, points of view or opinions.

Example : prendre

| **Present indicative** | **Present subjunctive** | |
|---|---|---|
| *ils prennent* | → *que je* ***prenne*** | |
| | → *que tu* ***prennes*** | |
| | → *qu'il* ***prenne*** | |
| | → *que nous* ***prenions*** | *(imperfect)* |
| | → *que vous* ***preniez*** | *(imperfect)* |
| | → *qu'ils* ***prennent*** | |

The forms of all three persons in the singular (**je, tu, il/elle**) and the third person plural (**ils/elles**) are based upon the third person plural (**ils/elles**) of the present indicative of the same verb (**ils prennent**).

For the first and second persons plural (**nous, vous**), the subjunctive is identical to the first and second persons plural of the imperfect tense.

▲ *Note that the verbs* ***être, avoir, aller, faire, vouloir, savoir*** *and* ***pouvoir*** *are irregular and do not obey this rule for the formation of the present subjunctive.*

## THE PASSIVE VOICE

The passive is used to highlight the object of the action, exactly the same as in English:

1 *Le Directeur invite Sylvie* (active)

2 *Sylvie est invitée par le Directeur* (passive)

The meaning of both sentences is identical but the direct object of the first sentence (Sylvie) is highlighted as the subject of the second sentence.

To obtain the passive voice, use :

> the verb **être** + the past participle
> (of the verb used in the active form)



*Louis XIV a construit Versailles. (Louis XIV built Versailles)*

*Versailles a été construit par Louis XIV. (Versailles was built by Louis XIV)*

▲ *Note that the verb **être** expresses the tense of the sentence in the passive voice.*

– The past participle agrees in gender and in number with the subject:

*Sylvie est invit**ée** par le directeur.*

– **par le**... (*by...*) is only used to be more precise (as in English) :

*Le voleur a été arrêté (par la police). (The thief was arrested by the police).*

| INFINITIVE | INDICATIVE | | |
|---|---|---|---|
| | **Present** | **Imperfect** | **Future** |
| être | je suis<br>tu es<br>il est<br>nous sommes<br>vous êtes<br>ils sont | j'étais<br>tu étais<br>il était<br>nous étions<br>vous étiez<br>ils étaient | je serai<br>je seras<br>il sera<br>nous serons<br>vous serez<br>ils seront |
| avoir | j'ai<br>tu as<br>il a<br>nous avons<br>vous avez<br>ils ont | j'avais<br>tu avais<br>il avait<br>nous avions<br>vous aviez<br>ils avaient | j'aurai<br>tu auras<br>il aura<br>nous aurons<br>vous aurez<br>ils auront |
| aimer | j'aime<br>tu aimes<br>il aime<br>nous aimons<br>vous aimez<br>ils aiment | j'aimais<br>tu aimais<br>il aimait<br>nous aimions<br>vous aimiez<br>ils aimaient | j'aimerai<br>tu aimeras<br>il aimera<br>nous aimerons<br>vous aimerez<br>ils aimeront |
| aller | je vais<br>tu vas<br>il va<br>nous allons<br>vous allez<br>ils vont | j'allais<br>tu allais<br>il allait<br>nous allions<br>vous alliez<br>ils allaient | j'irai<br>tu iras<br>il ira<br>nous irons<br>vous irez<br>ils iront |

| IMPERATIVE | CONDITIONAL | SUBJONCTIVE | PARTICIPLE |
|---|---|---|---|
| **Present** | **Present** | **Present** | **Past** |
| | je serais | que je sois | été |
| sois | tu serais | que tu sois | |
| | il serait | qu'il soit | |
| soyons | nous serions | que nous soyons | |
| soyez | vous seriez | que vous soyez | |
| | ils seraient | qu'ils soient | |
| | j'aurais | que j'aie | eu |
| aie | tu aurais | que tu aies | |
| | il aurait | qu'il aie | |
| ayons | nous aurions | que nous ayons | |
| ayez | vous auriez | que vous ayez | |
| | ils auraient | qu'ils aient | |
| | j'aimerais | que j'aime | aimé |
| aime | tu aimerais | que tu aimes | |
| | il aimerait | qu'il aime | |
| aimons | nous aimerions | que nous aimons | |
| aimez | vous aimeriez | que vous aimiez | |
| | ils aimeraient | qu'ils aiment | |
| | j'irais | que j'aille | allé |
| va | tu irais | que tu ailles | |
| | il irait | qu'il aille | |
| allons | nous irions | que nous allions | |
| allez | vous iriez | que vous alliez | |
| | ils iraient | qu'ils aillent | |

| INFINITIVE | INDICATIVE | | |
|---|---|---|---|
| | **Present** | **Imperfect** | **Future** |
| appeler | j'appelle<br>tu appelles<br>il appelle<br>nous appelons<br>vous appelez<br>ils appellent | j'appelais<br>tu appelais<br>il appelait<br>nous appelions<br>vous appeliez<br>ils appelaient | j'appellerai<br>tu appelleras<br>il appellera<br>nous appelleront<br>vous appellerez<br>ils appelleront |
| attendre | j'attends<br>tu attends<br>il attend<br>nous attendons<br>vous attendez<br>ils attendent | j'attendais<br>tu attendais<br>il attendait<br>nous attendions<br>vous attendiez<br>ils attendaient | j'attendrai<br>tu attendras<br>il attendra<br>nous attendrons<br>vous attendrez<br>ils attendront |
| boire | je bois<br>tu bois<br>il boit<br>nous buvons<br>vous buvez<br>ils boivent | je buvais<br>tu buvais<br>il buvait<br>nous buvions<br>vous buviez<br>ils buvaient | je boirai<br>tu boiras<br>il boira<br>nous boirons<br>vous boirez<br>ils boiront |
| commencer | je commence<br>tu commences<br>il commence<br>nous commençons<br>vous commencez<br>ils commencent | je commençais<br>tu commençais<br>il commençait<br>nous commencions<br>vous commenciez<br>ils commençaient | je commencerai<br>tu commenceras<br>il commencera<br>nous commencerons<br>vous commencerez<br>ils commenceront |

| IMPERATIVE | CONDITIONAL | SUBJONCTIVE | PARTICIPLE |
|---|---|---|---|
| **Present** | **Present** | **Present** | **Past** |
| | j'appellerais | que j'appelle | appelé |
| appelle | tu appellerais | que tu appelles | |
| | il appellerait | qu'il appelle | |
| appelons | nous appellerions | que nous appelions | |
| appelez | vous appelleriez | que vous appeliez | |
| | ils appelleraient | qu'ils appellent | |
| | j'attendrais | que j'attende | attendu |
| attends | tu attendrais | que tu attendes | |
| | il attendrait | qu'il attende | |
| attendons | nous attendrions | que nous attendions | |
| attendez | vous attendriez | que vous attendiez | |
| | ils attendraient | qu'ils attendent | |
| | je boirais | que je boive | bu |
| bois | tu boirais | que tu boives | |
| | il boirait | qu'il boive | |
| buvons | nous boirions | que nous buvions | |
| buvez | vous boiriez | que vous buviez | |
| | ils boiraient | qu'ils boivent | |
| | je commencerais | que je commence | commencé |
| commence | tu commencerais | que tu commences | |
| | il commencerait | qu'il commence | |
| commençons | nous commencerions | que nous commencions | |
| commencez | vous commenceriez | que vous commenciez | |
| | ils commenceraient | qu'ils commencent | |

| INFINITIVE | INDICATIVE | | |
|---|---|---|---|
| | **Present** | **Imperfect** | **Future** |
| comprendre | je comprends<br>tu comprends<br>il comprend<br>nous comprenons<br>vous comprenez<br>ils comprennent | je comprenais<br>tu comprenais<br>il comprenait<br>nous comprenions<br>vous compreniez<br>ils comprenaient | je comprendrai<br>tu comprendras<br>il comprendra<br>nous comprendrons<br>vous comprendrez<br>ils comprendront |
| conduire | je conduis<br>tu conduis<br>il conduit<br>nous conduisons<br>vous conduisez<br>ils conduisent | je conduisais<br>tu conduisais<br>il conduisait<br>nous conduisions<br>vous conduisiez<br>ils conduisaient | je conduirai<br>tu conduiras<br>il conduira<br>nous conduirons<br>vous conduirez<br>ils conduiront |
| connaître | je connais<br>tu connais<br>il connaît<br>nous connaissons<br>vous connaissez<br>ils connaissent | je connaissais<br>tu connaissais<br>il connaissait<br>nous connaissions<br>vous connaissiez<br>ils connaissaient | je connaîtrai<br>tu connaîtras<br>il connaîtra<br>nous connaîtrons<br>vous connaîtrez<br>ils connaîtront |
| croire | je crois<br>tu crois<br>il croit<br>nous croyons<br>vous croyez<br>ils croient | je croyais<br>tu croyais<br>il croyait<br>nous croyions<br>vous croyiez<br>ils croyaient | je croirai<br>tu croiras<br>il croira<br>nous croirons<br>vous croirez<br>ils croiront |

| IMPERATIVE | CONDITIONAL | SUBJONCTIVE | PARTICIPLE |
| --- | --- | --- | --- |
| **Present** | **Present** | **Present** | **Past** |
| | je comprendrais | que je comprenne | compris |
| comprends | tu comprendrais | que tu comprennes | |
| | il comprendrait | qu'il comprenne | |
| comprenons | nous comprendrions | que nous comprenions | |
| comprenez | vous comprendriez | que vous compreniez | |
| | ils comprendraient | qu'ils comprennent | |
| | je conduirais | que je conduise | conduit |
| conduis | tu conduirais | que tu conduises | |
| | il conduirait | qu'il conduise | |
| conduisons | nous conduirions | que nous conduisions | |
| conduisez | vous conduiriez | que vous conduisiez | |
| | ils conduiraient | qu'ils conduisent | |
| | je connaîtrais | que je connaisse | connu |
| connais | tu connaîtrais | que tu connaisses | |
| | il connaîtrait | qu'il connaisse | |
| connaissons | nous connaîtrions | que nous connaissions | |
| connaissez | vous connaîtriez | que vous connaissiez | |
| | ils connaîtraient | qu'ils connaissent | |
| | je croirais | que je croie | cru |
| crois | tu croirais | que tu croies | |
| | il croirait | qu'il croie | |
| croyons | nous croirions | que nous croyions | |
| croyez | vous croiriez | que vous croyiez | |
| | ils croiraient | qu'ils croient | |

| INFINITIVE | INDICATIVE | | |
|---|---|---|---|
| | **Present** | **Imperfect** | **Future** |
| dire | je dis<br>tu dis<br>il dit<br>nous disons<br>vous dites<br>ils disent | je disais<br>tu disais<br>il disait<br>nous disions<br>vous disiez<br>ils disaient | je dirai<br>tu diras<br>il dira<br>nous dirons<br>vous direz<br>ils diront |
| dormir | je dors<br>tu dors<br>il dort<br>nous dormons<br>vous dormez<br>ils dorment | je dormais<br>tu dormais<br>il dormait<br>nous dormions<br>vous dormiez<br>ils dormaient | je dormirai<br>tu dormiras<br>il dormira<br>nous dormirons<br>vous dormirez<br>ils dormiront |
| écrire | j'écris<br>tu écris<br>il écrit<br>nous écrivons<br>vous écrivez<br>ils écrivent | j'écrivais<br>tu écrivais<br>il écrivait<br>nous écrivions<br>vous écriviez<br>ils écrivaient | j'écrirai<br>tu écriras<br>il écrira<br>nous écrirons<br>vous écrirez<br>ils écriront |
| entendre | j'entends<br>tu entends<br>il entend<br>nous entendons<br>vous entendez<br>ils entendent | j'entendais<br>tu entendais<br>il entendait<br>nous entendions<br>vous entendiez<br>ils entendaient | j'entendrai<br>tu entendras<br>il entendra<br>nous entendrons<br>vous entendrez<br>ils entendront |

| IMPERATIVE | CONDITIONAL | SUBJONCTIVE | PARTICIPLE |
|---|---|---|---|
| **Present** | **Present** | **Present** | **Past** |
| | je dirais | que je dise | dit |
| dis | tu dirais | que tu dises | |
| | il dirait | qu'il dise | |
| disons | nous dirions | que nous disions | |
| dites | vous diriez | que vous disiez | |
| | ils diraient | qu' ils disent | |
| | je dormirais | que je dorme | dormi |
| dors | tu dormirais | que tu dormes | |
| | il dormirait | qu'il dorme | |
| dormons | nous dormirions | que nous dormions | |
| dormez | vous dormirez | que vous dormiez | |
| | ils dormiraient | qu'ils dorment | |
| | j'écrirais | que j'écrive | écrit |
| écris | tu écrirais | que tu écrives | |
| | il écrirait | qu'il écrive | |
| écrivons | nous écririons | que nous écrivions | |
| écrivez | vous écririez | que vous écriviez | |
| | ils écriraient | qu'ils écrivent | |
| | j'entendrais | que j'entende | entendu |
| entends | tu entendrais | que tu entendes | |
| | il entendrait | qu'il entende | |
| entendons | nous entendrions | que nous entendions | |
| entendez | vous entendriez | que vous entendiez | |
| | ils entendraient | qu'ils entendent | |

<table>
<tr><th rowspan="2">INFINITIVE</th><th colspan="3">INDICATIVE</th></tr>
<tr><th>Present</th><th>Imperfect</th><th>Future</th></tr>
<tr><td>envoyer</td><td>j'envoie<br>tu envoies<br>il envoie<br>nous envoyons<br>vous envoyez<br>ils envoyent</td><td>j'envoyais<br>tu envoyais<br>il envoyait<br>nous envoyions<br>vous envoyiez<br>ils envoyaient</td><td>j'enverrai<br>tu enverras<br>il enverra<br>nous enverrons<br>vous enverrez<br>ils enverront</td></tr>
<tr><td>essayer</td><td>j'essaie<br>tu essais<br>il essaie<br>nous essayons<br>vous essayez<br>ils essaient</td><td>j'essayais<br>tu essayais<br>il essayait<br>nous essayions<br>vous essayiez<br>ils essayaient</td><td>j'essaierai<br>tu essaieras<br>il essaiera<br>nous essaierons<br>vous essaierez<br>ils essaieront</td></tr>
<tr><td>faire</td><td>je fais<br>tu fais<br>il fait<br>nous faisons<br>vous faites<br>ils font</td><td>je faisais<br>tu faisais<br>il faisait<br>nous faisions<br>vous faisiez<br>ils faisaient</td><td>je ferai<br>tu feras<br>il fera<br>nous ferons<br>vous ferez<br>ils feront</td></tr>
<tr><td>falloir</td><td>il faut</td><td>il fallait</td><td>il faudra</td></tr>
</table>

| IMPERATIVE | CONDITIONAL | SUBJONCTIVE | PARTICIPLE |
|---|---|---|---|
| **Present** | **Present** | **Present** | **Past** |
| <br>envoie<br><br>envoyons<br>envoyez | j'enverrais<br>tu enverrais<br>il enverrait<br>nous enverrons<br>vous enverrez<br>ils enverraient | que j'envoie<br>que tu envoies<br>qu'il envoie<br>que nous envoyions<br>que vous envoyiez<br>qu'ils envoient | envoyé |
| <br>essaie<br><br>essayons<br>essayez | j'essaierai<br>tu essaierais<br>il essaierait<br>nous essaierions<br>vous essaieriez<br>ils essaieraient | que j'essaie<br>que tu essaies<br>qu'il essaie<br>que nous essayions<br>que vous essayiez<br>qu'ils essaient | essayé |
| <br>fais<br><br>faisons<br>faites | je ferais<br>tu ferais<br>il ferait<br>nous ferions<br>vous feriez<br>ils feraient | que je fasse<br>que tu fasses<br>qu'il fasse<br>que nous fassions<br>que vous fassiez<br>qu'ils fassent | fait |
| | il faudrait | qu'il faille | fallu |

| INFINITIVE | INDICATIVE | | |
|---|---|---|---|
| | **Present** | **Imperfect** | **Future** |
| finir | je finis<br>tu finis<br>il finit<br>nous finissons<br>vous finissez<br>ils finissent | je finissais<br>tu finissais<br>il finissait<br>nous finissions<br>vous finissiez<br>ils finissaient | je finirai<br>tu finiras<br>il finira<br>nous finirons<br>vous finirez<br>ils finiront |
| lire | je lis<br>tu lis<br>il lit<br>nous lisons<br>vous lisez<br>ils lisent | je lisais<br>tu lisais<br>il lisait<br>nous lisions<br>vous lisiez<br>ils lisaient | je lirai<br>tu liras<br>il lira<br>nous lirons<br>vous lirez<br>ils liront |
| manger | je mange<br>tu manges<br>il mange<br>nous mangeons<br>vous mangez<br>ils mangent | je mangeais<br>tu mangeais<br>il mangeait<br>nous mangions<br>vous mangiez<br>ils mangeaient | je mangerai<br>tu mangeras<br>il mangera<br>nous mangerons<br>vous mangerez<br>ils mangeront |
| mettre | je mets<br>tu mets<br>il met<br>nous mettons<br>vous mettez<br>ils mettent | je mettais<br>tu mettais<br>il mettait<br>nous mettions<br>vous mettiez<br>ils mettaient | je mettrai<br>tu mettras<br>il mettra<br>nous mettrons<br>vous mettrez<br>ils mettront |

| IMPERATIVE | CONDITIONAL | SUBJONCTIVE | PARTICIPLE |
|---|---|---|---|
| **Present** | **Present** | **Present** | **Past** |
| <br>finis<br><br>finissons<br>finissez | je finirais<br>tu finirais<br>il finirait<br>nous finirions<br>vous finiriez<br>ils finiraient | que je finisse<br>que tu finisses<br>qu'il finisse<br>que nous finissions<br>que vous finissiez<br>qu'ils finissent | fini |
| <br>lis<br><br>lisons<br>lisez | je lirais<br>tu lirais<br>il lirait<br>nous lirions<br>vous liriez<br>ils liraient | que je lise<br>que tu lises<br>qu'il lise<br>que nous lisions<br>que vous lisiez<br>qu'ils lisent | lu |
| <br>mange<br><br>mangeons<br>mangez | je mangerais<br>tu mangerais<br>il mangerait<br>nous mangerions<br>vous mangeriez<br>ils mangeraient | que je mange<br>que tu manges<br>qu'il mange<br>que nous mangions<br>que vous mangiez<br>qu'ils mangent | mangé |
| <br>mets<br><br>mettons<br>mettez | je mettrais<br>tu mettrais<br>il mettrait<br>nous mettrions<br>vous mettriez<br>ils mettraient | que je mette<br>que tu mettes<br>qu'il mette<br>que nous mettions<br>que vous mettiez<br>qu'ils mettent | mis |

| INFINITIVE | INDICATIVE | | |
|---|---|---|---|
| | **Present** | **Imperfect** | **Future** |
| neiger | il neige | il neigeait | il neigera |
| ouvrir | j'ouvre<br>tu ouvres<br>il ouvre<br>nous ouvrons<br>vous ouvrez<br>ils ouvrent | j'ouvrais<br>tu ouvrais<br>il ouvrait<br>nous ouvrions<br>vous ouvriez<br>ils ouvraient | j'ouvrirai<br>tu ouvriras<br>il ouvrira<br>nous ouvrirons<br>vous ouvrirez<br>ils ouvriront |
| partir | je pars<br>tu pars<br>il part<br>nous partons<br>vous partez<br>ils partent | je partais<br>tu partais<br>il partait<br>nous partions<br>vous partiez<br>ils partaient | je partirai<br>tu partiras<br>il partira<br>nous partirons<br>vous partirez<br>ils partiront |
| plaire | je plais<br>tu plais<br>il plaît<br>nous plaisons<br>vous plaisez<br>ils plaisent | je plaisais<br>tu plaisais<br>il plaisait<br>nous plaisions<br>vous plaisiez<br>ils plaisaient | je plairai<br>tu plairas<br>il plaira<br>nous plairons<br>vous plairez<br>ils plairont |

| IMPERATIVE | CONDITIONAL | SUBJONCTIVE | PARTICIPLE |
|---|---|---|---|
| **Present** | **Present** | **Present** | **Past** |
| | il neigerait | qu'il neige | neigé |
| <br>ouvre<br><br>ouvrons<br>ouvrez | j'ouvrirais<br>tu ouvrirais<br>il ouvrirait<br>nous ouvririons<br>vous ouvririez<br>ils ouvriraient | que j'ouvre<br>que tu ouvres<br>qu'il ouvre<br>que nous ouvrions<br>que vous ouvriez<br>qu'ils ouvrent | ouvert |
| <br>pars<br><br>partons<br>partez | je partirais<br>tu partirais<br>il partirait<br>nous partirions<br>vous partiriez<br>ils partiraient | que je parte<br>que tu partes<br>qu'il parte<br>que nous partions<br>que vous partiez<br>qu'ils partent | parti |
| <br>plais<br><br>plaisons<br>plaisez | je plairais<br>tu plairais<br>il plairait<br>nous plairions<br>vous plairiez<br>ils plairaient | que je plaise<br>que tu plaises<br>qu'il plaise<br>que nous plaisions<br>que vous plaisiez<br>qu'ils plaisent | plu |

| INFINITIVE | INDICATIVE | | |
| --- | --- | --- | --- |
| | **Present** | **Imperfect** | **Future** |
| pleuvoir | il pleut | il pleuvait | il pleuvra |
| pouvoir | je peux<br>tu peux<br>il peut<br>nous pouvons<br>vous pouvez<br>ils peuvent | je pouvais<br>tu pouvais<br>il pouvait<br>nous pouvions<br>vous pouviez<br>ils pouvaient | je pourrai<br>tu pourras<br>il pourra<br>nous pourrons<br>vous pourrez<br>ils pourront |
| préférer | je préfère<br>tu préfères<br>il préfère<br>nous préférons<br>vous préférez<br>ils préfèrent | je préférais<br>tu préférais<br>il préférait<br>nous préférions<br>vous préfériez<br>ils préféraient | je préférerai<br>tu préféreras<br>il préférera<br>nous préférerons<br>vous préférerez<br>ils préféreront |
| recevoir | je reçois<br>tu reçois<br>il reçoit<br>nous recevons<br>vous recevez<br>ils reçoivent | je recevais<br>tu recevais<br>il recevait<br>nous recevions<br>vous receviez<br>ils recevaient | je recevrai<br>tu recevras<br>il recevra<br>nous recevrons<br>vous recevrez<br>ils recevront |

| IMPERATIVE | CONDITIONAL | SUBJONCTIVE | PARTICIPLE |
|---|---|---|---|
| **Present** | **Present** | **Present** | **Past** |
| | il pleuvrait | qu'il pleuve | plu |
| | je pourrais | que je puisse | pu |
| | tu pourrais | que tu puisses | |
| | il pourrait | qu'il puisse | |
| | nous pourrions | que nous puissions | |
| | vous pourriez | que vous puissiez | |
| | ils pourraient | qu'ils puissent | |
| | je préférerais | que je préfère | préféré |
| préfère | tu préférerais | que tu préfères | |
| | il préférerait | qu'il préfère | |
| préférons | nous préférerions | que nous préférions | |
| préférez | vous préféreriez | que vous préfériez | |
| | ils préféreraient | qu'ils préfèrent | |
| | je recevrais | que je reçoive | reçu |
| reçois | tu recevrais | que tu reçoives | |
| | il recevrait | qu'il reçoive | |
| recevons | nous recevrions | que nous recevions | |
| recevez | vous recevriez | que vous receviez | |
| | ils recevraient | qu'ils reçoivent | |

| INFINITIVE | INDICATIVE | | |
| --- | --- | --- | --- |
| | **Present** | **Imperfect** | **Future** |
| répondre | je réponds<br>tu réponds<br>il répond<br>nous répondons<br>vous répondez<br>ils répondent | je répondais<br>tu répondais<br>il répondait<br>nous répondions<br>vous répondiez<br>ils répondaient | je répondrai<br>tu répondras<br>il répondra<br>nous répondrons<br>vous répondrez<br>ils répondront |
| rire | je ris<br>tu ris<br>il rit<br>nous rions<br>vous riez<br>ils rient | je riais<br>tu riais<br>il riait<br>nous riions<br>vous riiez<br>ils riaient | je rirai<br>tu riras<br>il rira<br>nous rirons<br>vous rirez<br>ils riront |
| savoir | je sais<br>tu sais<br>il sait<br>nous savons<br>vous savez<br>ils savent | je savais<br>tu sasais<br>il savait<br>nous savions<br>vous saviez<br>ils savaient | je saurai<br>tu sauras<br>il saura<br>nous saurons<br>vous saurez<br>ils sauront |
| sortir | je sors<br>tu sors<br>il sort<br>nous sortons<br>vous sortez<br>ils sortent | je sortais<br>tu sortais<br>il sortait<br>nous sortions<br>vous sortiez<br>ils sortaient | je sortirai<br>tu sortiras<br>il sortira<br>nous sortirons<br>vous sortirez<br>ils sortiront |

| IMPERATIVE | CONDITIONAL | SUBJONCTIVE | PARTICIPLE |
|---|---|---|---|
| Present | Present | Present | Past |
| | je répondrais | que je réponde | répondu |
| réponds | tu répondrais | que tu répondes | |
| | il répondrait | qu'il réponde | |
| répondons | nous répondrions | que nous répondions | |
| répondez | vous répondriez | que vous répondiez | |
| | ils répondraient | qu'ils répondent | |
| | je rirais | que je rie | ri |
| ris | tu rirais | que tu ries | |
| | il rirait | qu'il rie | |
| rions | nous ririons | que nous riions | |
| riez | vous ririez | que vous riiez | |
| | ils riraient | qu'ils rient | |
| | je saurais | que je sache | su |
| sache | tu saurais | que tu saches | |
| | il saurait | qu'il sache | |
| sachons | nous saurions | que nous sachions | |
| sachez | vous sauriez | que vous sachiez | |
| | ils sauraient | qu'ils sachent | |
| | je sortirais | que je sorte | sorti |
| sors | tu sortirais | que tu sortes | |
| | il sortirait | qu'il sorte | |
| sortons | nous sortirions | que nous sortions | |
| sortez | vous sortiriez | que vous sortiez | |
| | ils sortiraient | qu'ils sortent | |

# FRENCH/ENGLISH MINI-DICTIONARY

| | | Lessons | | See... |
|---|---|---|---|---|
| abandonner | leave, to | 13 | v. | |
| abîmé | damaged | 20 | adj. | |
| abondant | abundant, heavy | 23 | adj. | |
| absent | absent | 35 | adj. | |
| abuser | abuse, to | 33 | v. | |
| accepter | accept, to | 4 | v. | |
| accident | accident | 37 | n.m. | |
| accompagner | accompany, to | 44 | v. | |
| accord | agreement | 11 | n.m. | |
| achat | purchase | 17 | n.m. | |
| acheter | buy, to | 11 | v. | |
| acompte | deposit | 26 | n.m. | |
| acteur/actrice | actor/actress | 21 | n.m. | |
| actif | busy | 45 | adj. | |
| action | action | 29 | n.f. | |
| addition | bill | 14 | n.f. | |
| adorer | adore, to | 6 | v. | |
| adresse | address | 3 | n.f. | |
| affaire | business | 30 | n.f. | |
| agacement | annoyance | 38 | n.m. | |
| âge | age | 6 | n.m. | |
| agence | agency | 26 | n.f. | |
| agent | agent | 16 | n.m. | |
| agréable | pleasant | 20 | dj. | |
| agriculteur | farmer | 4 | n.m. | |
| aide | help | 16 | n.f. | |
| aider | help, to | 16 | v. | |
| aimer | like/love, to | 6 | v. | aimer |
| alcool | alcohol | 33 | .v | |
| aliment | food | 11 | n.m. | |
| allemand | German | 2 | adj. | |
| aller | go, to | 6 | v. | aller |
| allonger, s' | lie down, to | 32 | v. | manger |
| amabilité | kindness | 39 | n.f. | |
| ambassade | embassy | 45 | n.f. | |
| amende | fine | 37 | n.f. | |
| américain | American | 2 | adj. | |
| ami | friend | 4 | n.m. | |
| amitié | friendship/love | 6 | n.f. | |
| amour | love | 40 | n.m. | |
| amoureux | love, in | 40 | adj. | |
| an | year | 6 | n.m. | |
| analyse | test | 33 | n.f. | |

# A

*The verbs in the fourth column refer to the "Verb tables".*

| | | | | |
|---|---|---|---|---|
| ancien | old | 20 | adj. | |
| ancienneté | seniority | 31 | n.f. | |
| anglais | English | 2 | adj | |
| année | year | 9 | n.f. | |
| anniversaire | birthday | 17 | n.m. | |
| annonce | advertisement | 43 | n.f. | |
| annoncer | declare/announce, to | 24 | v. | |
| annuaire | telephone directory | 24 | n.m. | |
| anorak | anorak | 12 | n.m. | |
| antibiotique | antibiotics | 32 | n.m. | |
| août | August | 10 | n.m. | |
| apéritif | aperitif | 14 | n.m. | |
| appareil | device/telephone | 24 | n.m. | |
| appareil photo | camera | 12 | n.m. | |
| apparition | appearance | 23 | n.f. | |
| appartement | flat | 13 | n.m. | |
| appeler | call, to | 24 | v. | appeler |
| appeler, s' | called, to be | 4 | v. | appeler |
| appétissant | appetizing | 14 | adj. | |
| appétit | appetite | 36 | n.m. | |
| apporter | bring, to | 25 | v. | |
| après-midi | afternoon | 8 | n.m. | |
| argent | money | 11 | n.m. | |
| armoire | wardrobe | 34 | n.f. | |
| arrivée | arrival | 16 | n.f. | |
| arriver | arrive, to | 8 | v. | |
| art | art | 6 | n.m. | |
| aspirateur | hoover | 39 | n.m. | |
| assiette | plate | 22 | n.f. | |
| assurance | insurance | 17 | n.f. | |
| attendre | expect/wait, to | 8 | v. | attendre |
| attention | attention | 16 | n.f. | |
| attirer | attract, to | 16 | v. | |
| attrait | attraction | 45 | n.m. | |
| auditeur | listener | 18 | n.m. | |
| augmentation | increase | 31 | n.f. | |
| aujourd'hui | today | 21 | n.m. | |
| auteur | author | 21 | n.m. | |
| autobus | bus | 13 | n.m. | |
| automatique | automatic | 35 | adj. | |
| avantage | advantage | 26 | n.m. | |
| avenue | avenue | 7 | n.f. | |
| avion | plane | 10 | n.m. | |

# A-B

| | | | | |
|---|---|---|---|---|
| avis | opinion/view | 10 | n.m. | |
| avocat | lawyer | 2 | n.m. | |
| avoir l'air | seem, to | 14 | v. | |
| avouer | admit, to | 40 | v. | |
| bagages | luggage | 15 | n.m. | |
| bagnole* | car | 20 | n.f. | |
| baguette | stick of French bread | 11 | n.f. | |
| bain | bath | 17 | n.m. | |
| baisser | go down, to | 17 | v. | |
| bal | ball | 42 | n.m. | |
| banlieue | suburb(s) | 13 | n.f. | |
| banque | bank | 17 | n.f. | |
| baril | barrel | 25 | n.m. | |
| bateau | boat | 10 | n.m. | |
| batterie | battery | 38 | n.f. | |
| bavard | talkative | 44 | adj. | |
| beau | handsome | 6 | adj. | |
| beau-frère | brother-in-law | 29 | n.m. | |
| belle | beautiful | 6 | adj. | |
| belle-sœur | sister-in-law | 29 | n.f. | |
| besoin | need | 17 | n.m. | |
| bête | stupid | 42 | adj. | |
| bière | beer | 25 | n.f. | |
| bifteck | steak | 11 | n.m. | |
| billet | ticket | 16 | n.m. | |
| billet | note, (bank) | 17 | n.m. | |
| bise | kiss | 11 | n.f. | |
| bizarre | funny/strange | 20 | adj. | |
| blanc | white/blank | 10 | adj. | |
| blanche | white/blank | 10 | adj. | |
| blessure | injury | 33 | n.f. | |
| bleu | blue | 6 | adj. | |
| blond | fair-haired | 6 | adj. | |
| bois | wood | 20 | n.m. | |
| boisson | drink | 14 | n.f. | |
| boîte | box | 11 | n.f. | |
| boîte | tin | 34 | n.f. | |
| bon | good | 2 | adj. | |
| bonbon | sweet | 11 | n.m. | |
| bonheur | happiness | 36 | n.m. | |
| botte | boot | 12 | n.f. | |
| boucherie | butcher's | 11 | n.f. | |
| boulangerie | baker's | 11 | n.f. | |

| | | | | |
|---|---|---|---|---|
| boulevard | boulevard | 7 | n.m. | |
| boulot* | work | 31 | n.m. | |
| boum* | party | 42 | n.f. | |
| bouteille | bottle | 11 | n.f. | |
| bras | arm | 32 | n.m. | |
| bref | short | 30 | adj. | |
| bricolage | do-it-yourself | 43 | n.m. | |
| briller | shine, to | 23 | v. | |
| brochure | brochure | 45 | n.f. | |
| brosse | brush | 17 | n.f. | |
| brouillard | fog | 23 | n.m. | |
| bruit | noise | 20 | n.m. | |
| brûler | burn, to | 33 | v. | |
| brûlure | burn | 33 | n.f. | |
| brumeux | misty | 23 | adj. | |
| brun | dark-haired | 6 | adj. | |
| bruyant | noisy | 26 | adj. | |
| bulletin (météo) | forecast, (weather) | 23 | n.m. | |
| bureau | office | 19 | n.m. | |
| cabine | cabin | 24 | n.f. | |
| cable | wire | 20 | n.m. | |
| cafard | depression | 41 | n.m. | |
| café | coffee | 14 | n.m. | |
| café au lait | coffee, white | 25 | n.m. | |
| caisse | cash desk | 17 | n.f. | |
| calendrier | calendar | 9 | n.m. | |
| camarade | friend | 9 | n.m. | |
| caméra | camera | 12 | n.f. | |
| capot | bonnet | 20 | n.m. | |
| caractère | character | 6 | n.m. | |
| carré | square | 20 | n.m. | |
| carrefour | crossroads | 37 | n.m. | |
| carte | menu | 14 | n.f. | |
| carte (bancaire) | card (banker's/credit) | 17 | n.f. | |
| carte d'identité | identity card | 3 | n.f. | |
| carte postale | postcard | 10 | n.f. | |
| carton | cardboard | 20 | n.m. | |
| case | space | 10 | n.f. | |
| cassé | broken | 20 | adj. | |
| cause | cause | 38 | n.f. | |
| ceinture | belt | 37 | n.f. | |
| certificat | certificate | 37 | n.m. | |
| chaîne | channel | 18 | n.f. | |

# C

| | | | | |
|---|---|---|---|---|
| chaise | chair | 25 | n.f. | |
| chaleur | heat | 23 | n.f. | |
| chambre | bedroom | 26 | n.f. | |
| chance | luck | 36 | n.f. | |
| changer | change, to | 13 | v. | manger |
| charcuterie | delicatessen | 11 | n.f. | |
| charcuterie | cooked pork meats | 11 | n.f. | |
| chaud | hot | 23 | adj. | |
| chaussure | shoe | 12 | n.f. | |
| chauve | bald | 6 | adj. | |
| cheminée | fireplace | 34 | n.f. | |
| chemise | shirt | 28 | n.f. | |
| chemisier | blouse | 28 | n.m. | |
| chèque | cheque | 16 | n.m. | |
| cher | expensive | 11 | adj. | |
| chercher | look for, to | 6 | v. | |
| chéri | darling | 11 | n.m. | |
| cheveux | hair | 6 | n.m. | |
| chiffre | figure | 3 | n.m. | |
| chocolat | chocolate | 11 | n.m. | |
| choisir | choose, to | 18 | v. | finir |
| chose | thing | 27 | n.f. | |
| chute | fall | 23 | n.f. | |
| ciel | sky | 23 | n.m. | |
| cinéma | cinema | 6 | n.m. | |
| circuit | circuit | 45 | n.m. | |
| circulation | traffic | 37 | n.f. | |
| citron | lemon | 22 | n.m. | |
| classe | class | 16 | n.f. | |
| classique | classical | 6 | adj. | |
| clé | key | 26 | n.f. | |
| code | code | 37 | n.m. | |
| code postal | post code | 7 | n.m. | |
| cœur | heart | 36 | n.m. | |
| coiffeur | hairdresser | 19 | n.m. | |
| collègue | colleague | 4 | n. | |
| commander | order, to | 18 | v. | |
| commencer | begin, to | 3 | v. | commencer |
| commerçant | tradesman | 2 | n.m. | |
| commissariat | police station | 37 | n.m. | |
| commission | commission | 17 | n.f. | |
| communication | communications | 35 | n.f. | |
| compartiment | compartment | 16 | n.m. | |

| | | | | |
|---|---|---|---|---|
| complémentaire | complementary | 46 | adj. | |
| complet | sold out (theatre) | 21 | adj. | |
| composer | dial, to | 24 | v. | |
| comprendre | understand, to | 21 | v. | comprendre |
| compris | included | 25 | adj. | |
| compte | account | 17 | n.m. | |
| compter | count, to | 43 | v. | |
| compteur | meter | 15 | n.m. | |
| concierge | caretaker | 26 | n.m. | |
| conduire | drive, to | 29 | v. | conduire |
| conférence | conference | 30 | n.f. | |
| confirmer | confirm, to | 30 | v. | |
| confortable | comfortable | 26 | adj. | |
| connaître | know, to | 4 | v. | connaître |
| conseil | advice | 10 | n.m. | |
| conserver | keep, to | 42 | v. | |
| consulter | consult, to | 33 | v. | |
| contact | connection | 35 | n.m. | |
| content | happy | 15 | adj. | |
| continuer | continue/go on, to | 15 | v. | |
| contraire | opposite | 31 | n.m. | |
| contrat | contract | 35 | n.m. | |
| contrôleur | ticket inspector | 16 | n.m. | |
| convaincu | convinced | 28 | adj. | |
| copain* | friend | 42 | n.m. | copine |
| copine* | friend | 44 | n.f. | copain |
| costume | suit | 28 | n.m. | |
| coucher | put to bed, to | 13 | v. | |
| coucher, se | go to bed, to | 32 | v. | |
| couchette | berth | 16 | n.f. | |
| couleur | colour | 3 | n.f. | |
| coup de foudre | love at first sight | 40 | n.m. | |
| coupable | guilty | 41 | adj. | |
| coupé | cut | 24 | adj. | |
| couper, se | cut oneself, to | 17 | v. | |
| coupure | cut | 33 | n.f. | |
| cours | exchange rate | 17 | n.m. | |
| courses | shopping | 11 | n.f. | |
| cousin | cousin | 29 | n.m. | |
| couteau | knife | 22 | n.m. | |
| coûter | cost, to | 11 | v. | |
| couvert | overcast | 23 | adj. | |
| crédit | credit | 17 | n.m. | |

# C-D

| | | | | |
|---|---|---|---|---|
| crevaison | puncture | 20 | n.f. | |
| croire | believe, to | 40 | v. | croire |
| croissant | croissant | 25 | n.m. | |
| cuiller | spoon | 22 | n.f. | |
| cuir | leather | 20 | n.m. | |
| cuisine | cooking | 6 | n.f. | |
| cuisinière | cook | 22 | n.f. | |
| culturel | cultural | 45 | adj. | |
| dame | lady | 28 | n.f. | |
| dangereux | dangerous | 37 | adj. | |
| danser | dance, to | 42 | v. | |
| date | date | 3 | n.f. | |
| début | beginning | 23 | n.m. | |
| décidé | decided | 28 | adj. | |
| déclaration | declaration | 18 | n.f. | |
| décrire | describe, to | 20 | v. | |
| défendre | forbid, to | 39 | v. | attendre |
| degré | degree | 23 | n.m. | |
| déjeuner | lunch, to have | 12 | n.m. | |
| delco | distributor | 20 | n.m. | |
| délicat | delicate | 39 | adj. | |
| délice | delight | 22 | n.m. | |
| délicieux | delicious | 14 | adj. | |
| demander | wonder, to | 35 | v. | |
| demander | ask, to | 42 | v. | |
| démarrer | start, to | 20 | v. | |
| demi | half | 25 | n.m. | |
| dent | tooth | 17 | n.f. | |
| dentifrice | toothpaste | 17 | n.m. | |
| dentiste | dentist | 19 | n.m. | |
| départ | departure | 16 | n.m. | |
| département | department | 6 | n.m. | |
| dépasser | go beyond, to | 33 | v. | |
| dépêcher, se | hurry up, to | 17 | v. | |
| dépression | depression | 31 | n.f. | |
| déprimé | depressed | 41 | adj. | |
| dernier | last | 18 | adj. | |
| désaccord | disagreement/refusal | 11 | n.m. | |
| désespoir | despair | 41 | n.m. | |
| désolé | sorry | 12 | adj. | |
| dessert | dessert | 14 | n.m. | |
| destinataire | addressee | 7 | n.m. | |
| destination | destination | 16 | n.f. | |

| | | | | |
|---|---|---|---|---|
| détester | hate, to | 6 | v. | |
| devoir | must/have to | 14 | v. | |
| devoir | owe, to | 15 | v. | |
| différent | different | 31 | adj. | |
| différer | differ, to | 35 | v. | |
| difficile | difficult | 10 | adj. | |
| dimanche | Sunday | 9 | n.m. | |
| dîner | dinner, to have | 12 | v. | |
| dîner | dinner | 19 | n.m. | |
| dingue* | crazy | 40 | adj. | |
| diplôme | diploma | 31 | n.m. | |
| dire | say, to | 4 | v. | dire |
| directeur | manager (masc.) | 6 | n.m. | directrice |
| direction | direction | 15 | n.f. | |
| directrice | manager (fem.) | 6 | n.f. | directeur |
| discothèque | discothèque | 27 | n.f. | |
| disparaître | disappear, to | 19 | v. | |
| disponible | available | 30 | adj. | |
| distingué | distinguished | 45 | adj. | |
| divorce | divorce | 40 | n.m. | |
| divorcer | divorce, to | 40 | v. | |
| docteur | doctor | 32 | n.m. | |
| domicile | home | 3 | n.m. | |
| donner | give, to | 8 | v. | |
| dos | back | 32 | n.m. | |
| dose | dose | 33 | n.f. | |
| douane | customs | 10 | n.f. | |
| double | double | 26 | adj. | |
| douche | shower | 17 | n.f. | |
| douleur | pain | 32 | n.f. | |
| doux | sweet | 20 | adj. | |
| draguer | chat up, to | 42 | v. | |
| dragueur | flirt | 42 | n.m. | |
| eau | water | 11 | n.f. | |
| économies | savings | 11 | n.f. | |
| écouter | listen, to | 16 | v. | |
| écrire | write, to | 8 | v. | écrire |
| éditeur | editor | 43 | n.m. | |
| église | church | 15 | n.f. | |
| électrique | electric | 17 | adj. | |
| éloigné | far | 26 | adj. | |
| émission | programme | 18 | n.f. | |
| emmener | take, to | 44 | v. | |

# E

| | | | | |
|---|---|---|---|---|
| emploi | job | 31 | n.m. | |
| employé | employee | 2 | n.m. | |
| emprunt | loan (borrowed) | 17 | n.m. | |
| enfant | child | 13 | n.m. | |
| ennuyer, s' | bored, to get | 44 | v. | |
| enquête | inquiry | 19 | n.f. | |
| entendre | hear, to | 25 | v. | entendre |
| entrée | starter | 14 | n.f. | |
| entreprise | firm | 30 | n.f. | |
| entretien | interview | 43 | n.m. | |
| enveloppe | envelope | 7 | n.f. | |
| envie | desire | 33 | n.f. | |
| envoi | parcel | 10 | n.m. | |
| envoyer | send, to | 10 | v. | envoyer |
| épaule | shoulder | 28 | n.f. | |
| épicerie | grocer's | 11 | n.f. | |
| époque | time | 29 | n.f. | |
| épreuve | hardship | 36 | n.f. | |
| équipe | team | 30 | n.f. | |
| erreur | mistake | 43 | n.f. | |
| espagnol | Spanish | 2 | adj. | |
| espoir | hope | 41 | n.m. | |
| essayage | fitting (room) | 28 | n.m. | |
| essayer | try, to | 14 | v. | essayer |
| essence | petrol | 38 | n.f. | |
| estomac | stomach | 32 | n.m. | |
| étagère | shelf | 34 | n.f. | |
| état | condition | 20 | n.m. | |
| étonner | surprise | 42 | v. | |
| être | be, to | 2 | v. | être |
| étude | study | 35 | n.f. | |
| étudiant | student | 2 | n.m. | |
| évaluer | assess, to | 34 | v. | |
| évier | sink | 39 | n.m. | |
| exact | exact | 31 | adj. | |
| exagérer | exaggerate, to | 21 | v. | |
| examen | examination | 36 | n.m. | |
| excellent | excellent | 21 | adj. | |
| excuse | excuse | 17 | n.f. | |
| excuser | excuse, to | 25 | v. | |
| exemple | example | 42 | n.m. | |
| expéditeur | sender | 10 | n.m. | |
| exprimer | express, to | 11 | v. | |

F

| | | | | |
|---|---|---|---|---|
| facile | easy | 16 | adj. | |
| facteur | postman | 10 | n.m. | |
| faim | hunger | 22 | n.f. | |
| faire | do, to | 2 | v. | faire |
| falloir | have to/be needed, to | 11 | v. | falloir |
| famille | family | 13 | n.f. | |
| fatigant | tiring | 13 | adj. | |
| fauteuil | armchair | 34 | n.m. | |
| faux | false | 20 | adj. | |
| féliciter | congratulate, to | 22 | v. | |
| femme | woman/wife | 13 | n.f. | homme/mari |
| fenêtre | window | 34 | n.f. | |
| fer | iron | 20 | n.m. | |
| fermer | close, to | 17 | v. | |
| fermeté | firmness | 39 | n.f. | |
| fête | party | 36 | n.f. | |
| feu | traffic lights | 15 | n.m. | |
| fiancé | fiancé | 40 | n.m. | |
| fiche | form | 10 | n.f. | |
| fièvre | fever | 32 | n.f. | |
| fille | girl | 13 | n.f. | garçon |
| fille | daughter | 13 | n.f. | fils |
| film | film | 41 | n.m. | |
| fils | son | 13 | n.m. | fille |
| fin | end | 23 | n.f. | |
| fois | time | 40 | n.f. | |
| folle | mad | 20 | adj. | fou |
| fond | bottom/other end | 16 | n.m. | |
| forme | shape | 20 | n.f. | |
| formidable | formidable | 42 | adj. | |
| fort | strong | 24 | adj. | |
| fou | mad | 20 | adj. | folle |
| fourchette | fork | 22 | n.f. | |
| fraîche | fresh | 20 | adj. | frais |
| frais | fresh | 20 | adj. | fraîche |
| franc | franc | 10 | adj. | |
| français | French | 2 | adj. | |
| frein | brake | 20 | n.m. | |
| fréquent | frequent | 23 | adj. | |
| frère | brother | 4 | n.m. | sœur |
| frigo* | fridge | 34 | n.m. | |
| frisson | shiver | 32 | n.m. | |
| froid | cold | 23 | n.m. | |

F-H

| | | | | |
|---|---|---|---|---|
| fromage | cheese | 11 | n.m. | |
| fruit | fruit | 11 | n.m. | |
| fumeur | smoking | 16 | n.m. | |
| gagner | win, to | 13 | v. | |
| garage | garage | 34 | n.m. | |
| garçon | boy | 13 | n.m. | fille |
| gare | station | 16 | n.f. | |
| gastronomie | gastronomy | 45 | n. f | |
| gâteau | cake | 14 | n.m. | |
| gauche | left | 15 | n.f. | |
| geler | freeze, to | 23 | v. | |
| génial | great | 21 | adj. | |
| gentil | kind/nice | 12 | adj. | |
| gentillesse | kindness | 39 | n.f. | |
| glace | ice | 27 | n.f. | |
| gorge | throat | 32 | n.f. | |
| goût | taste | 6 | n.m. | |
| goûter | taste/try, to | 14 | v. | |
| grand | tall | 6 | adj. | |
| grand-mère | grandmother | 29 | n.f. | |
| grand-père | grandfather | 29 | n.m. | |
| grand-parents | grandparents | 29 | n.m. | |
| grave | serious | 43 | adj. | |
| grève | strike | 18 | n.f. | |
| grippe | flu | 32 | n.f. | |
| gris | grey | 6 | adj. | |
| gros | fat | 6 | adj. | |
| groupe | group | 45 | n.m. | |
| guérir | cure, to | 33 | v. | finir |
| guichet | ticket office | 10 | n.m. | |
| guide | guide | 45 | n.m. | |
| guitare | guitare | 42 | n.f. | |
| habiter | live, to | 6 | v. | |
| habitude | habit | 13 | n.f. | |
| haine | hatred | 40 | n.f. | |
| hall | hall, (departure) | 16 | n.m. | |
| hebdomadaire | weekly (newspaper) | 18 | n.m. | |
| hésiter | hesitate, to | 28 | v. | |
| heure | hour/time | 8 | n.f. | |
| heureux | happy | 20 | adj. | |
| histoire | story | 13 | n.f. | |
| homme | man | 13 | n.f. | femme |
| hôpital | hospital | 6 | n.m. | |

| | | | | |
|---|---|---|---|---|
| horaire | timetable | 16 | n.m. | |
| huile | oil | 11 | n.f. | |
| humeur | mood | 17 | n.f. | |
| idée | idea | 10 | n.f. | |
| identifier | identify, to | 35 | v. | |
| identité | identity/name | 2 | n.f. | |
| idiot | stupid | 42 | adj. | |
| immobilier | real-estate | 35 | n.m. | |
| impatience | impatience | 13 | n.f. | |
| impeccable | impeccable | 20 | adj. | |
| imperméable | raincoat | 12 | n.m. | |
| important | important | 31 | adj. | |
| impossible | impossible | 25 | adj. | |
| impôt | tax | 19 | n.m. | |
| imprimé | form | 10 | n.m. | |
| inadmissible | unacceptable | 25 | adj. | |
| inconnu | unknown | 18 | n.m. | |
| inconvénient | inconvenient | 26 | n.m. | |
| incroyable | incredible | 25 | adj. | |
| indécision | indecision | 44 | n. f | |
| indicatif | dialling code | 24 | n.m. | |
| indifférence | indifference | 24 | n.f. | |
| indiquer | show, to | 15 | v. | |
| information | information | 43 | n.f. | |
| informel | informal | 18 | adj. | |
| informer | inform, to | 43 | v. | |
| infraction | offense (driving) | 37 | n.f. | |
| inquiet | worried | 19 | adj. | |
| inspecteur | inspector | 19 | n.m. | |
| installer, s' | settle in, to | 34 | v. | |
| interdire | forbid | 22 | v. | dire |
| interdit | forbidden | 37 | adj. | |
| intéresser | interest, to | 44 | v. | |
| interlocuteur | interlocutor | 35 | n.m. | |
| international | international | 10 | adj. | |
| interroger | question, to | 32 | v. | manger |
| invitation | invitation | 12 | n.f. | |
| inviter | invite, to | 12 | v. | |
| isolé | isolated | 6 | adj. | |
| italien | Italian | 2 | adj. | |
| jambe | leg | 32 | n.f. | |
| jambon | ham | 11 | n.m. | |
| janvier | January | 10 | n.m. | |

# J-M

| | | | | |
|---|---|---|---|---|
| jardin | garden | 13 | n.m. | |
| jardinage | gardening | 44 | n.m. | |
| jaune | yellow | 20 | adj. | |
| jeune | young | 29 | adj. | |
| jeunesse | youth | 29 | n.f. | |
| joie | joy | 41 | n.f. | |
| joli | pretty | 6 | adj. | |
| jouer | play, to | 13 | v. | |
| jour | day | 8 | n.m. | |
| journal | newspaper | 18 | n.m. | |
| journaliste | journalist | 2 | n.m. | |
| journée | day | 2 | n.f. | |
| jupe | skirt | 28 | n.f. | |
| juste | just | 16 | adj. | |
| laisser | leave, to | 10 | v. | |
| lampe | lamp | 34 | n.f. | |
| lapin | rabbit | 22 | n.m. | |
| laver, se | washed, to get | 17 | v. | |
| lecture | reading | 44 | n. f | |
| léger | light | 22 | adj. | |
| légume | vegetable | 11 | n.m. | |
| lessive | soap powder | 11 | n.f. | |
| lettre | letter | 10 | n.f. | |
| lever, se | get up, to | 17 | v. | |
| libre | free | 15 | adj. | |
| lieu | place | 3 | n.m. | |
| ligne | line | 16 | n.f. | |
| linge | laundry | 39 | n.m. | |
| lire | read, to | 20 | v. | lire |
| lisse | smooth | 38 | adj. | |
| lit | bed | 16 | n.m. | |
| littérature | literature | 6 | n.f. | |
| livre | book | 13 | n.m. | |
| logement | accommodation | 45 | n.m. | |
| loisir | leisure | 21 | n.m. | |
| long | long | 20 | adj. | |
| loto | lottery | 13 | n.m. | |
| luge | toboggan | 27 | n.f. | |
| luxueux | luxurious | 26 | adj. | |
| machin | thingummyjig | 20 | n.m. | |
| machine à laver | washing machine | 39 | n.f. | |
| magasin | shop/store | 11 | n.m. | |
| main | hand | 32 | n.f. | |

| | | | | |
|---|---|---|---|---|
| maintenir | maintain, to | 35 | v. | |
| mairie | town hall | 15 | n.f. | |
| maison | house | 13 | n.f. | |
| malade | ill | 30 | | |
| maladie | illness | 32 | n.f. | |
| malheureux | unhappy | 41 | adj. | |
| mandat | money order | 10 | n.m. | |
| manger | eat, to | 13 | v. | |
| manière | manner | 18 | n.f. | |
| manque | lack | 17 | n.m. | |
| manteau | coat | 23 | n.m. | |
| maquiller, se | make-up, to put on | 17 | v. | |
| marchand de journaux | newsagent | 43 | n.m. | |
| marche | walking | 44 | n.f. | |
| mari | husband | 13 | n.m. | femme |
| mariage | marriage | 40 | n.m. | |
| marié | married | 6 | adj. | |
| marier, se | married, to get | 40 | v. | |
| marquer | mark, to | 15 | v. | |
| marron | brown | 6 | adj. | |
| matériel | equipment | 34 | n.m. | |
| matière | material | 20 | n.f. | |
| matin | morning | 13 | n.m. | |
| matinée | morning | 8 | n.f. | |
| mauvais | bad | 17 | adj. | |
| mécanicien | mechanic | 20 | n.m. | |
| médias | media | 18 | n.m. | |
| médecin | doctor | 19 | n.m. | |
| médicament | medicine | 32 | n.m. | |
| menu | menu | 14 | n.m. | |
| mépriser | despise, to | 40 | v. | |
| mer | sea | 26 | n.f. | |
| mère | mother | 4 | n.f. | père |
| message | message | 24 | n.m. | |
| météo | weather | 23 | adj. | |
| métier | profession/trade | 31 | n.m. | |
| mettre | put, to | 10 | v. | mettre |
| meuble | furniture, piece of | 34 | n.m. | |
| midi | midday | 13 | n.m. | |
| mince | slim | 6 | adj. | |
| minute | minute | 8 | n.f. | |
| moche* | ugly | 6 | adj. | |
| mode | fashion | 28 | n.f. | |

# M-N

| | | | | |
|---|---|---|---|---|
| modèle | model | 28 | n.m. | |
| modeste | modest | 13 | adj. | |
| mois | month | 8 | n.m. | |
| moment | moment | 29 | n.m. | |
| moniteur | monitor | 27 | n.m. | |
| monnaie | change (loose) | 17 | n.f. | |
| monotone | monotonous | 13 | adj. | |
| monsieur | mister | 2 | n.m. | |
| monsieur | sir | 16 | n.m. | |
| montagne | mountain | 6 | n.f. | |
| moral | morale | 41 | n.m. | |
| morceau | piece | 22 | n.m. | |
| mort | death | 44 | n.f. | |
| mot | word | 10 | n.m. | |
| moteur | engine | 20 | n.m. | |
| mourir | die, to | 44 | v. | |
| moutarde | mustard | 22 | n.f. | |
| moyens | means (financial) | 13 | n.m. | |
| musée | museum | 44 | n.m. | |
| musique | music | 6 | n.f. | |
| nager | swim, to | 44 | v. | manger |
| naissance | birth | 3 | n.f. | |
| natation | swimming | 44 | n.f. | |
| nationalité | nationality | 3 | n.f. | |
| nature | nature | 44 | n.f. | |
| nécessaire | necessary | 37 | adj. | |
| neige | snow | 23 | n.f. | |
| neiger | snow, to | 23 | v. | neiger |
| nettoyage | cleaning | 39 | n.m. | |
| nettoyer | clean, to | 39 | v. | |
| neuf | new | 20 | adj. | |
| niveau | level | 38 | n. m | |
| noir | black/dark | 6 | adj. | |
| nom | name | 7 | n.m. | |
| nombreux | numerous | 23 | adj. | |
| nord | north | 13 | n.m. | |
| note | bill | 25 | n.f. | |
| nouveau | new | 20 | adj. | |
| nouvelle | news, piece of | 8 | n.f. | |
| nuage | cloud | 23 | n.m. | |
| nuageux | cloudy | 23 | adj. | |
| nuit | night | 2 | n.f. | |
| nul | rubbish/useless | 21 | adj. | |

| | | | | |
|---|---|---|---|---|
| objet | object | 20 | n.m. | |
| obligation | obligation | 37 | n.f. | |
| obligatoire | compulsory | 37 | adj. | |
| obligé | obliged | 37 | adj. | |
| observer | observe, to | 23 | v. | |
| occupation | occupation, job | 44 | n. f | |
| occupé | busy | 12 | adj. | |
| occuper, s' | take care of, to | 42 | v. | |
| œil | eye | 6 | n.m. | yeux |
| officiel | official | 45 | adj. | |
| oncle | uncle | 29 | n.m. | tante |
| opinion | opinion | 14 | n.f. | |
| optimisme | optimism | 41 | n.m. | |
| orage | storm | 23 | n.m. | |
| orange | orange | 11 | n. f | |
| ordonnance | prescription | 32 | n.f. | |
| organisé | organized | 45 | adj. | |
| oublier | forget, to | 7 | v. | |
| ouvre-boîte | tin-opener | 11 | n.m. | |
| ouvrier | worker | 4 | n.m. | |
| ouvrir | open, to | 20 | v. | ouvrir |
| pain | bread | 11 | n.m. | |
| panne, en | broken down | 20 | n.f. | |
| panneau | display board | 15 | n.m. | |
| pantalon | trousers | 28 | n.m. | |
| papier | paper | 20 | n.m. | |
| papiers | documentation | 3 | n.m. | |
| paquet | parcel | 11 | n.m. | |
| paraître | seem, to | 18 | v. | |
| parapluie | umbrella | 12 | n.m. | |
| parc | park | 15 | n.m. | |
| pardonner | forgive, to | 17 | v. | |
| pareil | same | 31 | adj. | |
| parents | parents | 29 | n.m. | |
| parfait | perfect | 30 | adj. | |
| parler | speak, to | 6 | v. | |
| partir | leave/go, to | 8 | v. | partir |
| parvenir | reach, to | 45 | v. | |
| passer, se | happen, to | 8 | v. | |
| passer à | go to, to | 17 | v. | |
| passionné | enthusiastic | 44 | adj. | |
| patient | patient | 32 | n.m. | |
| patin | skate, (ice) | 27 | n.m. | |

# P

| | | | | |
|---|---|---|---|---|
| pâtisserie | cake shop | 11 | n.f. | |
| paye | pay | 31 | n.f. | |
| payer | pay, to | 13 | v. | essayer |
| pays | country | 7 | n.m. | |
| peigne | comb | 17 | n.m. | |
| peigner, se | comb one's hair, to | 17 | v. | |
| penser | think, to | 12 | v. | |
| pension | pension | 45 | n.f. | |
| père | father | 4 | n.m. | mère |
| périmé | out of date | 37 | adj. | |
| période | period | 45 | n.f. | |
| péripherique | ring road | 15 | n.m. | |
| permis | licence | 37 | n.m. | |
| personnel | personnel | 30 | n.m. | |
| pessimisme | pessimism | 41 | n.m. | |
| petit | small | 6 | adj. | |
| petit déjeuner | breakfast | 25 | n.m. | |
| phare | headlight | 38 | n.m. | |
| pharmacie | chemist's | 33 | n.f. | |
| photo | photograph | 29 | n.f. | |
| pièce | coin | 17 | n.f. | |
| pièce | part | 20 | n.f. | |
| pièce | play | 21 | n.f. | |
| pied | foot | 32 | n.m. | |
| pile | pile | 39 | n.f. | |
| piquer | sting, to | 33 | v. | |
| piqûre | injection | 33 | n.f. | |
| piscine | swimming pool | 27 | n.f. | |
| piste | ski slope | 27 | n.f. | |
| placard | cupboard | 34 | n.m. | |
| place | seat | 16 | n.f. | |
| place | position/place | 26 | n.f. | |
| place | square | 7 | n.f. | |
| plage | beach | 26 | n.f. | |
| plaindre, se | feel ill/complain, to | 33 | v. | |
| plaire | please, to | 12 | v. | plaire |
| plaisir | pleasure | 12 | n.m. | |
| plastique | plastic | 20 | n.m. | |
| plateau | tray | 22 | n.m. | |
| plein | full | 38 | n.m. | |
| pleuvoir | rain, to | 23 | v. | pleuvoir |
| pluie | rain | 23 | n.f. | |
| pneu | tyre | 20 | n.m. | |

| | | | | |
|---|---|---|---|---|
| point | point | 30 | n.m. | |
| poisson | fish | 14 | n.m. | |
| poissonnerie | fishmonger's | 11 | n.f. | |
| poivre | pepper | 22 | n.m. | |
| police | police | 19 | n.f. | |
| politesse | politeness | 39 | n.f. | |
| pomme | apple | 11 | n.f. | |
| ponctualité | punctuality | 17 | n.f. | |
| pont | bridge | 15 | n.m. | |
| porte | door | 34 | n.f. | |
| possibilité | possibility | 45 | n.f. | |
| poste | post office | 10 | n.f. | |
| poulet | chicken | 14 | n.m. | |
| pourboire | tip | 14 | n.m. | |
| pouvoir | be able, to | 14 | v. | pouvoir |
| preference | preference | 45 | n.f. | |
| préférer | prefer, to | 14 | v. | préférer |
| premier | first | 15 | adj. | |
| prendre | get/take/have, to | 10 | v. | comprendre |
| prénom | name, first | 7 | n.m. | |
| préparer | get ready/prepare, to | 12 | v. | |
| présentateur | presenter | 43 | n.m. | |
| présenter | present, to | 4 | v. | |
| presse | press | 18 | n.f. | |
| prêt | loan (lent) | 17 | n.m. | |
| prévenir | warn, to | 37 | v. | |
| prix | price | 25 | n.m. | |
| problème | problem | 38 | n.m. | |
| prochain | next | 30 | adj. | |
| produire | produce, to | 23 | v. | conduire |
| profession | occupation | 6 | n.f. | |
| programme | programme | 18 | n.m. | |
| projet | plan | 8 | n.m. | |
| promener, se | walk, to go for a | 27 | v. | |
| promettre | promise, to | 31 | v. | mettre |
| proposer | suggest/offer, to | 4 | v. | |
| propre | clean | 39 | adj. | |
| protester | protest, to | 25 | v. | |
| province | province | 6 | n.f. | |
| prudent | careful | 33 | adj. | |
| public | audience | 21 | n.m. | |
| pull-over | pullover | 12 | n.m. | |
| quai | platform | 16 | n.m. | |

| | | | | |
|---|---|---|---|---|
| qualité | quality | 38 | n.f. | |
| quartier | neighbourhood | 15 | n.m. | |
| quotidien | daily (newspaper) | 18 | n.m. | |
| radio | radio | 16 | n.f. | |
| raison | reason | 10 | n.f. | |
| rajeunir | younger, to grow | 44 | v. | finir |
| ranger | tidy, to | 39 | v. | manger |
| rappeler | remind, to | 33 | v. | appeler |
| raser, se | shave, to | 17 | v. | |
| réception | reception | 26 | n.f. | |
| recevoir | receive, to | 33 | v. | recevoir |
| réclamation | complaint | 14 | n.f. | |
| recommander | recommend, to | 33 | v. | |
| reconnaître | recognise, to | 33 | v. | connaître |
| rectangulaire | rectangular | 20 | adj. | |
| réfléchir | think, to | 28 | v. | finir |
| refuser | refuse, to | 10 | v. | |
| regarder | watch/look, to | 20 | v. | |
| région | region | 45 | n.f. | |
| regretter | sorry, to be | 12 | v. | |
| remarquer | notice, to | 31 | v. | |
| remplir | fill in, to | 10 | v. | |
| rendez-vous | rendez-vous | 33 | n.m. | |
| renseignement | information | 24 | n.m. | |
| rentrer | home, to arrive/go | 13 | v. | |
| réparation | repair | 20 | n.f. | |
| réparer | repair, to | 20 | v. | |
| repas | meal | 11 | n.m. | |
| repasser | iron, to | 39 | v. | |
| répéter | repeat, to | 24 | v. | |
| répondeur | answering machine | 35 | n.m. | |
| répondre | answer, to | 4 | v. | répondre |
| reposer, se | rest, to | 30 | v. | |
| reprendre | take again, to | 22 | v. | comprendre |
| reproche | reproach | 17 | n.m. | |
| réservation | reservation | 16 | n.f. | |
| réserve | uncertainty/reserve | 18 | n.f. | |
| réserver | reserve, to | 26 | v. | |
| résister | resist, to | 14 | v. | |
| responsabilité | responsibility | 31 | n.f. | |
| ressembler | look like, to | 28 | v. | |
| restaurant | restaurant | 14 | n.m. | |
| reste | rest | 17 | n.m. | |

| | | | | |
|---|---|---|---|---|
| retard, en | late | 17 | n.m. | |
| retarder | postpone/delay, to | 28 | v. | |
| retourner | return, to | 27 | v. | |
| retraite | retirement | 44 | n.f. | |
| réunion | meeting | 19 | n.f. | |
| réunir, se | meet, to | 30 | v. | finir |
| réussir | succeed, to | 36 | v. | finir |
| rêve | dream | 36 | n.m. | |
| réveiller, se | wake up, to | 17 | v. | |
| rêver | dream, to | 13 | v. | |
| revue | review | 18 | n. f | |
| rhume | cold (in the head) | 32 | n.m. | |
| rire | laugh, to | 42 | v. | rire |
| risque | risk | 23 | n.m. | |
| robe | dress | 28 | n.f. | |
| robinet | tap | 39 | n.m. | |
| rond | round | 20 | adj. | |
| rôti | roast | 14 | n.m. | |
| roue | wheel | 20 | n.f. | |
| rouge | red | 20 | adj. | |
| rousse | red-haired (fem.) | 6 | adj. | roux |
| route | road | 15 | n.f. | |
| roux | red-haired (masc.) | 6 | adj. | rousse |
| rue | street | 7 | n.f. | |
| sac | bag | 12 | n.m. | |
| sac à dos | rucksack | 12 | n.m. | |
| saigner | bleed, to | 33 | v. | |
| saison | season | 45 | n.f. | |
| salaire | salary | 31 | n.m. | |
| sale | dirty | 39 | adj. | |
| salle à manger | dining room | 29 | n.f. | |
| salle de bains | bathroom | 34 | n.f. | |
| salon | lounge | 39 | n.m. | |
| salutation | greeting | 1 | n.f. | |
| santé | health | 32 | n.f. | |
| sardine | sardine | 11 | n.f. | |
| satisfaction | satisfaction | 36 | n.f. | |
| savoir | know, to | 10 | v. | savoir |
| savon | soap | 17 | n.m. | |
| scandaleux | outrageous | 31 | adj. | |
| séance | performance | 21 | n.f. | |
| sec | dry (masc.) | 20 | adj. | sèche |
| sèche | dry (fem.) | 20 | adj. | sec |

# S

| | | | | |
|---|---|---|---|---|
| secouer | shake, to | 39 | v. | |
| secrétaire | secretary | 24 | n.m. | |
| séjour | stay | 45 | n.m. | |
| sel | salt | 11 | n.m. | |
| semaine | week | 8 | n.f. | |
| sensation | sensation | 23 | n.f. | |
| sentir | smell, to | 22 | v. | |
| sentir | feel, to | 32 | v. | |
| sérieux | serious | 23 | adj. | |
| serrer | tight, to be | 28 | v. | |
| serveur | waiter | 14 | n.m. | |
| serviette | napkin | 22 | n.f. | |
| serviette | towel | 34 | n.f. | |
| servir | serve, to | 20 | v. | |
| seul | alone | 6 | adj. | |
| signaler | point out, to | 33 | v. | |
| signature | signature | 3 | n.f. | |
| signe | sign | 23 | n.m. | |
| signer | sign, to | 10 | v. | |
| similitude | similarity | 31 | n.f. | |
| simple | simple | 13 | adj. | |
| sirop | syrup | 32 | n.m. | |
| ski | ski | 27 | n.m. | |
| skier | ski, to | 27 | v. | |
| skieur | skier | 27 | n.m. | |
| sœur | sister | 4 | n.f. | frère |
| soif | thirst | 22 | n.f. | |
| soigner | nurse/tend, to | 13 | v. | |
| soir | evening | 13 | n.m. | |
| soirée | evening | 19 | n.f. | |
| sol | ground | 39 | n.m. | |
| soleil | sun | 23 | n.m. | |
| sondage | opinion poll | 18 | n.m. | |
| sortie | exit | 15 | n.f. | |
| sortir | go out/take the exit, to | 15 | v. | sortir |
| souffrir | suffer, to | 33 | v. | |
| souhait | wish | 13 | n.m. | |
| soulager | to relieve/ease one's pain | 33 | v. | manger |
| soupe | soup | 14 | n.f. | |
| source | source | 36 | n.f. | |
| souvenir | memory | 29 | n.m. | |
| spécialité | speciality | 22 | n.f. | |
| spectacle | show | 21 | n.m. | |

| | | | | |
|---|---|---|---|---|
| splendide | splendid | 29 | adj. | |
| sport | sport | 6 | n.m. | |
| sportif | sportsman | 27 | n.m. | |
| sportif | sporty | 27 | adj. | |
| stade | stadium | 15 | n.m. | |
| stage | training course | 27 | n.m. | |
| standardiste | switchboard operator | 24 | n.m. | |
| standard | switchboard | 24 | n.m. | |
| station service | petrol station | 15 | n.f. | |
| stationnement | parking | 37 | n.m. | |
| sucre | sugar | 11 | n.m. | |
| suite | suite of rooms | 26 | n.f. | |
| suivant | next | 21 | adj. | |
| super* | super/fantastic | 42 | adj. | |
| supplément | extra charge | 15 | n.m. | |
| supporter | stand/tolerate, to | 40 | v. | |
| sûr | sure | 20 | adj. | |
| sympathique | nice | 6 | adj. | |
| symptôme | symptom | 32 | n.m. | |
| table | table | 22 | n.f. | |
| tablette | tablet | 11 | n.f. | |
| taille | size | 3 | n.f. | |
| tailleur | suit, (lady's) | 28 | n.m. | |
| tante | aunt | 29 | n.f. | oncle |
| tapis | carpet | 39 | n.m. | |
| tard | late | 17 | adj. | |
| tarif | price list | 15 | n.m. | |
| tarte | pie | 14 | n.f. | |
| taxi | taxi | 15 | n.m. | |
| technicien | technician | 13 | n.m. | |
| télégramme | telegram | 10 | n.m. | |
| téléphone | telephone | 24 | n.m. | |
| téléphoner | telephone, to | 8 | v. | |
| télévision | television | 16 | n.f. | |
| température | temperature | 23 | n. f | |
| tempête | storm | 23 | n.f. | |
| temps | time, weather | 8 | n.m. | |
| tenir à | insist, to | 35 | v. | |
| tenir dans | fit in, to | 12 | v. | |
| tennis | tennis | 19 | n.m. | |
| tente | tent | 12 | n.f. | |
| terrasse | pavement area (outside a café) | 25 | n.f. | |

# T-V

| | | | | |
|---|---|---|---|---|
| tête | head | 32 | n.f. | |
| thé | tea | 22 | n.m. | |
| théâtre | theatre | 6 | n.m. | |
| timbre | stamp | 10 | n.m. | |
| timide | shy | 23 | adj; | |
| toilettes | toilets | 33 | n.f. | |
| tonnerre | thunder | 23 | n.m. | |
| toucher | touch, to | 18 | v. | |
| touriste | tourist | 18 | n.m. | |
| touristique | touristic | 45 | adj. | |
| tourner | turn, to | 15 | v. | |
| toux | cough | 32 | n.f. | |
| train | train | 10 | n.m. | |
| tranche | slice | 11 | n.f. | |
| transmettre | transmit, to | 35 | v. | mettre |
| travail | work/job | 6 | n.m. | travaux |
| travailler | work, to | 6 | v. | |
| travaux | works | 24 | n.m. | travail |
| traverser | cross, to | 15 | v. | |
| triangulaire | triangular | 20 | adj. | |
| triste | sad | 41 | adj. | |
| tristesse | sorrow | 41 | n.f. | |
| tromper, se | mistaken, to be | 43 | v. | |
| troupe | theatrical company | 21 | n.f. | |
| trouver | find, to | 21 | v. | |
| truc* | thing/contraption | 20 | n.m. | |
| urgent | urgent | 10 | adj; | |
| utiliser | use, to | 10 | v. | |
| utilité | use | 10 | n. f | |
| vacances | holidays | 6 | n.f. | |
| vaisselle | washing up | 39 | n.f. | |
| valise | suitcase | 26 | n.f. | |
| valoir | worth, to be | 11 | v. | |
| vélo | bicycle | 14 | v | |
| vendeuse | sales assistant | 13 | n.f. | vendeur |
| venir | come, to | 12 | v. | |
| vent | wind | 23 | n.m. | |
| vente | sale | 17 | n.f. | |
| ventre | stomach | 32 | n.m. | |
| verglas | black ice | 23 | n.m. | |
| vérifier | check, to | 38 | v. | |
| verre | glass (material) | 20 | n.m. | |
| verre | glass (object) | 22 | n.m. | |

| | | | | |
|---|---|---|---|---|
| vert | green | 6 | adj. | |
| veste | jacket | 28 | n.f. | |
| vêtement | clothing, article of | 28 | n.m. | |
| viande | meat | 11 | n.f. | |
| vie | life | 13 | n.f. | |
| vieille | old (fem.) | 6 | adj. | vieux |
| vieux | old (masc.) | 6 | adj. | vieille |
| vif | alert | 20 | adj. | |
| ville | town, city | 6 | n.f. | |
| vin | wine | 14 | n.m. | |
| visite | visit | 8 | n.f. | |
| visiter | visit, to | 18 | v. | |
| vivre | live, to | 40 | v. | |
| vœux | wish | 36 | n.m. | |
| voie | track | 16 | n.f. | |
| voir | see, to | 15 | v. | |
| voisin | neighbour | 19 | n.m. | |
| voiture | car | 8 | n.f. | |
| voix | voice | 42 | n.f. | |
| vol | flight | 16 | n.m. | |
| vomir | vomit, to | 32 | v. | finir |
| vouloir | want, to | 10 | v. | |
| voyage | journey/travelling | 6 | n.m. | |
| voyager | travel, to | 6 | v. | manger |
| vrai | true | 31 | adj. | |
| vue | sight | 26 | n.f. | |
| vulgaire | vulgar | 21 | adj. | |
| wagon-restaurant | restaurant car | 16 | n.m. | |
| yeux | eyes | 3 | n.m. | œil |
| zone | area/region | 23 | n.f. | |

*familiar

# ENGLISH/FRENCH MINI-DICTIONARY

| | | Lessons | | See... |
|---|---|---|---|---|
| absent | absent | 35 | adj. | |
| abundant, heavy | abondant | 23 | adj. | |
| abuse, to | abuser | 33 | v. | |
| accept, to | accepter | 4 | v. | |
| accident | accident | 37 | n.m. | |
| accommodation | logement | 45 | n.m. | |
| accompany, to | accompagner | 44 | v. | |
| account | compte | 17 | n.m. | |
| action | action | 29 | n.f. | |
| actor/actress | acteur/actrice | 21 | n.m. | |
| address | adresse | 3 | n.f. | |
| addressee | destinataire | 7 | n.m. | |
| admit, to | avouer | 40 | v. | |
| adore, to | adorer | 6 | v. | |
| advantage | avantage | 26 | n.m. | |
| advertisement | annonce | 43 | n.f. | |
| advice | conseil | 10 | n.m. | |
| afternoon | après-midi | 8 | n.m. | |
| agency | agence | 26 | n.f. | |
| agent | agent | 16 | n.m. | |
| age | âge | 6 | n.m. | |
| agreement | accord | 11 | n.m. | |
| alcohol | alcool | 33 | .v | |
| alert | vif | 20 | adj. | |
| alone | seul | 6 | adj. | |
| American | américain | 2 | adj. | |
| annoyance | agacement | 38 | n.m. | |
| anorak | anorak | 12 | n.m. | |
| answer, to | répondre | 4 | v. | répondre |
| answering machine | répondeur | 35 | n.m. | |
| antibiotics | antibiotique | 32 | n.m. | |
| aperitif | apéritif | 14 | n.m. | |
| appearance | apparition | 23 | n.f. | |
| appetite | appétit | 36 | n.m. | |
| appetizing | appétissant | 14 | adj. | |
| apple | pomme | 11 | n.f. | |
| area/region | zone | 23 | n.f. | |
| arm | bras | 32 | n.m. | |
| armchair | fauteuil | 34 | n.m. | |
| arrival | arrivée | 16 | n.f. | |
| arrive, to | arriver | 8 | v. | |
| art | art | 6 | n.m. | |
| ask, to | demander | 42 | v. | |

*The verbs in the fourth column refer to the "Verb tables".*

| | | | | |
|---|---|---|---|---|
| assess, to | évaluer | 34 | v. | |
| attention | attention | 16 | n.f. | |
| attract, to | attirer | 16 | v. | |
| attraction | attrait | 45 | n.m. | |
| audience | public | 21 | n.m. | |
| August | août | 10 | n.m. | |
| aunt | tante | 29 | n.f. | oncle |
| author | auteur | 21 | n.m. | |
| automatic | automatique | 35 | adj. | |
| available | disponible | 30 | adj. | |
| avenue | avenue | 7 | n.f. | |
| back | dos | 32 | n.m. | |
| bad | mauvais | 17 | adj. | |
| bag | sac | 12 | n.m. | |
| baker's | boulangerie | 11 | n.f. | |
| bald | chauve | 6 | adj. | |
| ball | bal | 42 | n.m. | |
| bank | banque | 17 | n.f. | |
| barrel | baril | 25 | n.m. | |
| bath | bain | 17 | n.m. | |
| bathroom | salle de bains | 34 | n.f. | |
| battery | batterie | 38 | n.f. | |
| be able, to | pouvoir | 14 | v. | pouvoir |
| be, to | être | 2 | v. | être |
| beach | plage | 26 | n.f. | |
| beautiful | belle | 6 | adj. | |
| bedroom | chambre | 26 | n.f. | |
| bed | lit | 16 | n.m. | |
| beer | bière | 25 | n.f. | |
| begin, to | commencer | 3 | v. | commencer |
| beginning | début | 23 | n.m. | |
| believe, to | croire | 40 | v. | croire |
| belt | ceinture | 37 | n.f. | |
| berth | couchette | 16 | n.f. | |
| bicycle | vélo | 14 | v | |
| bill | addition | 14 | n.f. | |
| bill | note | 25 | n.f. | |
| birthday | anniversaire | 17 | n.m. | |
| birth | naissance | 3 | n.f. | |
| black ice | verglas | 23 | n.m. | |
| black/dark | noir | 6 | adj. | |
| bleed, to | saigner | 33 | v. | |
| blouse | chemisier | 28 | n.m. | |

# B-C

| | | | | |
|---|---|---|---|---|
| blue | bleu | 6 | adj. | |
| boat | bateau | 10 | n.m. | |
| bonnet | capot | 20 | n.m. | |
| book | livre | 13 | n.m. | |
| boot | botte | 12 | n.f. | |
| bored, to get | ennuyer, s' | 44 | v. | |
| bottle | bouteille | 11 | n.f. | |
| bottom/other end | fond | 16 | n.m. | |
| boulevard | boulevard | 7 | n.m. | |
| box | boîte | 11 | n.f. | |
| boy | garçon | 13 | n.m. | fille |
| brake | frein | 20 | n.m. | |
| bread | pain | 11 | n.m. | |
| breakfast | petit déjeuner | 25 | n.m. | |
| bridge | pont | 15 | n.m. | |
| bring, to | apporter | 25 | v. | |
| brochure | brochure | 45 | n.f. | |
| broken | cassé | 20 | adj. | |
| broken down | panne, en | 20 | n.f. | |
| brother-in-law | beau-frère | 29 | n.m. | |
| brother | frère | 4 | n.m. | sœur |
| brown | marron | 6 | adj. | |
| brush | brosse | 17 | n.f. | |
| burn | brûlure | 33 | n.f. | |
| burn, to | brûler | 33 | v. | |
| business | affaire | 30 | n.f. | |
| busy | actif | 45 | adj. | |
| bus | autobus | 13 | n.m. | |
| busy | occupé | 12 | adj. | |
| butcher's | boucherie | 11 | n.f. | |
| buy, to | acheter | 11 | v. | |
| cabin | cabine | 24 | n.f. | |
| cake | gâteau | 14 | n.m. | |
| cake shop | pâtisserie | 11 | n.f. | |
| calendar | calendrier | 9 | n.m. | |
| call, to | appeler | 24 | v. | appeler |
| called, to be | appeler, s' | 4 | v. | appeler |
| camera | appareil photo | 12 | n.m. | |
| camera | caméra | 12 | n.f. | |
| card (banker's/credit) | carte (bancaire) | 17 | n.f. | |
| car | bagnole* | 20 | n.f. | |
| cardboard | carton | 20 | n.m. | |
| careful | prudent | 33 | adj. | |

# C

| | | | | |
|---|---|---|---|---|
| caretaker | concierge | 26 | n.m. | |
| carpet | tapis | 39 | n.m. | |
| car | voiture | 8 | n.f. | |
| cash desk | caisse | 17 | n.f. | |
| cause | cause | 38 | n.f. | |
| certificate | certificat | 37 | n.m. | |
| chair | chaise | 25 | n.f. | |
| change (loose) | monnaie | 17 | n.f. | |
| change, to | changer | 13 | v. | manger |
| channel | chaîne | 18 | n.f. | |
| character | caractère | 6 | n.m. | |
| chat up, to | draguer | 42 | v. | |
| check, to | vérifier | 38 | v. | |
| cheese | fromage | 11 | n.m. | |
| chemist's | pharmacie | 33 | n.f. | |
| cheque | chèque | 16 | n.m. | |
| chicken | poulet | 14 | n.m. | |
| child | enfant | 13 | n.m. | |
| chocolate | chocolat | 11 | n.m. | |
| choose, to | choisir | 18 | v. | finir |
| church | église | 15 | n.f. | |
| cinema | cinéma | 6 | n.m. | |
| circuit | circuit | 45 | n.m. | |
| class | classe | 16 | n.f. | |
| classical | classique | 6 | adj. | |
| clean | propre | 39 | adj. | |
| clean, to | nettoyer | 39 | v. | |
| cleaning | nettoyage | 39 | n.m. | |
| close, to | fermer | 17 | v. | |
| clothing, article of | vêtement | 28 | n.m. | |
| cloudy | nuageux | 23 | adj. | |
| cloud | nuage | 23 | n.m. | |
| coat | manteau | 23 | n.m. | |
| code | code | 37 | n.m. | |
| coffee | café | 14 | n.m. | |
| coffee, white | café au lait | 25 | n.m. | |
| coin | pièce | 17 | n.f. | |
| cold (in the head) | rhume | 32 | n.m. | |
| cold | froid | 23 | n.m. | |
| colleague | collègue | 4 | n.m. | |
| colour | couleur | 3 | n.f. | |
| comb one's hair, to | peigner, se | 17 | v. | |
| comb | peigne | 17 | n.m. | |

# C-D

| | | | | |
|---|---|---|---|---|
| come, to | venir | 12 | v. | |
| comfortable | confortable | 26 | adj. | |
| commission | commission | 17 | n.f. | |
| communications | communication | 35 | n.f. | |
| compartment | compartiment | 16 | n.m. | |
| complaint | réclamation | 14 | n.f. | |
| complementary | complémentaire | 45 | adj. | |
| compulsory | obligatoire | 37 | adj. | |
| condition | état | 20 | n.m. | |
| conference | conférence | 30 | n.f. | |
| confirm, to | confirmer | 30 | v. | |
| congratulate, to | féliciter | 22 | v. | |
| connection | contact | 35 | n.m. | |
| consult, to | consulter | 33 | v. | |
| continue/go on, to | continuer | 15 | v. | |
| contract | contrat | 35 | n.m. | |
| convinced | convaincu | 28 | adj. | |
| cooked pork meats | charcuterie | 11 | n.f. | |
| cooking | cuisine | 6 | n.f. | |
| cook | cuisinière | 22 | n.f. | |
| cost, to | coûter | 11 | v. | |
| cough | toux | 32 | n.f. | |
| count, to | compter | 43 | v. | |
| country | pays | 7 | n.m. | |
| cousin | cousin | 29 | n.m. | |
| crazy | dingue* | 40 | adj. | |
| credit | crédit | 17 | n.m. | |
| croissant | croissant | 25 | n.m. | |
| cross, to | traverser | 15 | v. | |
| crossroads | carrefour | 37 | n.m. | |
| cultural | culturel | 45 | adj. | |
| cupboard | placard | 34 | n.m. | |
| cure, to | guérir | 33 | v. | finir |
| customs | douane | 10 | n.f. | |
| cut | coupé | 24 | adj. | |
| cut | coupure | 33 | n.f. | |
| cut oneself, to | couper, se | 17 | v. | |
| daily (newspaper) | quotidien | 18 | n.m. | |
| damaged | abîmé | 20 | adj. | |
| dance, to | danser | 42 | v. | |
| dangerous | dangereux | 37 | adj. | |
| dark-haired | brun | 6 | adj. | |
| darling | chéri | 11 | n.m. | |

# D

| | | | | |
|---|---|---|---|---|
| date | date | 3 | n.f. | |
| daughter | fille | 13 | n.f. | fils |
| day | journée | 2 | n.f. | |
| day | jour | 8 | n.m. | |
| death | mort | 44 | n.f. | |
| decided | décidé | 28 | adj. | |
| declaration | déclaration | 18 | n.f. | |
| declare/announce, to | annoncer | 24 | v. | |
| degree | degré | 23 | n.m. | |
| delicatessen | charcuterie | 11 | n.f. | |
| delicate | délicat | 39 | adj. | |
| delicious | délicieux | 14 | adj. | |
| delight | délice | 22 | n.m. | |
| dentist | dentiste | 19 | n.m. | |
| department | département | 6 | n.m. | |
| departure | départ | 16 | n.m. | |
| deposit | acompte | 26 | n.m. | |
| depressed | déprimé | 41 | adj. | |
| depression | cafard | 41 | n.m. | |
| depression | dépression | 31 | n.f. | |
| describe, to | décrire | 20 | v. | |
| desire | envie | 33 | n.f. | |
| despair | désespoir | 41 | n.m. | |
| despise, to | mépriser | 40 | v. | |
| dessert | dessert | 14 | n.m. | |
| destination | destination | 16 | n.f. | |
| device/telephone | appareil | 24 | n.m. | |
| dial, to | composer | 24 | v. | |
| dialling code | indicatif | 24 | n.m. | |
| die, to | mourir | 44 | v. | |
| differ, to | différer | 35 | v. | |
| different | différent | 31 | adj. | |
| difficult | difficile | 10 | adj. | |
| dining room | salle à manger | 29 | n.f. | |
| dinner | dîner | 19 | n.m. | |
| dinner, to have | dîner | 12 | v. | |
| diploma | diplôme | 31 | n.m. | |
| direction | direction | 15 | n.f. | |
| dirty | sale | 39 | adj. | |
| disagreement/refusal | désaccord | 11 | n.m. | |
| disappear, to | disparaître | 19 | v. | |
| discothèque | discothèque | 27 | n.f. | |
| display board | panneau | 15 | n.m. | |

# D-E

| | | | | |
|---|---|---|---|---|
| distinguished | distingué | 45 | adj. | |
| distributor | delco | 20 | n.m. | |
| divorce | divorce | 40 | n.m. | |
| divorce, to | divorcer | 40 | v. | |
| do, to | faire | 2 | v. | faire |
| do-it-yourself | bricolage | 43 | n.m. | |
| doctor | docteur | 32 | n.m. | |
| doctor | médecin | 19 | n.m. | |
| documentation | papiers | 3 | n.m. | |
| door | porte | 34 | n.f. | |
| dose | dose | 33 | n.f. | |
| double | double | 26 | adj. | |
| dream | rêve | 36 | n.m. | |
| dream, to | rêver | 13 | v. | |
| dress | robe | 28 | n.f. | |
| drink | boisson | 14 | n.f. | |
| drive, to | conduire | 29 | v. | conduire |
| dry (fem.) | sèche | 20 | adj. | sec |
| dry (masc.) | sec | 20 | adj. | sèche |
| easy | facile | 16 | adj. | |
| eat, to | manger | 13 | v. | |
| editor | éditeur | 43 | n.m. | |
| electric | électrique | 17 | adj. | |
| embassy | ambassade | 45 | n.f. | |
| employee | employé | 2 | n.m. | |
| end | fin | 23 | n.f. | |
| engine | moteur | 20 | n.m. | |
| English | anglais | 2 | adj | |
| enthusiastic | passionné | 44 | adj. | |
| envelope | enveloppe | 7 | n.f. | |
| equipment | matériel | 34 | n.m. | |
| evening | soir | 13 | n.m. | |
| evening | soirée | 19 | n.f. | |
| exact | exact | 31 | adj. | |
| exaggerate, to | exagérer | 21 | v. | |
| examination | examen | 36 | n.m. | |
| example | exemple | 42 | n.m. | |
| excellent | excellent | 21 | adj. | |
| exchange rate | cours | 17 | n.m. | |
| excuse | excuse | 17 | n.f. | |
| excuse, to | excuser | 25 | v. | |
| exit | sortie | 15 | n.f. | |
| expect/wait, to | attendre | 8 | v. | attendre |

| | | | | |
|---|---|---|---|---|
| expensive | cher | 11 | adj. | |
| express, to | exprimer | 11 | v. | |
| extra charge | supplément | 15 | n.m. | |
| eye | œil | 6 | n.m. | yeux |
| eyes | yeux | 3 | n.m. | œil |
| fair-haired | blond | 6 | adj. | |
| fall | chute | 23 | n.f. | |
| false | faux | 20 | adj. | |
| family | famille | 13 | n.f. | |
| farmer | agriculteur | 4 | n.m. | |
| far | éloigné | 26 | adj. | |
| fashion | mode | 28 | n.f. | |
| fat | gros | 6 | adj. | |
| father | père | 4 | n.m. | mère |
| feel ill/complain, to | plaindre, se | 33 | v. | |
| feel, to | sentir | 32 | v. | sentir |
| fever | fièvre | 32 | n.f. | |
| fiancé | fiancé | 40 | n.m. | |
| figure | chiffre | 3 | n.m. | |
| fill in, to | remplir | 10 | v. | |
| film | film | 41 | n.m. | |
| find, to | trouver | 21 | v. | |
| fine | amende | 37 | n.f. | |
| fireplace | cheminée | 34 | n.f. | |
| firm | entreprise | 30 | n.f. | |
| firmness | fermeté | 39 | n.f. | |
| first | premier | 15 | adj. | |
| fishmonger's | poissonnerie | 11 | n.f. | |
| fish | poisson | 14 | n.m. | |
| fitting (room) | essayage | 28 | n.m. | |
| fit in, to | tenir dans | 12 | v. | |
| flat | appartement | 13 | n.m. | |
| flight | vol | 16 | n.m. | |
| flirt | dragueur | 42 | n.m. | |
| flu | grippe | 32 | n.f. | |
| fog | brouillard | 23 | n.m. | |
| food | aliment | 11 | n.m. | |
| foot | pied | 32 | n.m. | |
| forbid | interdire | 22 | v. | dire |
| forbid, to | défendre | 39 | v. | attendre |
| forbidden | interdit | 37 | adj. | |
| forecast, (weather) | bulletin (météo) | 23 | n.m. | |
| forget, to | oublier | 7 | v. | |

# F-G

| | | | | |
|---|---|---|---|---|
| forgive, to | pardonner | 17 | v. | |
| fork | fourchette | 22 | n.f. | |
| form | fiche | 10 | n.f. | |
| formidable | formidable | 42 | adj. | |
| form | imprimé | 10 | n.m. | |
| franc | franc | 10 | adj. | |
| free | libre | 15 | adj. | |
| freeze, to | geler | 23 | v. | |
| French | français | 2 | adj. | |
| frequent | fréquent | 23 | adj. | |
| fresh | fraîche | 20 | adj. | frais |
| fresh | frais | 20 | adj. | fraîche |
| fridge | frigo* | 34 | n.m. | |
| friend | ami | 4 | n.m. | |
| friendship/love | amitié | 6 | n.f. | |
| friend | camarade | 9 | n.m. | |
| friend | copain* | 42 | n.m. | copine |
| friend | copine* | 44 | n.f. | copain |
| fruit | fruit | 11 | n.m. | |
| full | plein | 38 | n.m. | |
| funny/strange | bizarre | 20 | adj. | |
| furniture, piece of | meuble | 34 | n.m. | |
| garage | garage | 34 | n.m. | |
| garden | jardin | 13 | n.m. | |
| gardening | jardinage | 44 | n.m. | |
| gastronomy | gastronomie | 45 | n. f | |
| German | allemand | 2 | adj. | |
| get ready/prepare, to | préparer | 12 | v. | |
| get/take/have, to | prendre | 10 | v. | comprendre |
| get up, to | lever, se | 17 | v. | |
| girl | fille | 13 | n.f. | garçon |
| give, to | donner | 8 | v. | |
| glass (material) | verre | 20 | n.m. | |
| glass (object) | verre | 22 | n.m. | |
| go beyond, to | dépasser | 33 | v. | |
| go out/take the exit, to | sortir | 15 | v. | sortir |
| go, to | aller | 6 | v. | aller |
| good | bon | 2 | adj. | |
| go down, to | baisser | 17 | v. | |
| go to bed, to | coucher, se | 32 | v. | |
| go to, to | passer à | 17 | v. | |
| grandfather | grand-père | 29 | n.m. | |
| grandmother | grand-mère | 29 | n.f. | |

| | | | | |
|---|---|---|---|---|
| grandparents | grand-parents | 29 | n.m. | |
| great | génial | 21 | adj. | |
| green | vert | 6 | adj. | |
| greeting | salutation | 1 | n.f. | |
| grey | gris | 6 | adj. | |
| grocer's | épicerie | 11 | n.f. | |
| ground | sol | 39 | n.m. | |
| group | groupe | 45 | n.m. | |
| guide | guide | 45 | n.m. | |
| guilty | coupable | 41 | adj. | |
| guitare | guitare | 42 | n.f. | |
| habit | habitude | 13 | n.f. | |
| hair | cheveux | 6 | n.m. | |
| hairdresser | coiffeur | 19 | n.m. | |
| half | demi | 25 | n.m. | |
| hall, (departure) | hall | 16 | n.m. | |
| ham | jambon | 11 | n.m. | |
| handsome | beau | 6 | adj. | |
| hand | main | 32 | n.f. | |
| happen, to | passer, se | 8 | v. | |
| happiness | bonheur | 36 | n.m. | |
| happy | content | 15 | adj. | |
| happy | heureux | 20 | adj. | |
| hardship | épreuve | 36 | n.f. | |
| hate, to | détester | 6 | v. | |
| hatred | haine | 40 | n.f. | |
| have to/be needed, to | falloir | 11 | v. | falloir |
| headlight | phare | 38 | n.m. | |
| head | tête | 32 | n.f. | |
| health | santé | 32 | n.f. | |
| hear, to | entendre | 25 | v. | entendre |
| heart | cœur | 36 | n.m. | |
| heat | chaleur | 23 | n.f. | |
| help | aide | 16 | n.f. | |
| help, to | aider | 16 | v. | |
| hesitate, to | hésiter | 28 | v. | |
| holidays | vacances | 6 | n.f. | |
| home | domicile | 3 | n.m. | |
| home, to arrive/go | rentrer | 13 | v. | |
| hoover | aspirateur | 39 | n.m. | |
| hope | espoir | 41 | n.m. | |
| hospital | hôpital | 6 | n.m. | |
| hot | chaud | 23 | adj. | |

# H-J

| | | | | |
|---|---|---|---|---|
| hour/time | heure | 8 | n.f. | |
| house | maison | 13 | n.f. | |
| hunger | faim | 22 | n.f. | |
| hurry up, to | dépêcher, se | 17 | v. | |
| husband | mari | 13 | n.m. | femme |
| ice | glace | 27 | n.f. | |
| idea | idée | 10 | n.f. | |
| identify, to | identifier | 35 | v. | |
| identity card | carte d'identité | 3 | n.f. | |
| identity/name | identité | 2 | n.f. | |
| ill | malade | 30 | adj. | |
| illness | maladie | 32 | n.f. | |
| impatience | impatience | 13 | n.f. | |
| impeccable | impeccable | 20 | adj. | |
| important | important | 31 | adj. | |
| impossible | impossible | 25 | adj. | |
| included | compris | 25 | adj. | |
| inconvenient | inconvénient | 26 | n.m. | |
| increase | augmentation | 31 | n.f. | |
| incredible | incroyable | 25 | adj. | |
| indecision | indécision | 44 | n. f | |
| indifference | indifférence | 24 | n.f. | |
| inform, to | informer | 43 | v. | |
| informal | informel | 18 | adj. | |
| information | information | 43 | n.f. | |
| information | renseignement | 24 | n.m. | |
| injection | piqûre | 33 | n.f. | |
| injury | blessure | 33 | n.f. | |
| inquiry | enquête | 19 | n.f. | |
| insist, to | tenir à | 35 | v. | |
| inspector | inspecteur | 19 | n.m. | |
| insurance | assurance | 17 | n.f. | |
| interest, to | intéresser | 44 | v. | |
| interlocutor | interlocuteur | 35 | n.m. | |
| international | international | 10 | adj. | |
| interview | entretien | 43 | n.m. | |
| invitation | invitation | 12 | n.f. | |
| invite, to | inviter | 12 | v. | |
| iron | fer | 20 | n.m. | |
| iron, to | repasser | 39 | v. | |
| isolated | isolé | 6 | adj. | |
| Italian | italien | 2 | adj. | |
| jacket | veste | 28 | n.f. | |

| | | | | |
|---|---|---|---|---|
| January | janvier | 10 | n.m. | |
| job | emploi | 31 | n.m. | |
| journalist | journaliste | 2 | n.m. | |
| journey/travelling | voyage | 6 | n.m. | |
| joy | joie | 41 | n.f. | |
| just | juste | 16 | adj. | |
| keep, to | conserver | 42 | v. | |
| key | clé | 26 | n.f. | |
| kind/nice | gentil | 12 | adj. | |
| kindness | amabilité | 39 | n.f. | |
| kindness | gentillesse | 39 | n.f. | |
| kiss | bise | 11 | n.f. | |
| knife | couteau | 22 | n.m. | |
| know, to | connaître | 4 | v. | connaître |
| know, to | savoir | 10 | v. | savoir |
| lack | manque | 17 | n.m. | |
| lady | dame | 28 | n.f. | |
| lamp | lampe | 34 | n.f. | |
| last | dernier | 18 | adj. | |
| late | retard, en | 17 | n.m. | |
| late | tard | 17 | adj. | |
| laugh, to | rire | 42 | v. | rire |
| laundry | linge | 39 | n.m. | |
| lawyer | avocat | 2 | n.m. | |
| leather | cuir | 20 | n.m. | |
| leave, to | abandonner | 13 | v. | |
| leave, to | laisser | 10 | v. | |
| leave/go, to | partir | 8 | v. | partir |
| left | gauche | 15 | n.f. | |
| leg | jambe | 32 | n.f. | |
| leisure | loisir | 21 | n.m. | |
| lemon | citron | 22 | n.m. | |
| letter | lettre | 10 | n.f. | |
| level | niveau | 38 | n. m | |
| licence | permis | 37 | n.m. | |
| lie down, to | allonger, s' | 32 | v. | manger |
| life | vie | 13 | n.f. | |
| light | léger | 22 | adj. | |
| like/love, to | aimer | 6 | v. | aller |
| line | ligne | 16 | n.f. | |
| listen, to | écouter | 16 | v. | |
| listener | auditeur | 18 | n.m. | |
| literature | littérature | 6 | n.f. | |

# L-M

| | | | | |
|---|---|---|---|---|
| live, to | habiter | 6 | v. | |
| live, to | vivre | 40 | v. | |
| loan (borrowed) | emprunt | 17 | n.m. | |
| loan (lent) | prêt | 17 | n.m. | |
| long | long | 20 | adj. | |
| look for, to | chercher | 6 | v. | |
| look like, to | ressembler | 28 | v. | |
| lottery | loto | 13 | n.m. | |
| lounge | salon | 39 | n.m. | |
| love | amour | 40 | n.m. | |
| love at first sight | coup de foudre | 40 | n.m. | |
| love, in | amoureux | 40 | adj. | |
| luck | chance | 36 | n.f. | |
| luggage | bagages | 15 | n.m. | |
| lunch, to have | déjeuner | 12 | n.m. | |
| luxurious | luxueux | 26 | adj. | |
| mad | folle | 20 | adj. | fou |
| mad | fou | 20 | adj. | folle |
| maintain, to | maintenir | 35 | v. | |
| make-up, to put on | maquiller, se | 17 | v. | |
| manager (fem.) | directrice | 6 | n.f. | directeur |
| manager (masc.) | directeur | 6 | n.m. | directrice |
| man | homme | 13 | n.f. | femme |
| manner | manière | 18 | n.f. | |
| mark, to | marquer | 15 | v. | |
| marriage | mariage | 40 | n.m. | |
| married | marié | 6 | adj. | |
| married, to get | marier, se | 40 | v. | |
| material | matière | 20 | n.f. | |
| meal | repas | 11 | n.m. | |
| means (financial) | moyens | 13 | n.m. | |
| meat | viande | 11 | n.f. | |
| mechanic | mécanicien | 20 | n.m. | |
| media | médias | 18 | n.m. | |
| medicine | médicament | 32 | n.m. | |
| meet, to | réunir, se | 30 | v. | finir |
| meeting | réunion | 19 | n.f. | |
| memory | souvenir | 29 | n.m. | |
| menu | carte | 14 | n.f. | |
| menu | menu | 14 | n.m. | |
| message | message | 24 | n.m. | |
| meter | compteur | 15 | n.m. | |
| midday | midi | 13 | n.m. | |

| | | | | |
|---|---|---|---|---|
| minute | minute | 8 | n.f. | |
| mistake | erreur | 43 | n.f. | |
| mistaken, to be | tromper, se | 43 | v. | |
| mister | monsieur | 2 | n.m. | |
| misty | brumeux | 23 | adj. | |
| model | modèle | 28 | n.m. | |
| modest | modeste | 13 | adj. | |
| moment | moment | 29 | n.m. | |
| money | argent | 11 | n.m. | |
| money order | mandat | 10 | n.m. | |
| monitor | moniteur | 27 | n.m. | |
| monotonous | monotone | 13 | adj. | |
| month | mois | 8 | n.m. | |
| mood | humeur | 17 | n.f. | |
| morale | moral | 41 | n.m. | |
| morning | matinée | 8 | n.f. | |
| morning | matin | 13 | n.m. | |
| mother | mère | 4 | n.f. | père |
| mountain | montagne | 6 | n.f. | |
| museum | musée | 44 | n.m. | |
| music | musique | 6 | n.f. | |
| must/have to | devoir | 14 | v. | |
| mustard | moutarde | 22 | n.f. | |
| name, first | prénom | 7 | n.m. | |
| name | nom | 7 | n.m. | |
| napkin | serviette | 22 | n.f. | |
| nationality | nationalité | 3 | n.f. | |
| nature | nature | 44 | n.f. | |
| necessary | nécessaire | 37 | adj. | |
| need | besoin | 17 | n.m. | |
| neighbourhood | quartier | 15 | n.m. | |
| neighbour | voisin | 19 | n.m. | |
| newsagent | marchand de journaux | 43 | n.m. | |
| newspaper | journal | 18 | n.m. | |
| new | neuf | 20 | adj. | |
| new | nouveau | 20 | adj. | |
| news, piece of | nouvelle | 8 | n.f. | |
| next | prochain | 30 | adj. | |
| next | suivant | 21 | adj. | |
| nice | sympathique | 6 | adj. | |
| night | nuit | 2 | n.f. | |
| noise | bruit | 20 | n.m. | |
| noisy | bruyant | 26 | adj. | |

# N-P

| | | | | |
|---|---|---|---|---|
| north | nord | 13 | n.m. | |
| note, (bank) | billet | 17 | n.m. | |
| notice, to | remarquer | 31 | v. | |
| numerous | nombreux | 23 | adj. | |
| nurse/tend, to | soigner | 13 | v. | |
| object | objet | 20 | n.m. | |
| obligation | obligation | 37 | n.f. | |
| obliged | obligé | 37 | adj. | |
| observe, to | observer | 23 | v. | |
| occupation, job | occupation | 44 | n. f | |
| occupation | profession | 6 | n.f. | |
| offense (driving) | infraction | 37 | n.f. | |
| office | bureau | 19 | n.m. | |
| official | officiel | 45 | adj. | |
| oil | huile | 11 | n.f. | |
| old (fem.) | vieille | 6 | adj. | vieux |
| old (masc.) | vieux | 6 | adj. | vieille |
| old | ancien | 20 | adj. | |
| open, to | ouvrir | 20 | v. | ouvrir |
| opinion/view | avis | 10 | n.m. | |
| opinion | opinion | 14 | n.f. | |
| opinion poll | sondage | 18 | n.m. | |
| opposite | contraire | 31 | n.m. | |
| optimism | optimisme | 41 | n.m. | |
| orange | orange | 11 | n. f | |
| order, to | commander | 18 | v. | |
| organized | organisé | 45 | adj. | |
| out of date | périmé | 37 | adj. | |
| outrageous | scandaleux | 31 | adj. | |
| overcast | couvert | 23 | adj. | |
| owe, to | devoir | 15 | v. | |
| pain | douleur | 32 | n.f. | |
| paper | papier | 20 | n.m. | |
| parcel | envoi | 10 | n.m. | |
| parcel | paquet | 11 | n.m. | |
| parents | parents | 29 | n.m. | |
| parking | stationnement | 37 | n.m. | |
| party | boum* | 42 | n.f. | |
| party | fête | 36 | n.f. | |
| part | pièce | 20 | n.f. | |
| patient | patient | 32 | n.m. | |
| pavement area (outside a café) | terrasse | 25 | n.f. | |

P

| | | | | |
|---|---|---|---|---|
| pay | paye | 31 | n.f. | |
| pay, to | payer | 13 | v. | essayer |
| pension | pension | 45 | n.f. | |
| pepper | poivre | 22 | n.m. | |
| perfect | parfait | 30 | adj. | |
| performance | séance | 21 | n.f. | |
| period | période | 45 | n.f. | |
| personnel | personnel | 30 | n.m. | |
| pessimism | pessimisme | 41 | n.m. | |
| petrol | essence | 38 | n.f. | |
| petrol station | station service | 15 | n.f. | |
| photograph | photo | 29 | n.f. | |
| piece | morceau | 22 | n.m. | |
| pie | tarte | 14 | n.f. | |
| pile | pile | 39 | n.f. | |
| place | lieu | 3 | n.m. | |
| plane | avion | 10 | n.m. | |
| plan | projet | 8 | n.m. | |
| plastic | plastique | 20 | n.m. | |
| plate | assiette | 22 | n.f. | |
| platform | quai | 16 | n.m. | |
| play | pièce | 21 | n.f. | |
| play, to | jouer | 13 | v. | |
| pleasant | agréable | 20 | dj. | |
| please, to | plaire | 12 | v. | plaire |
| pleasure | plaisir | 12 | n.m. | |
| point out, to | signaler | 33 | v. | |
| point | point | 30 | n.m. | |
| police | police | 19 | n.f. | |
| police station | commissariat | 37 | n.m. | |
| politeness | politesse | 39 | n.f. | |
| position/place | place | 26 | n.f. | |
| possibility | possibilité | 45 | n.f. | |
| postcard | carte postale | 10 | n.f. | |
| post code | code postal | 7 | n.m. | |
| postman | facteur | 10 | n.m. | |
| post office | poste | 10 | n.f. | |
| postpone/delay, to | retarder | 28 | v. | |
| prefer, to | préférer | 14 | v. | préférer |
| preference | preference | 45 | n.f. | |
| prescription | ordonnance | 32 | n.f. | |
| present, to | présenter | 4 | v. | |
| presenter | présentateur | 43 | n.m. | |

# P-R

| | | | | |
|---|---|---|---|---|
| press | presse | 18 | n.f. | |
| pretty | joli | 6 | adj. | |
| price list | tarif | 15 | n.m. | |
| price | prix | 25 | n.m. | |
| problem | problème | 38 | n.m. | |
| produce, to | produire | 23 | v. | conduire |
| profession/trade | métier | 31 | n.m. | |
| programme | émission | 18 | n.f. | |
| programme | programme | 18 | n.m. | |
| promise, to | promettre | 31 | v. | mettre |
| protest, to | protester | 25 | v. | |
| province | province | 6 | n.f. | |
| pullover | pull-over | 12 | n.m. | |
| punctuality | ponctualité | 17 | n.f. | |
| puncture | crevaison | 20 | n.f. | |
| purchase | achat | 17 | n.m. | |
| put to bed, to | coucher | 13 | v. | |
| put, to | mettre | 10 | v. | mettre |
| quality | qualité | 38 | n.f. | |
| question, to | interroger | 32 | v. | manger |
| rabbit | lapin | 22 | n.m. | |
| radio | radio | 16 | n.f. | |
| raincoat | imperméable | 12 | n.m. | |
| rain | pluie | 23 | n.f. | |
| rain, to | pleuvoir | 23 | v. | pleuvoir |
| reach, to | parvenir | 45 | v. | |
| read, to | lire | 20 | v. | lire |
| reading | lecture | 44 | n. f | |
| real-estate | immobilier | 35 | n.m. | |
| reason | raison | 10 | n.f. | |
| receive, to | recevoir | 33 | v. | recevoir |
| reception | réception | 26 | n.f. | |
| recognise, to | reconnaître | 33 | v. | connaître |
| recommend, to | recommander | 33 | v. | |
| rectangular | rectangulaire | 20 | adj. | |
| red-haired (fem.) | rousse | 6 | adj. | roux |
| red-haired (masc.) | roux | 6 | adj. | rousse |
| red | rouge | 20 | adj. | |
| refuse, to | refuser | 10 | v. | |
| region | région | 45 | n.f. | |
| relieve/ease one's pain, to | soulager | 33 | v. | manger |
| remind, to | rappeler | 33 | v. | appeler |

| | | | | |
|---|---|---|---|---|
| rendez-vous | rendez-vous | 33 | n.m. | |
| repair | réparation | 20 | n.f. | |
| repair, to | réparer | 20 | v. | |
| repeat, to | répéter | 24 | v. | |
| reproach | reproche | 17 | n.m. | |
| reservation | réservation | 16 | n.f. | |
| reserve, to | réserver | 26 | v. | |
| resist, to | résister | 14 | v. | |
| responsibility | responsabilité | 31 | n.f. | |
| rest, to | reposer, se | 30 | v. | |
| restaurant car | wagon-restaurant | 16 | n.m. | |
| restaurant | restaurant | 14 | n.m. | |
| rest | reste | 17 | n.m. | |
| retirement | retraite | 44 | n.f. | |
| return, to | retourner | 27 | v. | |
| review | revue | 18 | n. f | |
| ring road | péripherique | 15 | n.m. | |
| risk | risque | 23 | n.m. | |
| road | route | 15 | n.f. | |
| roast | rôti | 14 | n.m. | |
| round | rond | 20 | adj. | |
| rubbish/useless | nul | 21 | adj. | |
| rucksack | sac à dos | 12 | n.m. | |
| sad | triste | 41 | adj. | |
| salary | salaire | 31 | n.m. | |
| sales assistant | vendeuse | 13 | n.f. | vendeur |
| sale | vente | 17 | n.f. | |
| salt | sel | 11 | n.m. | |
| same | pareil | 31 | adj. | |
| sardine | sardine | 11 | n.f. | |
| satisfaction | satisfaction | 36 | n.f. | |
| savings | économies | 11 | n.f. | |
| say, to | dire | 4 | v. | dire |
| sea | mer | 26 | n.f. | |
| season | saison | 45 | n.f. | |
| seat | place | 16 | n.f. | |
| secretary | secrétaire | 24 | n.m. | |
| see, to | voir | 15 | v. | |
| seem, to | avoir l'air | 14 | v. | |
| seem, to | paraître | 18 | v. | |
| send, to | envoyer | 10 | v. | envoyer |
| sender | expéditeur | 10 | n.m. | |
| seniority | ancienneté | 31 | n.f. | |

# S

| | | | | |
|---|---|---|---|---|
| sensation | sensation | 23 | n.f. | |
| serious | grave | 43 | adj. | |
| serious | sérieux | 23 | adj. | |
| serve, to | servir | 20 | v. | |
| settle in, to | installer, s' | 34 | v. | |
| shake, to | secouer | 39 | v. | |
| shape | forme | 20 | n.f. | |
| shave, to | raser, se | 17 | v. | |
| shelf | étagère | 34 | n.f. | |
| shine, to | briller | 23 | v. | |
| shirt | chemise | 28 | n.f. | |
| shiver | frisson | 32 | n.m. | |
| shoe | chaussure | 12 | n.f. | |
| shop/store | magasin | 11 | n.m. | |
| shopping | courses | 11 | n.f. | |
| short | bref | 30 | adj. | |
| shoulder | épaule | 28 | n.f. | |
| show | spectacle | 21 | n.m. | |
| show, to | indiquer | 15 | v. | |
| shower | douche | 17 | n.f. | |
| shy | timide | 23 | adj; | |
| sight | vue | 26 | n.f. | |
| signature | signature | 3 | n.f. | |
| sign | signe | 23 | n.m. | |
| sign, to | signer | 10 | v. | |
| similarity | similitude | 31 | n.f. | |
| simple | simple | 13 | adj. | |
| sink | évier | 39 | n.m. | |
| sir | monsieur | 16 | n.m. | |
| sister-in-law | belle-sœur | 29 | n.f. | |
| sister | sœur | 4 | n.f. | frère |
| size | taille | 3 | n.f. | |
| skate, (ice) | patin | 27 | n.m. | |
| skirt | jupe | 28 | n.f. | |
| ski | ski | 27 | n.m. | |
| ski slope | piste | 27 | n.f. | |
| ski, to | skier | 27 | v. | |
| skier | skieur | 27 | n.m. | |
| sky | ciel | 23 | n.m. | |
| slice | tranche | 11 | n.f. | |
| slim | mince | 6 | adj. | |
| small | petit | 6 | adj. | |
| smell, to | sentir | 22 | v. | |

S

| | | | | |
|---|---|---|---|---|
| smoking | fumeur | 16 | n.m. | |
| smooth | lisse | 38 | adj. | |
| snow | neige | 23 | n.f. | |
| snow, to | neiger | 23 | v. | neiger |
| soap powder | lessive | 11 | n.f. | |
| soap | savon | 17 | n.m. | |
| sold out (theatre) | complet | 21 | adj. | |
| son | fils | 13 | n.m. | fille |
| sorrow | tristesse | 41 | n.f. | |
| sorry | désolé | 12 | adj. | |
| sorry, to be | regretter | 12 | v. | |
| soup | soupe | 14 | n.f. | |
| source | source | 36 | n.f. | |
| space | case | 10 | n.f. | |
| Spanish | espagnol | 2 | | |
| speak, to | parler | 6 | v. | |
| speciality | spécialité | 22 | n.f. | |
| splendid | splendide | 29 | adj. | |
| spoon | cuiller | 22 | n.f. | |
| sport | sport | 6 | n.m. | |
| sportsman | sportif | 27 | n.m. | |
| sporty | sportif | 27 | adj. | |
| square | carré | 20 | n.m. | |
| square | place | 7 | n.f. | |
| stadium | stade | 15 | n.m. | |
| stamp | timbre | 10 | n.m. | |
| stand/tolerate, to | supporter | 40 | v. | |
| start, to | démarrer | 20 | v. | |
| starter | entrée | 14 | n.f. | |
| station | gare | 16 | n.f. | |
| stay | séjour | 45 | n.m. | |
| steak | bifteck | 11 | n.m. | |
| stick of French bread | baguette | 11 | n.f. | |
| sting, to | piquer | 33 | v. | |
| stomach | estomac | 32 | n.m. | |
| stomach | ventre | 32 | n.m. | |
| storm | orage | 23 | n.m. | |
| storm | tempête | 23 | n.f. | |
| story | histoire | 13 | n.f. | |
| street | rue | 7 | n.f. | |
| strike | grève | 18 | n.f. | |
| strong | fort | 24 | adj. | |
| student | étudiant | 2 | n.m. | |

# S-T

| | | | | |
|---|---|---|---|---|
| study | étude | 35 | n.f. | |
| stupid | bête | 42 | adj. | |
| stupid | idiot | 42 | adj. | |
| suburb(s) | banlieue | 13 | n.f. | |
| succeed, to | réussir | 36 | v. | finir |
| suffer, to | souffrir | 33 | v. | |
| sugar | sucre | 11 | n.m. | |
| suggest/offer, to | proposer | 4 | v. | |
| suit, (lady's) | tailleur | 28 | n.m. | |
| suit | costume | 28 | n.m. | |
| suitcase | valise | 26 | n.f. | |
| suite of rooms | suite | 26 | n.f. | |
| Sunday | dimanche | 9 | n.m. | |
| sun | soleil | 23 | n.m. | |
| super/fantastic | super* | 42 | adj. | |
| sure | sûr | 20 | adj. | |
| surprise | étonner | 42 | v. | |
| sweet | bonbon | 11 | n.m. | |
| sweet | doux | 20 | adj. | |
| swim, to | nager | 44 | v. | manger |
| swimming | natation | 44 | n.f. | |
| swimming pool | piscine | 27 | n.f. | |
| switchboard operator | standardiste | 24 | n.m. | |
| switchboard | standard | 24 | n.m. | |
| symptom | symptôme | 32 | n.m. | |
| syrup | sirop | 32 | n.m. | |
| tablet | tablette | 11 | n.f. | |
| table | table | 22 | n.f. | |
| take again, to | reprendre | 22 | v. | comprendre |
| take care of, to | occuper, s' | 42 | v. | |
| take, to | emmener | 44 | v. | |
| talkative | bavard | 44 | adj. | |
| tall | grand | 6 | adj. | |
| tap | robinet | 39 | n.m. | |
| taste | goût | 6 | n.m. | |
| taste/try, to | goûter | 14 | v. | |
| tax | impôt | 19 | n.m. | |
| taxi | taxi | 15 | n.m. | |
| team | équipe | 30 | n.f. | |
| tea | thé | 22 | n.m. | |
| technician | technicien | 13 | n.m. | |
| telegram | télégramme | 10 | n.m. | |
| telephone directory | annuaire | 24 | n.m. | |

# T

| | | | | |
|---|---|---|---|---|
| telephone | téléphone | 24 | n.m. | |
| telephone, to | téléphoner | 8 | v. | |
| television | télévision | 16 | n.f. | |
| temperature | température | 23 | n. f | |
| tennis | tennis | 19 | n.m. | |
| tent | tente | 12 | n.f. | |
| test | analyse | 33 | n.f. | |
| theatre | théâtre | 6 | n.m. | |
| theatrical company | troupe | 21 | n.f. | |
| thing | chose | 27 | n.f. | |
| thing/contraption | truc* | 20 | n.m. | |
| thingummyjig | machin | 20 | n.m. | |
| think, to | penser | 12 | v. | |
| think, to | réfléchir | 28 | v. | finir |
| thirst | soif | 22 | n.f. | |
| throat | gorge | 32 | n.f. | |
| thunder | tonnerre | 23 | n.m. | |
| ticket | billet | 16 | n.m. | |
| ticket inspector | contrôleur | 16 | n.m. | |
| ticket office | guichet | 10 | n.m. | |
| tidy, to | ranger | 39 | v. | manger |
| tight, to be | serrer | 28 | v. | |
| time | époque | 29 | n.f. | |
| time | fois | 40 | n.f. | |
| time, weather | temps | 8 | n.m. | |
| timetable | horaire | 16 | n.m. | |
| tin | boîte | 34 | n.f. | |
| tin-opener | ouvre-boîte | 11 | n.m. | |
| tip | pourboire | 14 | n.m. | |
| tiring | fatigant | 13 | adj. | |
| toboggan | luge | 27 | n.f. | |
| today | aujourd'hui | 21 | n.m. | |
| toilets | toilettes | 33 | n.f. | |
| tooth | dent | 17 | n.f. | |
| toothpaste | dentifrice | 17 | n.m. | |
| touch, to | toucher | 18 | v. | |
| tourist | touriste | 18 | n.m. | |
| touristic | touristique | 45 | adj. | |
| towel | serviette | 34 | n.f. | |
| town, city | ville | 6 | n.f. | |
| town hall | mairie | 15 | n.f. | |
| track | voie | 16 | n.f. | |
| tradesman | commerçant | 2 | n.m. | |

# T-W

| | | | | |
|---|---|---|---|---|
| traffic | circulation | 37 | n.f. | |
| traffic lights | feu | 15 | n.m. | |
| training course | stage | 27 | n.m. | |
| train | train | 10 | n.m. | |
| transmit, to | transmettre | 35 | v. | mettre |
| travel, to | voyager | 6 | v. | manger |
| tray | plateau | 22 | n.m. | |
| triangular | triangulaire | 20 | adj. | |
| trousers | pantalon | 28 | n.m. | |
| true | vrai | 31 | adj. | |
| try, to | essayer | 14 | v. | essayer |
| turn, to | tourner | 15 | v. | |
| tyre | pneu | 20 | n.m. | |
| ugly | moche* | 6 | adj. | |
| umbrella | parapluie | 12 | n.m. | |
| unacceptable | inadmissible | 25 | adj. | |
| uncertainty/reserve | réserve | 18 | n.f. | |
| uncle | oncle | 29 | n.m. | tante |
| understand, to | comprendre | 21 | v. | comprendre |
| unhappy | malheureux | 41 | adj. | |
| unknown | inconnu | 18 | n.m. | |
| urgent | urgent | 10 | adj; | |
| use, to | utiliser | 10 | v. | |
| use | utilité | 10 | n. f | |
| vegetable | légume | 11 | n.m. | |
| visit, to | visiter | 18 | v. | |
| visit | visite | 8 | n.f. | |
| voice | voix | 42 | n.f. | |
| vomit, to | vomir | 32 | v. | finir |
| vulgar | vulgaire | 21 | adj. | |
| waiter | serveur | 14 | n.m. | |
| wake up, to | réveiller, se | 17 | v. | |
| walk, to go for a | promener, se | 27 | v. | |
| walking | marche | 44 | n.f. | |
| want, to | vouloir | 10 | v. | |
| wardrobe | armoire | 34 | n.f. | |
| warn, to | prévenir | 37 | v. | |
| washed, to get | laver, se | 17 | v. | |
| washing machine | machine à laver | 39 | n.f. | |
| washing up | vaisselle | 39 | n.f. | |
| watch/look, to | regarder | 20 | v. | |
| water | eau | 11 | n.f. | |
| weather | météo | 23 | adj. | |

| | | | | |
|---|---|---|---|---|
| weekly (newspaper) | hebdomadaire | 18 | n.m. | |
| week | semaine | 8 | n.f. | |
| wheel | roue | 20 | n.f. | |
| white/blank | blanc | 10 | adj. | |
| white/blank | blanche | 10 | adj. | |
| win, to | gagner | 13 | v. | |
| window | fenêtre | 34 | n.f. | |
| wind | vent | 23 | n.m. | |
| wine | vin | 14 | n.m. | |
| wire | cable | 20 | n.m. | |
| wish | souhait | 13 | n.m. | |
| wish | vœux | 36 | n.m. | |
| woman/wife | femme | 13 | n.f. | homme/mari |
| wonder, to | demander | 35 | v. | |
| wood | bois | 20 | n.m. | |
| word | mot | 10 | n.m. | |
| work | boulot* | 31 | n.m. | |
| work, to | travailler | 6 | v. | |
| work/job | travail | 6 | n.m. | travaux |
| worker | ouvrier | 4 | n.m. | |
| works | travaux | 24 | n.m. | travail |
| worried | inquiet | 19 | adj. | |
| worth, to be | valoir | 11 | v. | |
| write, to | écrire | 8 | v. | écrire |
| year | an | 6 | n.m. | |
| year | année | 9 | n.f. | |
| yellow | jaune | 20 | adj. | |
| young | jeune | 29 | adj. | |
| younger, to grow | rajeunir | 44 | v. | finir |
| youth | jeunesse | 29 | n.f. | |

*familiar

# GRAMMAR INDEX

# INDEX OF LANGUAGE FUNCTIONS

*(The entries refer to the different functions presented in the "Variations" section of each lesson)*

# INDEX OF THEMES

# LIST OF IDIOMATIC EXPRESSIONS

The French say things differently from the English ! A blinding flash of the obvious ? Perhaps. But worth repeating to remind people learning the language that the French consider it perfectly natural to use certain strings of words in certain situations that, translated literally, seem rather strange (or even humorous) to English speakers. Imagine how expressions such as "What about a coffee ?" or "I'd sooner you didn't seem obscure to French speakers (What approximately a coffee/I'd earlier you didn't!!). This section is intended to make these differences explicit, and to help you memorize them by providing **literal** translations of the more important expressions found in the book. (The list is chronological in the order of the lessons)

*The sign (!) indicates a rather surprising literal translation.*

* **Bonjour, monsieur :** it sounds terribly proper to say *Hello, sir* in English, but the French usually add *madame, mademoiselle, monsieur* when they say "Bonjour" or "Au revoir" to someone they do not know very well.

* **Je suis avocat :** *I'm lawyer.*

* **Papa, Maman, je vous présente Louis, un ami :** *Dad, Mum, I present you Louis, a friend.*

* **Comment allez-vous ? :** *How do you go ?*

* **Vous connaissez ? :** *You know ?*
It is clear from the context that the subject is the city of Namur, so no reference is made to it in French.

* **On se dit tu:** *one says tu to one another.*

* **J'ai trente-six ans :** *I have thirty-six years.*

* **Nous n'avons pas de nouvelles :** *We haven't any news.*

* **... le 5 août :** *... the five August.*

* **Mais avant nous attendons votre visite :** *but before we are waiting (for) your visit.*

* **Un timbre, s'il vous plaît :** *a stamp, if it pleases you.*

* **C'est combien le mot ? :** *it's how much the word.*

* **Il faut du pain :** *it is necessary some bread (!).*



* **Prends :** *take.*

* **Un pain complet :** *a complete bread.*

* **Dis, ça vous plairait de venir en week-end avec nous ? :** *Say, it would please you to come on weekend with us ?*

* **Qu'est-ce qu'on prend ? :** *what is it that one takes ?*

* **On tient tous dans le minibus :** *one holds all in the minibus (!).*

* **À demain :** *to tomorrow.*

* **Leurs enfants les attendent avec impatience :** *their children wait for them with impatience*

* **Monsieur prendra le menu ou la carte ? :** *Sir will take the menu (limited choice) or the card (wider choice).*

* **Comme entrée vous me mettrez une salade de crudités :** *As starter, you will put me a salad of raw vegetables (!).*

* **Ouais :** "oui" is to "ouais" as "yes" is to "yeah".

* **Attention, vous sortirez après la Porte d'Asnières :** *Attention, you will leave after the Porte d'Asnières.*

* **Excusez-moi, monsieur, les guichets des grandes lignes ? :** *Excuse me, sir, the ticket offices of the big lines ?*

* **... j'irais à la mer :** *I would go to the sea.*

* **Ce n'est pas grave :** *it isn't serious.*

* **Je vous prie de bien vouloir me faire parvenir des informations sur votre ville afin d'y organiser un voyage l'été prochain :** *I beg you to want well to make to send to me information on your city in order to organize there a trip next summer (!).*

* **Je vous prie d'accepter, Monsieur, l'expression de mes salutations les plus distinguées :** *I beg you to accept, Sir, the expression of my most distinguished greetings.*

Imprimé en France par I.M.E. - 25110 Baume-les-Dames
Dépôt légal n° 9630-07/1992 - Collection n° 45 - Edition n° 02
15/4892/4